Gender, Catholicism and Spirituality

'The introduction and essays provide nuanced and stimulating treatments of their topics [...] this volume promises to stimulate thought and debate.' – **Claire Sahlin**, *Texas Woman's University*

This timely collection of essays on British and European Catholic spiritualities explores how ideas of the sacred have influenced female relationships with piety and religious vocations over time. Each of the studies focuses on specific persons or groups within the varied contexts of England, France, Italy, the Netherlands and Spain, together spanning the medieval period through to the nineteenth century.

Examining the interplay between women's religious roles and patriarchal norms, the volume highlights the relevance of gender and spirituality over a wide geographical and chronological spectrum. It is an essential resource for students of Gender History, Women's Studies and Religious Studies, introducing a wealth of new research and providing an approachable guide to current debates and methodologies.

Contributions by: Nancy Jiwon Cho, Frances E. Dolan, Rina Lahav, Jenna Lay, Laurence Lux-Sterritt, Carmen M. Mangion, Querciolo Mazzonis, Marit Monteiro, Elizabeth Rhodes, Kate Stogdon and Anna Welch.

Laurence Lux-Sterritt is Lecturer in British History at the University of Aix-Marseille. She is the author of *Redefining Female Religious Life* (2005).

Carmen M. Mangion is Honorary Research Fellow at Birkbeck College, University of London. Her publications include *Contested Identities: Catholic Women Religious in Nineteenth-Century England and Wales* (2008).

D1612571

Gender and History

Series editors: Amanda Capern and Louella McCarthy

Published

Ann Taylor Allen	*Women in Twentieth-Century Europe*
Trev Lynn Broughton and	
Helen Rogers (eds)	*Gender and Fatherhood in the Nineteenth Century*
Krista Cowman	*Women in British Politics c. 1689–1979*
Shani D'Cruze and Louise A. Jackson	*Women, Crime and Justice in England since 1660*
William Henry Foster	*Gender, Mastery and Slavery: From European to Atlantic World Frontiers*
Rachel G. Fuchs and	
Victoria E. Thompson	*Women in Nineteenth-Century Europe*
Laurence Lux-Sterritt and	
Carmen Mangion (eds)	*Gender, Catholicism and Spirituality: Women and the Roman Catholic Church in Britain and Europe, 1200–1900*
Perry Willson	*Women in Twentieth-Century Italy*
Angela Woollacott	*Gender and Empire*

Forthcoming

Paul Bailey	*Women and Gender in Twentieth-Century China*
Ana Carden-Coyne	*Gender and Conflict since 1914*
Natasha Hodgson	*Gender and the Crusades*

Gender and History Series
Series Standing Order ISBN 978–14039–9374–8 hardback
(outside North America only)

You can receive future titles in this series as they are published by placing a standing order. Please contact your bookseller or, in case of difficulty, write to us at the address below with your name and address, the title of the series and the ISBN quoted above.

Customer Services Department, Macmillan Distribution Ltd

Gender, Catholicism and Spirituality

Women and the Roman Catholic Church in Britain and Europe, 1200–1900

Edited by

LAURENCE LUX-STERRITT

and

CARMEN M. MANGION

Selection, editorial matter and Introduction © Laurence Lux-Sterritt and Carmen M. Mangion 2011. Individual chapters (in order) © Anna Welch; Rina Lahav; Querciolo Mazzonis; Elizabeth Rhodes; Laurence Lux-Sterritt; Jenna Lay; Marit Monteiro; Nancy Jiwon Cho; Kate Stogdon; Carmen M. Mangion; Frances E. Dolan 2011.

All rights reserved. No reproduction, copy or transmission of this publication may be made without written permission.

No portion of this publication may be reproduced, copied or transmitted save with written permission or in accordance with the provisions of the Copyright, Designs and Patents Act 1988, or under the terms of any licence permitting limited copying issued by the Copyright Licensing Agency, Saffron House, 6–10 Kirby Street, London EC1N 8TS.

Any person who does any unauthorized act in relation to this publication may be liable to criminal prosecution and civil claims for damages.

The authors have asserted their rights to be identified as the authors of this work in accordance with the Copyright, Designs and Patents Act 1988.

First published 2011 by
PALGRAVE MACMILLAN

Palgrave Macmillan in the UK is an imprint of Macmillan Publishers Limited, registered in England, company number 785998, of Houndmills, Basingstoke, Hampshire RG21 6XS.

Palgrave Macmillan in the US is a division of St Martin's Press LLC, 175 Fifth Avenue, New York, NY 10010.

Palgrave Macmillan is the global academic imprint of the above companies and has companies and representatives throughout the world.

Palgrave® and Macmillan® are registered trademarks in the United States, the United Kingdom, Europe and other countries.

ISBN 978–0–230–57760–2   hardback
ISBN 978–0–230–57761–9   paperback

This book is printed on paper suitable for recycling and made from fully managed and sustained forest sources. Logging, pulping and manufacturing processes are expected to conform to the environmental regulations of the country of origin.

A catalogue record for this book is available from the British Library.

A catalog record for this book is available from the Library of Congress.

10   9   8   7   6   5   4   3   2   1
20   19   18   17   16   15   14   13   12   11

Printed in China

Gender, Catholicism and Spirituality is dedicated to
Marie Cariani (1919–1988)
and
Sharon Torick Stewart (1962–2008)

Contents

List of Figures

Acknowledgements

When we began to discuss the possibilities of an edited collection on Roman Catholic women's spiritualities in 2006, the task seemed daunting. We owe a great deal of thanks to Claire Renkin and Katherine Massam, who were generous enough to share with us some of the fruits of their 2007 Melbourne conference on 'The Spirituality of Religious Women: From the Old World to the Antipodes, 1400–1900'. We approached those speakers whose remit seemed to mesh well with the parameters of this edited collection and solicited other historians within our own networks to give this volume the desired geographical and chronological depth. We are thankful to these authors for their patience during the numerous starts and stops that have punctuated this project. Although finding the right palette of European experiences and balancing that with periodicity provided more of a challenge than we had bargained for, we are pleased to have nurtured essays from a geographically diverse group of scholars who function in various disciplines and address the themes of gender, Catholicism and spirituality from the medieval to the modern period in England, France, Italy, the Netherlands and Spain.

We have accumulated many collegial debts along the way. The intellection process of bringing together an edited collection of this scope made it necessary to gather a panel of academic experts to review and critique each essay. Despite their busy schedules, they readily agreed to read various essay drafts and generously gave our authors thoughtful feedback. They have made us more confident in those areas that were not necessarily our expertise and added great value to the essays. On our behalf, and on behalf of the authors, we would like to thank: Gillian Ahlgren, Caroline Bowden, Claire Cross, Kimm Curran, Sylvia Evangelisti, Julian Haseldine, Peter Howard, Andrew Jotischky, S. Karly Kehoe, James Kelly, Phil Kilroy, Judith Lancaster, Rosa MacGinley, Sue Morgan, Susan Mumm, Michael Questier, Glyn Redworth, Joos van Vugt, Claire Walker, Alison Weber and Elizabeth West.

Throughout this process, we found a supportive team at Palgrave. Sonya Barker as Commissioning Editor shepherded the project and fielded numerous queries, while series editors Amanda Capern and Louella McCarthy guided us through the challenges of editing an interdisciplinary text.

Family and friends were often an integral part of the process of bringing us back to earth when the intensity of our teaching and research responsibilities were making it difficult for us to see the forest through the trees. We are thankful for their patience and good will. However our special appreciation goes to Rich Wagner for an unending supply of love and support and to Simon Sterritt for his constancy, his humour and his ability to see the glass half full.

The editors and publisher wish to thank the following for permission to reproduce the following material in the chapter by Nancy Jiwon Cho:

Society of the Holy Child Jesus (charity reg. no. 223035), for permission to reproduce the hymn 'I am a little Catholic' by Mother Maria Joseph (born Elizabeth) Buckle;

The Sisters of Notre Dame de Namur, for permission to reproduce lines from the hymns, 'Martyrs of England! Standing on high!' and 'To Venerable Margaret Clitheroe (Martyr)' by Sister M.X. (Sybil Farish Partridge).

Every effort has been made to trace the copyright holders but if any have been inadvertently overlooked the publishers will be pleased to make the necessary arrangements at the first opportunity.

List of Contributors

Nancy Jiwon Cho's research is located in the intersection of literature, gender and religion during the long nineteenth century. She is a Visiting Research Professor in English at Seoul National University. She has been a postdoctoral research fellow in English at Nottingham Trent University working on the life and prophetic writings of Dorothy Gott (1748–1812). Her PhD in English Studies (thesis entitled: 'The Ministry of Song: Unmarried British Women's Hymn Writing, 1760–1936') was awarded by Durham University in 2007. She is a Fellow of the Oxford Centre for Christianity and Culture at Regent's Park College, Oxford, and a research assistant working on the *Canterbury Dictionary of Hymnology* (c. 2010) Project at Durham University. She has published journal articles on Anne Steele, Amy Carmichael, Dorothy Gott and late-Georgian women's millennial writing, and women hymn-writers' use of metre.

Frances E. Dolan is Professor of English at the University of California, Davis. She is the author of *Whores of Babylon: Gender, Catholicism, and Seventeenth-Century Print Culture* (1999), as well as *Marriage and Violence: The Early Modern Legacy* (2008) and *Dangerous Familiars: Representations of Domestic Crime in England, 1550–1700* (1994). She has published numerous articles on early modern Catholicism and anti-Catholicism in collections and journals, including essays on Catholic women's biographies (in *English Literary Renaissance*), why nuns are found funny (in the *Huntington Library Quarterly*), the gendering of Catholic space (in the *Journal of Interdisciplinary History*), attempts to blame Catholics for the Great Fire of London (in the *Journal of Medieval and Early Modern Studies*), the association of witchcraft with Catholicism (in *differences*) and Catholicism as the undead (in *The Impact of Feminism in English Renaissance Studies*, ed. Dympna Callaghan).

Rina Lahav is a PhD student at Monash University, looking into the personal history of Marguerite Porete and especially her trial. Her research interests include the monastic experience and specifically the fathers of the desert. She holds a B.A. in Israeli Studies and Comparative Literature and a Tour Guide diploma from Haifa University. She has held positions as a museum research assistant and manager of the Archaeological & Historical Museum of Kfar-Saba, Israel, where she was responsible for creating and maintaining contacts with relevant scientists, conducting research and developing exhibition tools and educational programmes.

Jenna Lay is an assistant professor in the English Department at Lehigh University, Pennsylvania. She received her PhD in English Literature from Stanford University in 2009. Her first book project, *Beyond the Cloister: Catholic Englishwomen and*

Early Modern Book Culture, explores the role of English nuns and recusant women in the development of early modern literary history. The archival work for this project has been supported by fellowships from Stanford University, the Institute for Historical Research, the Huntington Library and the Renaissance Society of America. Her research and teaching interests include early modern religious politics, women's writing, book history and post-Restoration republicanism.

Laurence Lux-Sterritt is a lecturer in British History at the University of Aix-Marseille. Her work focuses particularly upon a comparative analysis of female Catholic endeavours in early modern England and France. She obtained her PhD in History at the University of Lancaster, UK, with her thesis 'Soldiers of God: Aspects of Female Involvement in the Catholic Reformation in England and France, 1604–1685', and she is the author of *Redefining Female Religious Life: French Ursulines and English Ladies in Seventeenth Century Catholicism* (Ashgate, 2005). She has published various articles in English and in French, exploring such issues as the governance, spirituality and missionary involvement of both the Ignatian Institute founded by the Yorkshire woman Mary Ward (1585–1645) and the French teaching Order of the Ursulines. She is currently working on recusancy and especially on the place of women in Protestant representations of Catholicism.

Carmen M. Mangion's research focuses on the history of nineteenth-century Britain, concentrating on gender and religion. Her current research looks at nineteenth-century British women religious, Catholicism and healthcare, using faith and philanthropy as frameworks to study the development of Catholic healthcare. She has published several chapters, essays and book reviews on women and religion in nineteenth-century Britain and Ireland, and her book *Contested Identities: Catholic Women Religious in Nineteenth-century England and Wales* was published by Manchester University Press in 2008. She is also co-organizer of the History of Women Religious of Britain and Ireland (H-WRBI), a vibrant international research network connected via an electronic list and a website which acts as a research portal. She holds an honorary research fellowship at Birkbeck College, University of London.

Querciolo Mazzonis is a Lecturer in History at the Università degli Studi di Teramo. He received his degree from the University of Rome 'La Sapienza' in 1990. In 1998 he was awarded the Isobel Thornley Research Fellowship at the Institute of Historical Research, University of London, and in 1999 he completed his PhD in History at Royal Holloway, University of London. He then taught Early Modern European History in several universities in England, Ireland and Italy. His research focuses on religious mentality in the sixteenth century, and in particular on female spirituality, which he studies through a cultural perspective. He is author of *Spirituality, Gender and the Self in Renaissance Italy: Angela Merici and the Company of St. Ursula (1474–1540)* (Catholic University of America Press 2007, also published in Italian) and of a number of articles in English and Italian journals. He is currently working on a project on the spirituality of some male and female protagonists of the so-called 'Catholic Reformation'.

Marit Monteiro is full professor in the History of Dutch Catholicism at the Faculty of Arts of the Radboud University Nijmegen. She specializes in the history of religious institutes, as well as in the fields of confessional heritage, memory studies, gender and religion. She is project manager of the research programme 'Catholic Intellectual Vanguards: Bearers of Tradition and Modernity' (facilitated by the Dutch Ministry of Education). Her recent publications include a monumental study on the history of the Dominicans in the Netherlands, *Gods Predikers* (2008), and a co-edited volume, *Mannen Gods* (*Men of God*, 2007), that addresses the transformations of clerical culture in the Netherlands.

Elizabeth Rhodes teaches in the graduate and advanced undergraduate programme of Hispanic Studies at Boston College. Her recent publications include a translation/edition of selected tales by baroque author, María de Zayas y Sotomayor, *Exemplary Tales of Love and Tales of Disillusion* (with Margaret Greer, University of Chicago Press, 2009); a study and translation/edition of works by Catholic activist Luisa de Carvajal, *This Tight Embrace: Luisa de Carvajal y Mendoza (1566–1614)* (Marquette University Press, 2000); and an analytic overview of early modern Spanish religious culture: 'Mysticism and History: The Case of Spain's Golden Age', in *Teresa of Avila and Spanish Mysticism*, edited by Alison Weber (MLA Press, 2009, pp. 47–56). She is currently polishing a monograph on the second collection of novellas by María de Zayas and has begun a project on the lives of saints, particularly how the *vitae* of female sinner saints change across the early modern period. Her pedagogical areas of expertise include early modern Hispanic literature and culture, Hispanic film and religious culture and history.

Kate Stogdon completed her doctorate on the notion of self-surrender in the life of Thérèse Couderc at the University of Manchester in 2005. She teaches courses in theology, spirituality and pastoral formation at Birkbeck College (University of London), Education for Parish Service (St Mary's University College, Twickenham, London) and the Ignatian Spirituality Course (London). She has spent several years working as a spiritual director and trainer within the Ignatian tradition. Her recent publications include an examination of the Spiritual Exercises: 'Life, Death and Discernment: Ignatian Perspectives' in *Grace Jantzen: Redeeming the Present* edited by Elaine L. Graham (Ashgate, 2009, pp. 141–55).

Anna Welch has recently submitted her doctoral thesis, 'Franciscan Liturgy and Identities: Networks of Manuscript Production in Umbria, 1280–1350' (Melbourne College of Divinity, 2010). Funding from the Australian Province of the Order of Friars Minor, an Australian Postgraduate Award and a postgraduate fellowship from the Australian European University Institute Fellowship Association Inc. (AEUIFAI) supported the research for this dissertation. Her research interests include thirteenth- and fourteenth-century Umbrian Franciscan Liturgy and manuscripts, early visual and textual representations of Francis of Assisi's stigmata, constructions of communal religious identity, material history and museum studies.

Preface

This volume emerged from the realization that the history of women religious[1] was attracting the interest of an increasing number of scholars. We noticed the steady growth of the History of Women Religious of Britain and Ireland (H-WRBI), a network of scholars initiated by Carmen Mangion and Caroline Bowden in 2001 to encourage research in the history of women religious.[2] Their annual conferences are consistently well attended and gather scholars from all parts of the globe. Recently, other major conferences have testified to the vigour of research in women's spirituality. Claire Renkin and Katherine Massam's 2007 conference in Melbourne (Australia) focused on 'The Spirituality of Religious Women: From the Old World to the Antipodes, 1400–1900'. In 2009, Sarah Apetrei and Hannah Smith organized a conference on 'Women and Religion in Britain c. 1660–1760' in Oxford (UK), while Laurence Lux-Sterritt and Claire Sorin welcomed over 40 speakers from 13 countries to speak on 'Women and Spirituality' in Aix-en-Provence (France).

Noticing the efflorescence of research in this field did, in turn, raise questions on how to place our own work within the history of European Catholic women's spirituality over the *longue durée*. We became curious about overarching themes which could apply to the study of female roles within the Catholic Church in the varied circumstances of their countries and times. What were the continuities and discontinuities that influenced, hindered and spurred on women whose spirituality became the core of their many identities? This collective publication, which federates the efforts of academics and specialists in this field, provides some revealing insights into the factors which affected the relationships of Catholic women with their Church; it shows that female spirituality was not isolated by national contexts, but rather influenced by the passage of time as well as shifting understandings of gender. Contributors utilize a mix of sources, including liturgical manuscripts, devotional texts, prescriptive literature, biographies, autobiographies, correspondence and hymns. They approach the investigation of gender, spirituality and Catholicism from varied vantage points and methodologies, which provides an interdisciplinary lens that highlights insights into the diverse dimensions of spiritualities. These varied outlooks include post-structural analysis and textual archaeology as well as liturgical, cultural, Church and gender history, and allow for a fuller understanding of the interplay at work between femininities and spiritualities in Britain and Europe.

Note that terms in the glossary are shown in **bold** on their first appearance in each chapter.

Notes

1. Women religious is the term used to refer to both contemplative nuns, who took solemn vows and lived a life of prayer within an enclosed community, and active sisters, who took simple vows and whose apostolic work, typically teaching or nursing, occurred outside convent walls.
2. Their website is located at http://www.rhul.ac.uk/Bedford-Centre/history-women-religious/.

Introduction: Gender, Catholicism and Women's Spirituality over the *Longue Durée*

Laurence Lux-Sterritt and Carmen M. Mangion

Derived from St Paul's reference to 'spiritual persons' as those 'influenced by the Holy Spirit of God',[1] the term spirituality became linked to seventeenth-century French spiritual writers and clergy. In subsequent centuries, the general understanding of spirituality became increasingly non-denominational. Today, spirituality is broadly understood to give meaning and purpose to life and to provide a transcendental experience to those in search of the sacred. It can be attained through meditation, prayer or communion with the natural world. This transcendence can lead to a sense of connectedness with something greater than oneself, such as nature, the universe or a higher being. For some, spirituality is thoughtful and passive, while for others it is emotional or action-oriented. Notions of spirituality are not fixed, but rather culturally derived and constantly shifting, fashioned by myriad forces including gender, ethnicity and class. Since spirituality mirrors specific times, places and cultures, it can be used as an analytic tool to examine various facets of society.

Each of the ten essays gathered here focuses on specific persons or groups within the cultural milieus of England, France, Italy, the Netherlands and Spain between the thirteenth and the nineteenth centuries. Of course, we cannot hope to present in this volume an all-inclusive overview of how such complex concepts as gender and spirituality interact with the history of Catholicism, but each piece should be seen as a small contribution towards a greater under-standing of their interactions. These essays, exploring female relationships with piety and religious vocations in their various contexts, raise similar questions. It appears that, when studying the religious endeavours of women within the Catholic Church, regardless of time and place, one is confronted with issues concerning norms and margins, be they vocational, social or institutional. Authors therefore question whether or not female agents for the Church differentiated themselves from male religious, and whether they considered their strengths and failings as defined or influenced by their sex. In studying women's voluntary contributions to the Catholic Church, each chapter engages with the gendered preconceptions within which they operated. To what extent were female contributions to the Catholic Church limited by socially defined gendered acceptability? Such considerations, in turn, lead to the questioning of the relationship of these women's vocations with the (male) institutional orthodoxy of the Church they aimed to serve. Indeed, the success or failure of female movements was often decided by women's positions regarding canonical conformity, religious rules and clerical authority. Yet did success depend upon institutional orthodoxy?

The following chapters consider a denominational, Roman Catholic spirituality. Despite their varied geographical and chronological contexts, all are linked to a shifting theological vision. Moreover, our understanding of the gendered nature of spirituality and Catholicism is informed by our designation of gender as a category of analysis which allows the development of diverse observations of femininities and masculinities. Consequently, this collection of essays reflects the gendering of both women and men as spiritualities shift over time and place.[2] As can be seen in this collection, women did not confine themselves to operating within official boundaries.[3] Their faith legitimated actions which were often unconventional. The underlying tension between the authority women believed came from God and the (male) ecclesiastical view of this authority sprang partly from gendered discourses.

Gender and religious status: women in the institutional Church

Until the thirteenth century, women enjoyed a certain amount of freedom in the ways they were allowed to express their spirituality. For instance, the Flemish Mary of Oignies (1177–1213) was one of the most famous living saints, yet she was not a nun. Though married, she and her spouse consensually vowed to live together in chastity and converted their home into a leper hospital. Free from the constraints of a religious establishment, with its rules, its strict *horarium*, its **enclosure** and its male authority, Mary of Oignies was able to develop a spirituality which was flexible, in direct personal interaction with the world but also with the divine. When she quickly became renowned, it was not simply as a charitable soul whose apostolate brought much-needed succour to her neighbours, but also as a mystic and a saint who enjoyed unmediated spiritual communion with God. Her a-institutional choice of life was translated into greater spiritual freedom, a **mysticism** which allowed her – despite her status as a laywoman – to wield great influence even over clerics such as her **confessor**, and later hagiographer, Bishop Jacques de Vitry (d. 1240).[4]

Although the Catholic Church was initially benevolent towards unorthodox avenues for female spirituality, issues of control were always present. When Clare of Assisi aligned her Poor Ladies of San Damiano (later known as the Poor Clares) with the Franciscan family recently approved by Innocent III, she was perceived to borrow from male expressions of spirituality, since she assumed the ideal of absolute poverty, a new feature of religious life spearheaded by Francis of Assisi (1181–1226). This unorthodox choice met with clerical opposition and in 1215–16, Clare went directly to the pope to seek his help. In response, her Poor Clares were granted a rare papal favour, the unique Privilege of poverty, in which Innocent III recognized their right to remain in poverty in imitation of Christ. The Poor Clares were the only female Order to be able to secure such a thorough endorsement from the papacy, and to gain such protection. Such success reflected Clare's charisma and power. Yet, despite initially supporting Clare's ideal, the clergy – including Francis himself – became uncomfortable with what it entailed. Clare was to fight for the rest of her life for what she saw as the initial *raison d'être* of her Order, poverty and the imitation of Christ, against a clerical hierarchy for whom neither was appropriate as a defining trait of the Poor Clares. The decades of conflict which peppered Clare's experience testify to the difficulties which faced women whose vocation did not fit clerical definitions of acceptable female religious life. Later still, after the deaths of both Francis and Clare, the spirituality of the female Order was deeply transformed.[5] Anna Welch's chapter demonstrates that Clare's status in the Franciscan movement was muted by subsequent leaders, which reflected the lack of clarity and unity amongst the friars themselves.

Although the varied ways of life of spiritual women at times provoked the suspicion of their secular neighbours and local divines, Pope Gregory IX's 1233 bull *Glorium virginalem* offered informal religious groups a measure of papal protection, since it no longer suspected quasi-religious women of heresy. However, by the end of the century, concerns arose about the status of woman in the institutional Church. Pope Boniface VIII's 1298 decree *Periculoso* reduced the temporal power of abbesses and demanded the complete separation of religious women from the outside world.[6] Although the Bull was applied only loosely for a long period of time, it was a sign of things to come, as it reflected the Church's growing desire to contain the women in its midst through the imposition of walls, **Rules** and ecclesiastical control.[7] After several decades of relative disregard, this initial movement of conventualization was followed by a wave of inner reforms when Church officials, helped by zealous **nuns** and abbesses, attempted to impose higher standards of spirituality and purer moral values to fight the perceived slackness of certain convents. The observance of the same *horarium* and of identical Rules in daily life created a strong sense of cohesion within communities and dynamized the intensity of their spiritual lives as a group. However, as the reformed communities were placed more directly under the control of bishops and ordinaries, the powers of female governance and the convents' contacts with the outside world were subject to further erosion.[8]

Yet the relationship between male representatives of the Church and the women who sought to serve it was not always tense or confrontational. Many religious institutes adopted male-defined Rules and conditions willingly and viewed a cloistered life in contemplation, following episcopal guidance, as the most holy path to spiritual perfection. Many women never questioned increasing institutionalization and some welcomed it whole-heartedly. It is difficult to assess, over a period of several centuries, the level of resistance or compliance with which female groups encountered male control. The cloistered existence of two of the most renowned religious women studied in this volume, Clare of Assisi (1194–1253) and Teresa of Àvila (1515–82, in religion Teresa de Jesús), points to the continued attraction of an institutional life supported and encouraged by the Church. For many women, and their families, this was the most viable option of lived spirituality, and they celebrated the benefits of *clausura*. Institutional religious life represented an important connection to their Church as well as a source of authority. This fed their spirituality and allowed them to become spiritual leaders within the convent.[9]

The Protestant Reformation heralded another period of increased episcopal control over the women who wished to be recognized officially as religious. In order to offset Protestant advances, the Catholic Church implemented a two-pronged strategy. First, it embarked upon a vigorous effort of reform from within, a Catholic Reformation meant to eradicate the abuses of the Church, to purify its practice and strengthen its spirituality. Second, an aggressive missionary movement was launched as a counter-attack against the progress of Protestantism, focused on re-conquering territory and souls. Whilst many enclosed institutions, both male and female, offered their prayers as a means of religious action to further the success of the Catholic offensive against the spread of Protestantism, Ignatius Loyola founded his **Society of Jesus**, the Constitutions of which were approved in 1540 by Paul III. The **Jesuits'** mission was to catechize and proselytize in the world, focusing in great part on the education of boys and the conversion of men. They were to be soldiers of God, **regular clergy** unconfined by enclosure. Their mobility and flexibility enabled them to work effectively to re-establish the spiritual authority of Rome, and their apostolate appealed greatly to both lay and religious women.

Despite this appeal, ecclesiastical authorities were unwilling to apply a similar line of action across the boundaries of gender. Rather than open female religious life to action in the world, the Church embraced Boniface VIII's *Periculoso* when, in 1563, the Council of Trent defined **women religious** as strictly enclosed, denying them the chance of an **apostolic** mission outside the cloister: 'After religious profession no nun may go out of her monastery on any pretext even for short time, except for a legitimate reason approved by the bishop [...].'[10] This was followed by decrees crystallizing the Church's rigidity towards what it deemed acceptable for women in the institutional Church: according to Pius V's *Circa Pastoralis* (1566) and *Lubricum Vitae Genitus* (1568), enclosure was a prerequisite for female communities claiming religious status.[11]

Despite their usefulness given the disputed circumstances of sixteenth-century religious strife, women who embraced vocations which differed from this model were to remain secular. Militant apostolic work, catechesis and the salvation of souls were considered better suited for men, since women were deemed physically, morally and spiritually unable to endure the difficulties awaiting them when faced with such duties.[12] One of the main obstacles hindering women's participation in the active work of the Catholic offensive resided in the belief that women were, by nature, flawed and therefore unsuitable for such missionary ventures.[13] This combination of religious tradition and vivid suspicion of female constancy made the idea of women missionaries unacceptable to Church authorities.

Men of the Church, in their capacities as chroniclers, **spiritual directors** or administrators, often de-emphasized the multifaceted and flexible nature of female movements. As they named them, defined them as groups, sometimes even attributed male founders for them and imposed established conventual Rules upon them, they sought to keep control of female movements. As shown in Querciolo Mazzonis's chapter on Angela Merici's Italian Ursulines, unrequited clerical control could change the initial essence of female religious endeavours. Initially, Merici's lay women were responsible for their own lives, and their Company was managed by women for women. Yet issues of authority and control created tensions between the congregations and both their secular and religious neighbours. Although Angela Mericihad obtained Paul III's approval in 1544, in 1582 the Milan Archbishop Carlo Borromeo (1538–1584) reorganized the Ursulines into religious congregations where the members lived together as laywomen with an apostolic and educational focus.[14] As they spread to the rest of Italy, then France in the seventeenth century, they deviated from the religious type of life initially envisaged by Angela Merici.

The Englishwoman Mary Ward (1585–1645) encountered a similar struggle to persuade the Church to validate her proposed Institute modelled on the Society of Jesus. As Laurence Lux-Sterritt's chapter explains, even Mary Ward's Jesuit confessor Roger Lee was intimidated by her vocation: in the Rules he had penned for her in 1612, the English Ladies were to be a teaching and enclosed, not a militant, missionary cohort. Mary Ward's continued search for papal approval and her determination to apply the Ignatian Rules to her Institute led to her ultimate trial in 1631, when her English Ladies were ordered to disband and the **foundress** was labeled a heretic.

The tension between the cloister and the world has always been at the very core of monastic life; yet recent influential studies have convincingly argued that enclosure was not so hermetic as to prevent all communication between the two worlds.[15] Convents had a deep impact upon the societies in which they operated, and conversely were influenced by them too. Claire Walker's *Gender and Politics in Early Modern Europe* explores English convents in France and the Low Countries and shows that enclosed English nuns transcended the boundaries of their physical claustration: their religious vocations stemmed from the troubled context of English Catholicism. The taking of **vows** became a complex act, both spiritually intimate and very public, as a political gesture. The spirit of the English mission was present at the heart of spiritual life, since these houses constantly evoked the sufferings of their coreligionists at home. The same was true of the aristocratic nuns of Naples discussed by Hills in *Invisible City*, though sometimes enclosed to suit their families' economic circumstances, these women's influence went further than the thick walls of their convents and they enjoyed a certain authority in the city.

Therefore, as noted in *Nuns: A History of Convent Life*, general debates over issues such as monastic observance or strict enclosure were influenced by the varied local circumstances of each convent.[16] Local conditions invariably influenced life in religious houses and softened the Tridentine spirit of uniform *clausura* with more nuanced realities, leading at times to a rather more flexible model of female monastic life. With time, papal attitudes slowly shifted to take into account the achievements of women who, through their work outside the cloister, emerged as successful Christian missionaries. Yet this evolution was not straightforward, and did not willingly concede religious status to these pious workers. In his 1727 *Pretiosus*, Pope Benedict XIII gave his approbation to women who took simple vows and appeared outside convent walls; but if this edict allowed tertiaries to exist, it pointedly ignored the issue of religious status. Later, in *Romanus Pontifex* (1732), Benedict XIII reversed *Pretiosus* and insisted that religious status for women implied strict separation from the world.[17]

Despite papal hesitations, lay and clerical support for women religious living religious life outside the cloister became more encouraging by the eighteenth century. This support was based on the practical needs of a parish or a diocese, as simple-vowed women religious provided much-needed education, health care and parish assistance. Recent research on eighteenth-century French women religious asserts that their institutions, charity schools, nursing homes and hospitals, were tolerated and encouraged for pragmatic reasons: they filled a need.[18] Rome's acceptance of simple-vowed women religious was reflected in *Quamvis Justo* (1749), which gave women's religious congregations legitimate and juridical authority although their members were not considered 'true nuns'.[19] As Laurence Lux-Sterritt's essay establishes, such times offered Mary Ward's eighteenth-century successors a welcome window of opportunity: they negotiated with Rome and gained approval as an enclosed Institute, accepting traditional conventual hierarchy and ecclesiastical control. When they became devoted to the education of girls, they endorsed a role which the Church deemed better suited to women, but in so doing they created a community which diverged greatly from Mary Ward's initial ideals.[20]

Gender and forms of religious life: multifarious female organizations

The historiography of female Catholic spiritualities illustrates that women's expressions of piety have tended, across the ages, to take less institutional forms than those of their male counterparts.[21] As Caroline Walker Bynum explained:

> the basic characteristics of women's piety cut across the lines between lay and monastic, heterodox and orthodox, churchly and sectarian. Although women were found in all institutions – Church, monastery and sect – their mystical, charismatic piety seemed to express itself most comfortably in amorphous groups, such as beguine or tertiary communities, or in friendship networks within religious houses.[22]

Indeed, since the Church was embodied by its male clergy, women were to some extent excluded, and even those who most wished to serve the Church would never be part of it in the same way as men. Women's piety expressed itself in modes which bypassed male institutional forms, and resisted external pressures towards institutionalization.

As shown in *Sisters in Arms*, despite the Church's attempts at controlling female religious life, the avenues chosen by Catholic women remained, through the ages, extremely varied, nuanced and difficult to categorize neatly.[23] The labels which helped categorize women religious into enclosed nuns, recluses, tertiaries or lay **sisters** did not encompass the variety of female religious identities, and women's endeavours often blurred clerically given theoretical definitions. In keeping with this seemingly adaptable, flexible nature which centred on experience rather than structure, female organizations often seemed less preoccupied by their religious status than by a personal dedication to God and to the Church. Their outlook reintroduced the self at the core on their relationship with the divine, giving an important place to self-surrender and mysticism as privileged vectors of their experience of the sacred.

Indeed, not all religiously inclined women entered the convent: some were married, others were widows, whilst others still, remaining single, preferred to serve the Church from outside its ranks, in a secular capacity. The reasons for such choices were varied, sometimes linked to a refusal by cloistered institutions, at other times owing to more pragmatic considerations linked to property ownership. The Italian Angela Merici (c. 1470–1540) first founded her Ursulines as a community of secular women, serving the Church and the community outside the convent and without clerical control. Querciolo Mazzonis's chapter illustrates that, as spiritual laywomen, the Ursulines' 'third status' remained somewhat vague. Yet since their roles did not compete with male institutional roles, they gained papal approval in 1546. Merici's original idea of a female laity 'free to follow their personal inspiration' gave women a new space to develop their spirituality outside the traditional '*aut maritus, aut murus*', a husband or a cloister. These women were offered a degree of religious freedom more associated with a-institutional structures than with Rule-oriented religious Orders.

In the sixteenth century, the confessional crisis of the Reformation created a new environment in which female religious life rapidly acquired 'distinct configurations responding to the new circumstances'.[24] A specifically female type of active, uncloistered spiritual existence developed to such an extent that it became a feature of Catholic social and religious life by the seventeenth century. In the Netherlands, the religious movement of *Devotio Moderna* gave rise to the Sisters of the Common Life, who lived together bound by a private promise.[25] Moreover, some spiritual women chose a-institutional forms which were neither cloistered nor communal, neither nuns nor **beguines**, but operated on a more independent level, one that required the balancing of diverse roles. Yet these **spiritual virgins** did not count themselves as part of the laity, but rather as part of the Church. As both spiritual daughters and spiritual mothers, Dutch spiritual virgins had to manoeuvre delicately between obedience and authority, balancing sometimes conflicting responsibilities.

The paradox of submission which Monteiro identifies is an important feature in many of the essays in this collection. The institutional Church relegated religious women as subordinate to religious men, and reminded them of this through prescriptive literature which gendered ideals such as obedience and submission as feminine. Yet religious women used their faith to create for themselves a measure of authority and a mode of action by creating a-institutional cohorts. These forms of actions were not without gendered boundaries, but within those boundaries women had latitude to be both spiritual and temporal leaders. Unlike women religious, they did not cling to the visible signs and symbols of institutional recognition. Their spirituality was fluid and less constrained by the requirements of the Church.

In France, the *filles séculieres* (single laywomen who practised a religious lifestyle in the world) became educators, nurses and catechists, and lived in communities; yet they took only simple vows, since their unenclosed apostolate differentiated them from the solemn-vowed contemplative Orders. Apostolic, charitable vocations soon came to be construed as a typically female form of involvement in the service of the Church. By the eighteenth-century, Italian 'lay congregations' such as *Maestre Pie*, or 'Pious schoolmistresses', formed a bridge between new and old forms of religious life and were precursors to the congregations of the nineteenth century.[26] Many founders in the late eighteenth and nineteenth century were like Thérèse Couderc (1805–1885), whose experience of the French Revolution informed her passion for what she saw as the 'work of the Lord'. As Kate Stogdon demonstrates, Couderc and her Sisters of Our Lady of the Retreat in the Cenacle sought to 're-construct and re-invigorate Roman Catholicism' in France.[27]

The amorphous groups and communities that emerged gave women opportunities to practise their devotion together without entering recognized convents. Such groups sometimes gathered single women, virgins and widows only, whilst others accepted married women. These cohorts did not feel the need to answer to a precise name, to pay deference to a specific founder or figure of authority, or to observe strict rules. They existed purely to allow women of a spiritual nature to dedicate themselves to their faith through the practice of charity, and a life of apostolate action was at the core of their lived spiritual experience, whilst a corporate identity remained relatively unimportant. Yet despite these women's dedication to the Church, Rome and the ecclesiastical hierarchy remained ambivalent about them.[28]

The essays in this volume show that female forms of religious life escape classification and boundaries. Not only do they appear to defy Church definitions which differentiated between religious and secular, they also blurred the boundaries between action and contemplation and transcended geographical determinism. The influential *La sainteté en Occident*[29] proposed a typology of medieval sainthood which was defined geographically. It presented a North/ South dichotomy according to which nearly all northern European saints came from an aristocratic background and extolled virtues such as austerity and separation from the world. In southern Europe sainthood took on a less elitist face; sanctity was granted to more popular, often urban figures who generally were actively involved in the apostolate and charitable works.

Although this theory was also endorsed by the authors of *Saints and Society*,[30] it has since been challenged by Caroline Walker Bynum, who argues that northern women did not always embrace the more reclusive forms of piety by becoming nuns, contemplatives or mystics and rejecting the world; conversely, she shows that not all southern women worked in the world and dedicated their piety to others in their active, neighbourly apostolate as tertiaries. In agreement with this interpretation, this volume argues that female forms of religious life escape attempts to reduce them to categories or binary classifications. Bynum rehabilitates the under-studied functions of religious or quasi-religious women who combined the roles of both Martha and Mary, valuing forms of contemplation and mystical life whilst at the same time extending their apostolate and charity in the world. Therefore, the model presented by the Low Country beguines 'raise[s] doubts both about the north/south dichotomy and about the innerworldly-active/world-fleeing-contemplative dichotomy'.[31] In the thirteenth and fourteenth centuries, the same region had witnessed the development of the beguinages, informal communities of women who chose to live together whilst retaining their secular freedom.[32]

The essays contained in this volume come to a similar conclusion with regards to the dichotomy of action and contemplation. The female movements studied here tend to support Bynum's conclusion that 'in the women's self-understanding, there is in general no contrast between action in the world and contemplation (or discipline) that flees the world.'[33] The case studies offered, which span both northern and southern Europe and Britain over the *longue durée*, highlight how even nuns who accepted and treasured claustration as holy nevertheless considered themselves as active through their writings, their prayers and their devotions.[34] Conversely, active women also cherished contemplative elements of their lives and spent much time in prayer and communion with the divine. The roles of Martha and of Mary seemed intertwined rather than mutually exclusive.

As echoed in the chapters of this collection, the active impetus which was already present from the early modern era in female Catholic spiritualities intensified with time, and although its gradual acceptance was subject to variations in different countries or regions, by the nineteenth century the 'mixed life' of active spirituality had become more commonplace. Active women in this era of the nun[35] were credited for the development of a distinctly Catholic spiritual ethos promulgated through their schools, orphanages, reformatories and hospitals. In France, female religious associations, both religious and lay, were among most characteristic forms of female religiosity in the first half of the nineteenth century and were in the forefront in providing welfare services.[36] Convent networks made 'the most profound impact on the provision of charity' in Ireland.[37] In Spain, the resurgence of women religious occurred in the last quarter of the century, but they also became the 'unrivalled spearhead of Catholic revival'.[38]

The tension between a Jesuit-like vocation and a more gendered (and clerically acceptable) educational sphere of activity was a common pattern in innovative female endeavours. It affected various groups, including the Cenacle Sisters, who in the nineteenth century incorporated the Jesuit *Spiritual Exercises* as a foundation for their own spiritual life and also employed them in retreats given to women. This was a new domain of apostolic ministry; no other female congregation had ever given the *Spiritual Exercises* in France. The death of the congregation's male co-founder put their endeavours at risk of failure. Founder Thérèse Couderc was aware that male support was necessary for this new venture to succeed, especially since such work could be construed as an infringement upon ministerial responsibilities and a possible trespass on the work of male clergy. In 1836, she successfully defended this vocation against some of her sisters who, supported by local clergy, wished to steer away from their Ignatian undertakings and prioritize the education of girls.

Indeed, by the nineteenth century, the need to catechize, to teach and to nurse was unremitting, and this work became integrated with the spirituality of simple-vowed women religious. Religious congregations became the foot soldiers of Rome as the practical needs of the Church far outweighed some gendered limitations of femininity. In nineteenth-century Italy there was an explosion of women's groups active in the welfare and education of poor girls, linked by a 'powerful need for community and solidarity'. Many were trans-formed into active religious congregations such as the Servants of Charity in Brescia (1844) or the Canossian Daughters of Charity in Verona (1808), whose remit was to form 'good, Christian mothers'. Between 1800 and 1860, at least 127 new foundations were approved in Italy.[39]

Yet, as Carmen Mangion's chapter argues, prayer remained the core of this 'mixed life', but balancing the contemplative with the active required constant attention. There were those, from both within and without the convent, who saw the 'mixed' life as too contemplative and others who saw it as too utilitarian. Yet, action was construed as a pathway towards sanctity, and for the Church, active religious life was an important means of re-Catholicizing the masses of unchurched Catholics. Interestingly, much of the nineteenth-century historiography of female laity and religious focuses less on spirituality *per se* than on the charitable features influenced by a robust Catholic faith. This reflects the dominance of social and cultural studies but perhaps also is symptomatic of the perceived a-historicism of religion and spirituality.

However, freedom from the cloister did not necessarily lead to a more flex-ible understanding of spirituality. As congregations grew in size, their missions expanded and cloistered walls were replaced by an invisible cloister, a strict morality codified in Rules and constitutions. Though imposed by the Church, these strictures were endorsed by women's congregations. Carmen Mangion's chapter explains that after their founder's death the Sisters of Mercy were not content with a simple Rule and constitutions but implemented a guide which included more complex regulations to monitor religious life and encourage uniformity. The addition of Rule upon Rule increased the distance between the religious sisters themselves, and separated them also from their charges and co-workers. Prayer life was strictly defined and timed, as were all aspects of religious life; these changes met with clerical approval and were confirmed with the codification of canon law in 1917.

Gender and spiritual expressions: the authority of female piety and writings

The essays in this volume show the complex realities of Catholic female spiritualities: they illustrate how women involved in important religious endeavours could be secular or religious, active or contemplative, northern or southern European. Yet more importantly, they also demonstrate that these female movements escape such classifications or binary definitions, since they often reconciled modes of spirituality which they did not see as antithetical but rather as complementary. The outward configurations which female religious groups adopted expressed their religious spirit, one which was less preoccupied with status or propriety than with efficacy. These women sought to further the faith, and to contribute to the broad mission of their Church; as individuals, rather than institutions, they offered their services to God in a manner which was not always mediated by male clerical input. The essays in this volume all agree that female piety in many ways bypassed clerically imposed rules, structures, vows or hierarchy. In their individual religious endeavours, women often claimed to obey the revealed will of God, and referred to a mystical closeness with the divine. Indeed, a tradition of female mystics, prophets and visionaries was already well established in the thirteenth century. For instance, Mechtild of Magdeburg (1207–82), as a beguine, had written *The Flowing Light of the Godhead* to describe how she was filled with God's presence from the age of 12. The avenue of mysticism, buttressed by the Mendicant Orders, offered opportunities for female piety increasingly to differentiate itself from men's, favouring a direct rapport with the divine. Famous figures of medieval mysticism, such as the recluse Benedictine Julian of Norwich (1342–1416), voiced their intimate relationship with the divine: in her *Relevations of Divine Love*, or *Showings*, Julian recorded the visions she received in May 1373 and insisted upon the unmediated nature of her relationship with God. Distinct from theologians of her time, she emphasized the human nature of God. Thus comforted by her faith in a kind and loving God, she suggested that Christians must surrender their souls to God in their quest for divine presence. This philosophy of hope, love and self-surrender was shared by many of the prominent women considered in this collection.

The spiritual women studied in this volume illustrate the importance of mysticism in the female experience of the divine. Clare of Assisi, even before meeting Francis, had already acquired a reputation as a mystic, dedicating much of her time to contemplation, meditation and prayer; her deep conviction that her vocation was the will of God gave her the strength to struggle against all opposition to see her Franciscan ideal accepted. Similarly, Frenchwoman Marguerite Porete (c.1250–1310) wrote her *Mirror of Simple Annihilated Souls* in order to convey to others the lights she claimed she had received directly from God; she did not present herself as the self-willed author of the book, but rather, as Rina Lahav's chapter reveals, 'as an annihilated self which ha[d] become the vessel of God's message'. Not unlike Clare of Assisi, Porete refused to stop pursuing her religious goals, and did not hesitate to disregard ecclesiastic censorship in order to be true to what she saw as her Godly duty to proselytize.

The motif of mystical revelation is problematic, since self-surrender to the perceived will of God could become the very cornerstone of female resistance to male authority. Women who, when speaking in their own names, self-consciously acknowledged the normative feminine ideals which subordinated them to the authority of clerics, became much less pliable when invested with what they saw as a divine mission. The language of self-surrender could be used as a discursive tool to deflect criticism or perhaps exhibit agency. In Spain, Teresa de Jesús's writings testified to her direct knowledge of God and edified not only her female followers but also her spiritual director and the clerics who surrounded her. Using what one literary scholar has called her 'pragmatic stylistics', she subtly turned the tables on the perceived spiritual weakness of women, in order to make it an asset.[40] Teresa claimed that, since a woman's judgement was indeed feeble, she needed God's direct guidance. Therefore, when she obeyed His commands, all opposition was bound to be futile or misdirected.

Such convictions were to be found across Europe. Mary Ward's endeavours for the recatholicization of England following the Ignatian model found their source in a series of visions culminating in 1611 with what she described as the divine commandment to 'Take the Same of the Society' (in other words to imitate the Ignatians as faithfully as possible).[41] It was this revelation which gave her the determination to struggle against much opposition to see her Society of Jesus for women established and recognized, since such was the will of God. Mary Ward described the feelings that compelled her, almost against her will, to leave behind the ideal of the so-called perfect life of monastic contemplation and forsake her personal inclinations in a gesture of self-offering.[42] Although the path indicated to her was not one which she had spontaneously chosen, she resolved to embrace it as her godly duty, and would not hear clerical injunctions to abandon her mission.

Such rhetoric of empowerment through mystical self-surrender was typically feminine and it persisted, although it became rarer, into the nineteenth century. Kate Stogdon's chapter demonstrates that in France Thérèse Couderc used the motif of self-surrender to challenge ecclesial responses to her requests when she disagreed with the nature of the response. Couderc used the language of obedience and humility but remained insistent that the work of the congregation, giving retreats, needed guidance not from diocesan priests, but from the Jesuits.[43]

Over the chronological span of this volume, the female spiritual voice was to be subject to increasing attempts at clerical control. Women's mysticism became the object of suspicion, especially after the confessional crisis of the sixteenth century when the developments of the Protestant Reformation:

> led ecclesiastical figures to rally to the defence of their institutions, deflected the attention of many members of religious orders from promoting the cult of the 'living saint' to the doctrinal controversy, and increased caution in preaching and in publicizing visions and spiritual doctrines that would soon come to seem suspect.[44]

Following both the Enlightenment's dedication to reason and the Catholic Church's efforts to contain modes of spirituality which evaded its control, the status of mysticism gradually diminished. Although forms of female mysticism survived into the nineteenth and even the twentieth centuries, they did not enjoy the same kudos as in centuries past, and were neither celebrated nor publicized. The mystic visions and revelations of women such as Mary Potter (1847–1913), founder of the Little Company of Mary, were dismissed by otherwise supportive clergy as 'bouts of imagination'.[45]

As the essays in this collection affirm, many women upset the gendered preconceptions and role-distributions of their age when they defended their religious writings or their apostolic works. Church authorities were unsettled by the unmediated nature of their expressions of piety, which sometimes bypassed its control or usurped the perceived preserves of the clergy. Hence, women's choices in their modes of spiritual experience came under close scrutiny.

Women's religious writings and teachings were particularly subject to caution; those who did not gain clerical support were to face insurmountable difficulties, trials, and sometimes condemnation.[46] As Rina Lahav's chapter shows, Marguerite Porete had chosen to write her *Mirror of Simple Annihilated Souls* using the form of a sermon. As she aimed to edify her audience, she followed typical prescriptions in sermon writing, and in so doing she contravened several of the Church's conventions. Here was a woman who flouted the Pauline decree against women speaking publicly on religious subjects; moreover, what she taught was the result of her own immediate experience of God, and was not approved by Church officials. Finally, and perhaps even more importantly, she had used 'male' means of instructing. Porete therefore challenged gender norms: she not only altered traditional exegesis to fit her new theology, which in itself threatened the teachings of the Church, but did this using a typically clerical standard of expression, the formulaic sermon. Yet Porete did not seem to accept the gendered limitations imposed upon her work, and she defended her right to speak in public. When her work was condemned by the **Inquisition**, she refused to stop her teaching. For refusing to heed the Pauline order enjoining women to be silent, and for transgressing perceived female religious limitations, she paid the ultimate price and was executed in 1310.

In the context of the so-called Counter-Reformation, Mary Ward also believed that her divine revelations empowered her to speak and act despite the social and religious restrictions imposed upon women. Her uncompromising stance regarding the capabilities of the female self lends itself to a radical understanding of the agency of women. Ward identified women's abilities and failings and saw them as no different from men's. She wrote: 'There is no such difference between men and women, that women may not do great matters, as we have seen by the example of many Saints who have done great things, and I hope in God it will be seen that women in time to come will do much.'[47] Clearly, she saw no issue with women's agency, autonomy and leadership, especially in the urgent circumstances of the Catholic struggle against Protestant progress.

Ward's subordinating of gendered limitations to pragmatic efficacy in times of crisis echoed the famous words of one she would have recognized as a female exemplar, the Spanish Teresa de Jesús. Even as a recognized mystic, Teresa de Jesús required male approval for her writings, although they were directed at her female subordinates and aimed to teach and inspire other women. In the *Way to Perfection*, Teresa defended women's spiritual rights, reminding her readers that Jesus gave women as much love as he did men, and even credited them with more faith. Empowered by her direct, mystical 'knowledge of God', she used her authoritative voice to share her knowledge with religious men. She denounced men's despotism over the religious endeavours of women, which she claimed went contrary to God's will: 'I see that times are so bad that it is not right to reject virtuous and strong spirits, even if they be women.' These words are highly reminiscent of those written by Mary Ward in the seventeenth century. Yet, as Elizabeth Rhodes's chapter demonstrates, Teresa went further than to claim the recognition of female worth in the Church: she actually critiqued male spiritual guidance, which she argued led to risks to the souls of women. She criticized their lack of confidentiality (which if gendered female would be identified as gossiping) and pointed out their need for humility in accepting God's will when they were not favoured with spiritual gifts. She actively attempted to redefine masculinity by transmitting her spiritual values to men. In leaving this book as a legacy to her sisters, she was expecting them also to play a role in the 'management of masculinity'.

Yet Teresa was ever cautious when she dealt with the religious politics of gender: aware of gendered constraints imposed upon female religious writing, she used 'a pattern of linguistic choice motivated by deliberate strategies and constrained by social roles'.[48] By appropriating what male authorities defined as the acceptable language of women, a low-key, humble style, she appeared both unpresumptuous and unthreatening. Such precaution, she knew, was essential since, to men such as the nuncio Felipe Sega, she was guilty of teaching others against the Pauline prohibition.[49] Yet when she spoke as a 'little woman', she deflected opposition by endorsing patriarchal preconceptions of female accept-ability as a vehicle for a message which remained, nevertheless, very personal, unorthodox and powerful.

As Jenna Lay's essay also illustrates, female writings could wield considerable charismatic authority. Reading was an important form of spirituality which fed the spiritual life of contemplative sisters, and women such as Barbara Constable (1617–1684) contributed to the corpus of reading material available for nuns to study. Thus, communal spirituality was shared through 'learning, example and instruction'. Spiritual reading and **contemplative prayer** acted as an inter-mediary between God and the reader, and when Constable established her own 'interpretative authority', her writings came to play an important mediating role between the penitent and the divine, a role which would normally have been the preserve of the clergy. However, Lay also notes that Constable employed the modesty topos to disguise her authority. Moreover, Barbara Constable's advice 'to Preachers' and 'for missioners' added her voice to discourses of 'contempo-rary religious politics and spiritual controversies'. Her work was not simply for private convent consumption; she meant it for a wider audience. Like Teresa de Jesús, she wanted to influence those outside the convent with her ideas on spiritual direction and her theories on the nature of religious authority.

As the chapters on Barbara Constable and Teresa de Jesús illustrate, women's religious writings could sometimes become effective forms of communication which breached the divide between the convent and the world. However, such female writings were rarely allowed to become authoritative, since women's use of 'male' modes of expression continued to be condemned by the Church throughout the ages. Women were therefore forced to create their own avenues of expression. In the nineteenth-century, they circumvented their exclusion from the pulpit and from formalized theological training by utilizing other forms of literary genres to develop and communicate theological ideas. Since formal sermons and treatises were declared masculine theological discourses, women used the language of more acceptable literary devices, such as the essay or article which appeared in the periodical press, the letter, the novel or the devotional manual, to assert their theology.[50] Nancy Cho's essay establishes that women also communicated their faith through vernacular hymn-writing which, as an acceptable form of feminine labour, provided a versatile means of communicating complex theology in more accessible language. Cho suggests Catholic women appropriated this medium and used it not only to explain theological precepts, but also to raise awareness of social concerns and to educate Catholics, particularly children, about their faith. Female Catholic hymn-writers were both lay women and religious and their hymns served to document their Catholic spirituality. These hymns were used to advocate Catholic devotions, instruct about doctrinal ideas, commemorate the English **recusant** past and, controversially, to pray for the conversion of England. Cho suggests that Catholic female hymn-writers used the Virgin Mary as a frequent *topos*. Mary was the archetype of the feminine divine and provided for a more gynocentric spirituality that enabled hymn singers to reflect on the valuable female roles in the history of Catholicism. So Catholic women, barred from other avenues of expression reserved to the clergy, found in hymn-writing a means to disseminate their own approach to spirituality.

Conclusions

Spirituality represents an important nexus through which women have been socially constituted and ideologically stimulated. The essays in this volume highlight the diversity of women's spiritualities, showing that Catholic women were not always satisfied with the normative modes of spirituality defined by the Church. Religious women throughout history expanded the boundaries of institutional and spiritual life, creating for themselves new, flexible identities. Authorities in Rome attempted to organize, to control and to standardize. Female responses to such normative control varied greatly. Some women needed to be true to their spiritual identities, or to follow their personal message from God, while others adapted their ideals to conform to Church standards. Whilst some, such as Mary Ward, claimed institutional boundaries, others such as the Dutch spiritual virgins and widows refused them. Yet, although ultimate 'success' did depend on a measure of institutional orthodoxy, the continuous pressures of testing the boundaries slowly altered the parameters of religious life.

The women discussed in this volume therefore share much in common, despite the specificities of their national contexts , and many of these distinctive features have remained evident throughout the changes which transformed female Catholic life over time. Considered together, these case studies indicate that women did not shrink from facing overwhelming odds to achieve their goals and determine their own spiritual lives. In the process, they developed an expertise in certain areas such as charity, schooling or nursing, and they found a specifically female voice through gendered modes of spiritual expression.

Yet women's tendency to disregard considerations of status or gendered role distributions, and their ability to respond to particular sets of circumstances in a pragmatic way, may invite us to reconsider the very paradigm of gender in female Catholic life. In the same way as they transcend the binary oppositions between enclosed and non-enclosed, contemplation and action, religious and secular, these women somewhat point to a spirituality of a 'third gender', one in which the dichotomy between male and female was seen as reductive.[51] Women often went beyond this rigid gendered separation to undertake whatever form of religious life they believed to be suited to themselves and to their particular, local circumstances. When they bemoaned ecclesiastical control or denounced rules imposed by men, did they seek to rehabilitate the feminine, or did they indicate that they preferred an inclusive view of spirituality, free of gendered divisions?

In this introduction, we have attempted to sketch out what we see as the parameters of women's spirituality; in so doing, we were influenced by the steadily growing body of research on Catholic women's spirituality. Yet, we are also aware that there is much more research that needs to be completed. We hope this volume encourages others to question and explore the dynamic qualities of women's spiritualities.

Notes

1. *St James Bible*, 1 Cor. 2:13, 15; Eph. 1:3.
2. U. King, 'Religion and Gender: Embedded Patterns, Interwoven Frameworks', in T. A. Meade and M. E. Weisner-Hanks (eds) *A Companion to Gender History* (Oxford: Blackwell, 2004), pp. 72, 76.
3. P. Crawford, *Women and Religion in England 1500–1720* (London and New York: Routledge, 1993), p. 210.
4. A. B. Mulder-Bakker (ed.), *Mary of Oignies, Mother of Salvation* (Turnhout: Brepols, 2006).
5. P. Ranft, *Women and the Religious Life in Premodern Europe* (New York: St Martin's Press, 1996), pp. 65–7.
6. M. E. Weisner, *Women and Gender in Premodern Europe* (Cambridge: Cambridge University Press, 1993), p. 216.
7. F. Medioli, 'An Unequal Law: The Enforcement of Clausura before and after the Council of Trent', in C. Meek (ed.), *Women in Renaissance and Early Modern Europe* (Dublin: Four Courts Press, 2000), pp. 136–52.
8. M. Weisner, *Women and Gender*, p. 217.
9. E. Power, *Medieval English Nunneries c. 1275 to 1535* (Cambridge: Cambridge University Press, 1922).
10. Session 25, 3–4 December 1563, in N. Tanner (ed.) *Decrees of the Ecumenical Councils* (London: Sheed and Ward, 1990), vol. 2 p. 778. Also, E. Makowski, *Canon Law and Cloistered Women: Periculoso and its Commentators, 1298–1545* (Washington D.C.: The Catholic University of America Press, 1997).
11. On the tensions between the cloister and the apostolate for religious women, see E. Rapley, *The Dévotes: Women and Church in Seventeenth-century France* (Kingston, Ont.: McGill, Queen's University Press, 1990) and R. Liebowitz, 'Virgins in the Service of Christ: The Dispute over an Active Apostolate for Women during the Counter-Reformation', in R. Radford Ruether (ed.) *Women of Spirit* (New York: Simon and Schuster, 1979), pp. 131–52.
12. Liebowitz, 'Virgins in the Service of Christ', pp. 31–52, and E. Rapley, 'Women

and the Religious Vocation in Seventeenth-Century France', *French Historical Studies*, 18:3 (1994), pp. 613–31.

13. J. O'Faolain and L. Martines, *Not in God's Image* (London: Virago, 1979).

14. T. Ledochowska, *Angèle Merici et la compagnie de sainte Ursule à la lumière des documents*, 2 vols (Rome: Ancora Press, 1967).

15. For a sweeping study, see J. A. K. McNamara, *Sisters in Arms: Catholic Nuns through Two Millennia* (Cambridge, Mass.: Harvard University Press, 1996). For the early modern era, see L. Evangelisti, *Nuns: A History of Conventual Life, 1450–1700* (Oxford: Oxford University Press, 2007), and C. Van Wyhe, *Female Monasticism in Early Modern Europe: An Interdisciplinary View* (Aldershot: Ashgate, 2008). For influential analyses of monastic life in specific countries, see H. Hills, *Invisible City: The Architecture of Devotion in Seventeenth-Century Neapolitan Convents* (Oxford: Oxford University Press, 2004) and C. Walker, *Gender and Politics in Early Modern Europe: English Convents in France and the Low Countries* (Houndmills: Palgrave, 2003).

16. Evangelisti, *Nuns*.

17. L. Jarrell, OSU, *The Development of Legal Structures for Women Religious Between 1500 and 1900: A Study of Selected Institutes of Religious Life for Women* (unpublished doctoral thesis, Catholic University of America, 1984), pp. 26–8.

18. Rapley, *The Dévotes*, pp. 41 and 195.

19. C. Orth, *The Approbation of Religious Institutes* (Washington, D.C.: Catholic University of America, 1931), p. 54. The Munich convent of the English Ladies clashed with the Bishop of Augsburg over issues of authority. The matter was adjudicated by Pope Benedict XIV (1740–1758), whose response in *Quamvis Justo* served to give tacit approval to congregations and recognised the authority of the superior of a congregation in certain matters.

20. J. Coakley, *Women, Men, and Spiritual Power: Female Saints and Their Male Collaborators* (New York: Columbia University Press, 2006).

21. Weisner, *Women and Gender*.

22. C. Walker Bynum, *Fragmentation and Redemption: Essays on Gender and the Human Body in Medieval Religion* (New York: Zone Books, 1992), p. 63.

23. McNamara, *Sisters in Arms*.

24. G. Zarri, 'The Third Status', in A. Jacobson Schutte, T. Kuehn and S. Seidel Menchi (eds), *Time, Space and Women's Lives in Early Modern Europe* (Kirksville: Truman State University Press, 2001), p. 182.

25. W. Sheepsma and D. F. Johnson, *Medieval Religious Women in the Low Countries: The Modern Devotion, the Canonesses of Windesheim, and their Writings* (Woodbridge: Boydell, 2004).

26. M. Caffiero, 'From the Late Baroque Mystical Explosion to the Social Apostolate, 1650–1850', in L. Scaraffia and G. Zarri (eds), *Women and Faith: Catholic Religious Life in Italy from Late Antiquity to the Present* (Cambridge, Mass.: Harvard University Press, 1999), p. 193.

27. K. Stogdon, 'A Journey with Thérèse Couderc: Inspiration, Liability or Possibility for Change?', *Feminist Theology*, 16:2 (2008), p. 211.

28. Rapley, *The Dévotes*, p. 16.

29. A. Vauchez, *La sainteté en Occident aux derniers siècles du Moyen Age d'après les procès de canonisation et les documents hagiographiques* (Rome: Ecole française de Rome, 1981).

30. D. Weinstein and R. M. Bell, *Saints and Society: The Two Worlds of Western Christendom, 1000–1700* (Chicago and London: University of Chicago Press, 1982).

31. Bynum, *Fragmentation and Redemption*, p. 68.
32. See F. W. J. Koorn, 'Women without Vows: The Case of the Beguines and the Sisters of the Common Life in the Northern Netherlands', in E. Schulte van Kessel (ed.), *Women and Men in Spiritual Culture, XV–XVII Centuries, A Meeting of North and South* (The Hague: Netherlands Government Publishing Office, 1986). Male communities formed in this model did exist, but they were not numerous.
33. Bynum, *Fragmentation and Redemption*, p. 69.
34. Walker, *Gender and Politics in Early Modern Europe*.
35. C. Langlois, *Le catholicisme au fêminin: les congrégations francaises à supérieure générale au XIX e siècle* (Paris: Les Editions du Cerf, 1984).
36. H. Mills. '"Saintes soeurs" and "femmes fortes": Alternative Accounts of the Route to Womanly Civic Virtue, and the History of French Feminism', in C. Campbell Orr (ed.), *Wollstonecraft's Daughters: Womanhood in England and France 1780–1920* (Manchester and New York: Manchester University Press, 1996), pp. 145–6.
37. M. Luddy, 'Religion, Philanthropy and the State in Eighteenth- and Early Nineteenth-Century Ireland', in H. Cunningham and J. Innes (eds), *Charity, Philanthropy and Reform from the 1690s to 1850* (London: Macmillan, 1998), p. 49.
38. F. Lannon, *Persecution, Privilege, and Prophecy: The Catholic Church in Spain, 1875–1975* (Oxford: Clarendon, 1987), p. 61.
39. Caffiero, 'From the Late Baroque Mystical Explosion', p. 204.
40. A. Weber, *Teresa of Àvila and the Rhetoric of Femininity* (Princeton: Princeton University Press, 1990).
41. Letter to the Nuncio Antonio Albergati, c.1621, in C. Kenworthy-Browne (ed.), *Mary Ward, 1585–1645: A Briefe Relation with Autobiographical Fragment and a Selection of Letters* (Woodbridge: Boydell, 2008), p. 146.
42. *Ibid.*
43. Langlois, *Le catholicisme au fêminin*.
44. G. Zarri, 'Living Saints: A Typology of Female Sanctity in the Early Sixteenth Century', in D. Bornstein and R. Rusconi (eds), *Women and Religion in Medieval and Renaissance Italy* (Chicago and London: University of Chicago Press, 1996), p. 248.
45. E. A. West, *One Woman's Journey: Mary Potter Founder – Little Company of Mary* (Richmond, Victoria, Australia: Spectrum Publications, 2000), pp. xii, 42, 103.
46. D. Elliott, *Proving Woman: Female Spirituality and Inquisitional Culture in the Later Middle Ages* (Princeton: Princeton University Press, 2004).
47. *Three speeches of our Reverend Mother Chief Superior made at St Omer having been long absent*, in U. Dirmeier, CJ (ed.), *Mary Ward, und ihre Gründung. Die Quellentexte bis 1645*, 4 vols (Münster: Aschendorff Verlag, 2007), vol. 1, p. 358.
48. Weber, *Teresa of Àvila*, p. 15.
49. *Ibid.*, p. 18.
50. J. Melnyk, 'Introduction', in J. Melnyk (ed.), *Women's Theology in Nineteenth-Century Britain: Transfiguring the Faith of Their Fathers* (New York and London: Garland Publishing, 1998), pp. xii–xvi.
51. McNamara, *Sisters in Arms*.

1

Presence and Absence: Reading Clare of Assisi in Franciscan Liturgy and Community[1]

Anna Welch

Introduction

The historiography of the Order of Friars Minor and its founder, St Francis of Assisi (1181/82–1226), is long and complex. Scholars have written volumes about this charismatic man, searching for new understandings of his spirituality and that of his powerful yet divided Order.[2] However, it is only more recently that scholars have given this same level of attention to St Clare of Assisi (1194–1253), first abbess and namesake of the Second Order of Franciscans, the Poor Ladies of San Damiano (at other times, the Poor Clares or the Order of St Clare). It was not until the early twentieth century that the early sources pertaining to Clare were first transcribed and translated from their manuscript originals.[3] Clare was canonized with great speed in 1255, two years after her death, and the office for her *dies natalis* (the day she died and was born into eternal life) was added to the Franciscan liturgy in 1260.[4] This chapter will examine whether or not the feasts of Clare – her *dies natalis* on 12 August and her *translatio* (the moving of her body from the church of San Giorgio to the newly built Basilica di Santa Chiara, which occurred in 1260) on 2 October – are present in the calendar, **litany** and **sanctoral cycle** of five thirteenth and fourteenth-century Franciscan liturgical manuscripts from Umbria (Figure 1.1). Also present within the selected manuscripts are the same feasts for Francis and Anthony of Padua (Figures 1.2 and 1.3). This evidence will be discussed with a view to possible reasons for the form, presence or absence of Clare's feasts, and the way in which they compare with the parallel feasts for Francis and Anthony.

This discussion will address a broader issue – the relationship between the Franciscan friars and the Poor Ladies of San Damiano in the thirteenth century. Given the very complicated development of the Order of St Clare, only Clare's original community at San Damiano can be discussed. Even to set this limitation involves considering significant complexities, given the differences of opinion amongst the thirteenth-century Franciscan friars regarding the authentic intentions of their founder, both towards women and concerning broader issues such as poverty and learning. It is within these complexities and differences that a more subtle reading of Clare's status in the liturgical life of the friars can be found. To recognize the community of San Damiano as an exception to the normative modes of communal female religious life in the thirteenth century, both Franciscan and non-Franciscan, is to acknowledge the extraordinary strength of Clare as an individual, and to challenge the idea, supported by historians such as Catherine Mooney and Marco Bartoli, that she was marginalized by the Order as a whole during her lifetime.[5] Instead, it is here suggested that Clare's marginalization occurred both at the hands of the mainstream Order in the later thirteenth century, from the Minister Generalship of Bonaventure (1257–74) onwards, and of modern historians.

The historiography of Clare and her community is an example of the limitations of previous gender history scholarship and illustrates the need for a fresh reading both of the primary sources and of our own biases as historians. The selected approach combines the discipline of liturgical history with the broader approaches of cultural and Church history, and an awareness of the implications, limitations and potential in the application of gender history for subjects such as medieval spirituality and liturgy.

In building a picture of the spiritual relationship between the Poor Ladies and the Friars Minor, liturgical evidence has traditionally been under-utilized, perhaps due to historians' unwillingness to cross what is perceived as a firm disciplinary boundary. While the concept of women in liturgy has attracted much scholarly attention in recent decades, many such studies, particularly those which posit contemporary liturgical practice as the descendent of a linear past, approach their subject using the same binary model that they critique – that is, a model which positions women's experiences of liturgy in opposition to men's experiences. They thus suggest a fundamental, conceptual division of gender in liturgy which, I propose, is neither applicable nor productive in the context of medieval understandings of the mechanics and function of liturgy.[6] Teresa Berger's work, for example, raises important questions about the future directions of liturgical history and historiography and its relationship to feminist and gender theory. However, the complex interplay of gender and identity politics represented in any liturgical manuscript suggests that a more inclusive approach (one that considers male and female liturgical activity as interrelated, rather than as oppositional) will be of greater benefit in constructing an understanding of communal identity as it is expressed in liturgy. Therefore, this study will draw together liturgical evidence and non-liturgical textual sources to build a picture of the relationship between the Friars and Poor Ladies in the first century of the Order of friars Minor's existence, adding depth and texture to the picture of both the friars' daily spiritual rituals and the Poor Ladies' struggle for recognition within the Order.

Clare in Franciscan liturgy

A selection of evidence drawn from five liturgical texts of the late thirteenth and early fourteenth centuries is presented below. The texts themselves are **missals** and **breviaries** used by Friars Minor in Umbria.[7] The manuscripts have been selected from a wider group currently under research, and have been chosen as a representative sample of the trends observed in this larger group.[8] These manuscripts were made and used in the heartland of Franciscan Umbria, in Perugia, Assisi and Gubbio. Each manuscript has been studied in its original.[9] The information is drawn from the calendar (of feast days), the litany (a prayer used in the celebration of the mass, formulated as a list of petitions to particular saints) and the sanctoral cycle (the section of a liturgical book which contains the text for the celebration of specific saints' feasts) of each liturgical text. Some technical notes for reading the tables:

- A ✓ indicates the feast is present, a ✖ indicates it is not.
- Text in round brackets is the English translation of the saint's description, e.g. 'virgin', 'confessor'.
- Entries followed by [R] are **rubricated** in the original (that is, written in red ink).
- Where a feast is an addition, it is noted as such in square brackets.
- 'n/a' indicates the necessary folios are missing from the manuscript.

Given the possibility of variation between what was written and what was actually performed, it is not wise to view this liturgical data as indisputable evidence of a community's liturgical activity. However, despite its pitfalls, this evidence remains essential to scholars wishing to build an accurate picture of the liturgical life of a community, both in terms of what was included in the community's rituals and what was not.

The manuscripts[10]

A. *Codex Sancti Paschalis*. Franciscan missal, c. 1270–97, Perugia. State Library of Victoria, Melbourne[11]

The *Codex Sancti Paschalis* is a Franciscan missal originally from Perugia, dated c. 1270–97 (due to the addition of the Office for Louis of Toulouse at the end of the missal). Art historians have argued convincingly for a Perugian **provenance**, given the similarity of the *Codex's* decorative programme to those of other late-thirteenth-century Perugian manuscripts.[12]

B. Ms. 13. Roman missal, before 1297, Gubbio (Biblioteca Comunale e dell'Accademia Etrusca di Cortona)[13]

This Roman missal is believed to have been made for use in Gubbio, due to the prominence of St Ubaldo (bishop and patron saint of Gubbio) in the calendar.[14] The missal lacks a litany.

	Calendar– *Dies natalis*	Calendar – *Translatio*	Litany	Sanctoral – *Dies natale*	Sanctoral – *Translatio*
Ms. A (1270–97)	✓ (virgin)	✗	[addition]	✓	✗
Ms. B (1270–97)	✓ (first virgin of the order of ladies)	✗	n/a	✓ [marginal addition in variety of hands]	✗
Ms. C (1280–90)	✗	✗	✓	✓	✗
Ms. D (after 1317)	✓ (virgin)	✗	✗	✓	✗
Ms. E (1322)	✓ [R] (virgin) **Octave** also present	[R addition; virgin]	✓	✓	✗

Figure 1.1   Feasts of St Clare

C. Ms. 262. Franciscan missal, 1280–90, Sacro Convento, Assisi (Bib. Sacro Convento, Assisi)[15]

This missal, sometimes known as the 'Messale Sancte Elizabeth', has suffered many additions and re-bindings. Unusually (and unrelated to the re-bindings), its original contents are somewhat disordered – the missal begins with the litany, which is followed by the calendar. The missal's *incipit* specifies it as Franciscan: 'Incipit ordo missalis fratrum minorum' (f. 9r).

D. Ms. 8. Franciscan missal, post-1317, possibly used in Santa Maria del Verzaro in Perugia (Capitolo di San Lorenzo, Perugia)[16]

As the calendar of this Franciscan missal includes the feast of Louis of Toulouse, who was canonized in 1317, the missal as a whole dates from after that year.

	Calendar– *Dies natalis*	Calendar – *Translatio*	Litany	Sanctoral – *Dies natale*	Sanctoral – *Translatio*
Ms. A (1270–97)	✓ (institutor and rector of the order of friars minor)	✓	✓	✓	✓
Ms. B (1270–97)	✓ [R] (blessed)	✓ [R]	n/a	✓ (**confessor**)	✓
Ms. C (1280–90)	✓ (confessor)	[addition]	✓	✓	✓
Ms. D (after 1317)	✓ (confessor)	✓	✓	✓	✓
Ms. E (1322)	✓ (blessed francis, founder and first minister of the order of friars minor)	✓ [R]	✓	✓	✓

Figure 1.2   Feasts of St Francis

E. Ms. 265. Franciscan breviary, 1322, Sacro Convento in Assisi (Bib. Sacro Convento, Assisi)[17]

This Franciscan breviary has the distinction of being one of the few dated medieval liturgical manuscripts in existence. On f. 171r is a note by the scribe indicating the work was completed in 1322.[18] The breviary's *incipit* leaves no room to doubt its Franciscan use, which is made clear by the many additions to the calendar of later Franciscan saints and feasts.

In the calendars of the five selected manuscripts, the main feast of Clare (her *dies natalis*) is not uniformly represented, despite being officially included in Franciscan liturgy some 30 years before any of these manuscripts were

	Calendar– *Dies natalis*	Calendar – *Translatio*	Litany	Sanctoral – *Dies natale*	Sanctoral – *Translatio*
Ms. A (1270–97)	✓ (confessor of the order of friars minor)	✗	✓	✓	✗
Ms. B (1270–97)	✓ [R] (confessor of the order of friars minor)	✗	n/a	✓	✗
Ms. C (1280–90)	✓ (of the order minor)	✗	✓	✓ (confessor)	✗
Ms. D (after 1317)	✓ (of the order of friars minor)	✗	✓	✓	✗
Ms. E (1322)	✓ (confessor)	[R addition]	✓ [but absent from Greater Litany]	✓	✗

Figure 1.3 Feasts of St Anthony of Padua

produced. Mss A, D and E include this feast of Clare's death in their calendars, and in Ms. D the feast is rubricated (that is, written in red ink as a method of highlighting the entry's importance – from the Latin *ruber*, red). Only Ms. E includes the octave of this feast, in which it is rubricated. Ms. E is also the only one to include the feast of Clare's *translatio* (the relocation of her body), as a rubricated addition in a later hand (and thus no corresponding office in the sanctoral of the missal). Ms. C does not include any feasts of St Clare, despite its unequivocally Franciscan nature.

Similarly, we may note the disparity of the wording of these entries. Mss A, D and E refer to Clare simply as 'virgin'. Ms. B includes the most unusual phrasing from within this selection of manuscripts, referring to Clare as 'first virgin of the order of ladies', a direct and unexpected (in light of the other manuscripts) reference to Clare's community, the Poor Ladies of San Damiano.[19] In most cases there was little effort made to denote Clare as specifically Franciscan. That Clare's feasts could be entirely lacking from a missal of undoubted Franciscan use

(Ms. C) while being emphasized with specific reference to her community in another (Ms. B) underscores the inconsistent attitude which the friars of Umbria seem to have displayed in regard to Clare's feasts, and suggests a link between liturgical practice and wider debates within the Franciscan Order during this period.

The representation of Clare's feasts in the sanctoral cycles of these manuscripts reaffirms this point. Mss A, C, D and E include the feast of Clare's death in their sanctoral cycles, in the original scribal hands.[20] Ms. B again stands out as the most unusual: the scribe has not written the office, but has noted in the margin (perhaps as an afterthought) that the feast ought to be there. The office has been added in the margin, in a variety of later hands. It is correct and complete, but strikes the reader as haphazard at best. None of the manuscripts include the feast of Clare's *translatio* in their sanctoral cycles. It would appear that this feast was not regularly included in Franciscan liturgy until the fourteenth century. One reason for this may be that the Franciscans evidently re-used the text from the office for Clare's *dies natalis* to celebrate her *translatio*;[21] without the impetus of having a new office to write into liturgical texts, the feast was more easily overlooked by scribes.

This seems a perplexing situation. Ms. E does not include Clare in its calendar, and yet her office occurs in its sanctoral cycle in the original hand. Ms. B includes a specific reference to Clare as 'virgin of the First Order of the Ladies' of San Damiano, and yet the scribe has neglected to write out her office in the sanctoral cycle, merely signalling its correct place with a marginal note. The office has not been written out in full by a second scribe, but filled in over time in many different hands. Clare's *translatio* is not accorded the same importance as her *dies natalis,* and is not routinely included in Franciscan liturgy of the period, despite the initial speed of her canonization and the significance of the new basilica (Santa Chiara, completed in 1260) constructed to house her body.

The evidence drawn from the litanies of these liturgical texts underlines the discrepancies regarding Clare in the Franciscan liturgy. In Mss C and E, Clare is present in the litany, alongside the other major Franciscan saints. In Ms. A, she has been added to the litany in a later (though probably still thirteenth-century) hand. In Ms. D, Clare is absent entirely from the litany. These four manuscripts (the litany of Ms. B being unavailable for study, as noted) provide a representative spread of the trends in Franciscan liturgical manuscripts across a 50–year time period, and again we notice that there is little uniformity amongst them. The General Chapter of Narbonne in 1260 had ruled that Clare was to be included in the litany, and yet even by the early fourteenth century this was not always the case.

All of this evidence might suggest confusion or even antagonism on the part of the Friars Minor regarding the feasts of Clare and her role as an important early Franciscan figure. The picture of inconsistency it presents sits at odds with the medieval Franciscans' reputation for liturgical uniformity – even the rubrication of a feast seems to be a matter of individual preference (either for the scribe and/or the Franciscan community using the book). In the 1240s, the Minister General of the Franciscan Order, Haymo of Faversham (died ca. 1243), revised and shortened the rubrics for the missal and breviary, at the request of the papacy and for the use of the busy Papal Curia in Rome. The Franciscan Order also officially adopted this reformed liturgy, and it has long been the contention of modern liturgical historians from S. J. P. van Dijk onwards that the missionary activity of the Franciscans played a large role in assisting the papacy to spread a uniform Roman rite through the medieval Church.[22] Historians' tendency has been to note, as van Dijk did, the repeated reinforcements of Haymo's revisions at Franciscan General Chapters throughout the middle and later thirteenth century, but not to acknowledge the necessary implication that these reinforcements suggest: that the revisions were not being used in Franciscan communities.[23] It would seem that close examination of Franciscan liturgical sources suggests a greater level of variability and flexibility within Franciscan liturgy than has usually been acknowledged by historians of the Order, provoking a re-assessment of standard assumptions about the construction and maintenance of communal identity through liturgy.

The ongoing schism within the Franciscan Order over the production, ownership and use of books must be considered as a weighty factor in the discrepancies observed in the selected manuscripts. Francis included specific prohibitions about the production of books in his **Rule** for the Order (1209) and in his *Testament* (1226).[24] As mendicants, Franciscan friars were required to maintain absolute poverty – that is, both personal and corporate. One might expect this poverty would exclude the possibility of *scriptoria* in Franciscan friaries, but in fact evidence that friars were copying their own theological and liturgical texts occurs very early in the Order's history, as Bert Roest's authoritative study of Franciscan education has suggested.[25] Whether Franciscan friaries contained *scriptoria* in a formal sense remains a matter for debate, but liturgical books seem to have been viewed by the friars themselves as a special case: in 1260, Minister General Bonaventure of Bagnoregio issued his *Statutum*, an instruction manual for scribes which indicated that the copying of liturgical texts was a task for friars, too important to be left to secular scribes.[26] It is quite possible, even likely, that the scribes of the manuscripts selected by this study were friars. However, the fact of their membership of the Order does not imply a uniform approach: the many divisions within the Order and the variability of access to the most current liturgical *exempla* are vital factors in considering the importance of scribal identity to the liturgical variations within these five manuscripts. It must also be remembered that the selected manuscripts date from the period which saw the rise of commercial artists and ateliers, and that the manuscript production networks included lay as well as religious people. These liturgical manuscripts are multi-layered, and their production was a joint enterprise; their use was in some measure affected by this fact. We do not know who decided which feasts should be entered or highlighted, who decided upon the exact wording of each entry or on what basis these decisions were made (whether ideological differences and/or practical lack of access to the 'correct' *exempla*, or a combination of these factors).

A challenge to the friars' reputation for liturgical uniformity can be seen clearly in Figures 1.1, 1.2 and 1.3 and their evidence regarding the treatment of Francis and Anthony compared with that of Clare. Though there is uniformity in the inclusion of Francis's feasts across all five manuscripts (as one would expect), there was not a uniform phrase recording each feast. Francis is named in a variety of ways: two drawing attention to his status as founder (Mss A and E) and one referring to him simply as 'blessed' (Ms. B) and two citing him as a confessor (Mss C and D). Only Ms. B has Francis's *dies natalis* as a rubric, while it and Ms. E include his *translatio* as a rubric. Though Francis's feasts are unanimously included, their wording and rubrication is subject to the same variation as was seen in the case of Clare's liturgical feasts.

The feasts of Anthony of Padua (d. 1231) provide a very interesting comparison with Clare, given the role of both as important but secondary figures (that is, of lesser status than Francis) in the early Franciscan movement. Mss A, B, C and D are all at pains to emphasize Anthony's connection to the Order of Friars Minor. Only Ms. E refers to him simply as '*confessoris*'. Unlike Clare, Anthony is included in the litany in every instance (though it cannot be verified in the case of Ms. B, which lacks a litany). Again unlike Clare, the office for Anthony's *dies natalis* is always included in the sanctoral cycles of our selected manuscripts. However, in common with Clare, Anthony's *translatio* (both its calendar entry and its office in the sanctoral cycle) is almost always excluded (being included only in Ms. E's calendar as an addition), despite the fact that the translation of Anthony's relics had occurred in 1263, some 20 to 30 years before these manuscripts were written.[27] In fact, historians have noted that, working from the evidence available, the feast of Anthony's translation seems not to have entered the Franciscan liturgical calendar until 1350, 113 years after the event occurred.[28]

In the light of this, it is unsurprising that Anthony's *translatio* is not entered in the original hand of any of the manuscripts considered in this chapter (which date between 1270 and 1322), but what remains surprising is the long delay between the event and its inclusion in the calendar. As with Clare, it appears that no new office was written for Anthony's *translatio*, but instead the office for his *dies natalis* was re-used.[29] One might suppose that Anthony's *translatio*, which was presided over by St Bonaventure himself and which included the discovery of Anthony's miraculously incorrupt tongue, would have quickly entered Franciscan liturgy and perhaps even with its own original office; the fact that this did not occur further underlines the prosaic Franciscan attitude to liturgical feasts, even those of saints important to the Order, be they male or female. A comparison of the feasts of Clare and Anthony suggests that, rather than gender, a main factor in understanding perceived discrepancies is the nature of Franciscan liturgical practice itself, and the recording of this practice.

Franciscan liturgy in context

It is tempting to believe that Clare was diminished and even occasionally excluded from Franciscan liturgy by virtue of her gender, as the actions of some friars and popes regarding care of the Poor Clare sisters during this period do not indicate sympathy for Clare, her community or their claim to be part of the Franciscan family, despite Francis's evident acknowledgement of this. Clare was received into religious life by Francis himself, and was finally settled by him at the newly restored church of San Damiano, the site of his own conversion. There she was joined by many of her female relatives, and the community of the Poor Ladies was formed.[30] That Clare's community intended to live a life along the lines formulated by Francis and his friars, and that Francis supported them in doing this, is evident from the *formula vivendi* (form of life) which Francis wrote for the Poor Ladies in 1212–13, in which he made them an important assurance: 'I resolve and promise for myself and for my brothers to always have that same loving care and solicitude for you as [I have] for them.'[31]

In 1215, Francis had personally requested (through 'prayers and insistence'[32]) that Clare assume the role of abbess at San Damiano.[33] In Francis's actions we see that the friars (or at least Francis) were involved in the administration of the Poor Ladies at this point, fulfilling Francis's earlier promise to the community. With the prohibitive rulings of the Fourth Lateran Council (1215) regarding new religious communities, the Poor Ladies did, however, have to accept life under the Benedictine Rule.[34] This setback was softened in 1216, when Pope Innocent III granted Clare's community the unprecedented *privilegium paupertatis* (Privilege of poverty), upholding their right to live as Francis lived, albeit within an **enclosed** space.[35] In 1217, Cardinal Ugolino (the future Pope Gregory IX and a long-time supporter of Francis) was appointed as Cardinal Bishop of Ostia, giving him authority over the Poor Ladies, amongst other communities.[36] In 1219, Ugolino composed a Rule for the use of female religious communities under his authority. Ratified by Honorius III's **papal bull** *Sacrosancta* on 9 December 1219, Ugolino's work was based on the Benedictine Rule and removed the right of absolute poverty for **women religious**.[37] Ugolino envisaged that the Poor Ladies would accept this Rule, thus solving the complex issue of both their spiritual character and their administration: as a community living under the Benedictine Rule and the protection of a cardinal bishop, they would no longer be reliant on the Order of Friars Minor, nor have any real claim to be part of the Franciscan movement.

When the new pope Gregory IX (formerly Ugolino) came to the papal throne in 1227, one year after Francis's death, Clare appealed to him to renew her community's Privilege of poverty, which he did (somewhat reluctantly) in 1228.[38] The new pope also removed the Friars Minor as **chaplains** to the Poor Ladies, an administrative change with wider implications for the two groups' relations.[39] In requesting a renewal of the Privilege, Clare showed a deep awareness of the problems which had been simmering amongst the friars, who found themselves struggling to agree on and maintain their founder's ideals in the face of their order's rapid growth. As the Order's membership began to include more clerics and intellectuals than lay brothers (such as Francis himself had been) and its horizons correspondingly expanded, it came into sharp conflict with **secular clergy** as well as monastic and fellow mendicant communities over its role within universities and its pastoral activities.[40] Indeed, Francis had perceived these threats to his **apostolic** ideal for the Order before his death in 1226: in his short will to the Poor Ladies, which Clare eventually included in her own Rule of 1253, Francis exhorted them to 'live always in this most holy life and poverty [and] keep most careful watch that you never depart from this by reason of teaching or advice of anyone.'[41] The ideal of absolute poverty was continuously in jeopardy, most especially in the case of the Poor Ladies, as they were continually prompted by Gregory IX and other Church leaders to give up this aspect of their communal life.

Absolute poverty was perhaps the most distinguishing feature of Clare's community and its strongest claim to being Franciscan. Regis Armstrong's sensitive exploration of the daily spiritual life of the Poor Ladies, in the introduction to his critical edition of the primary sources, underscores the radical nature of Clare's commitment to living the holy poverty espoused by Francis: never before had absolute, corporate poverty been attempted by an enclosed female community. The apostolic poverty Francis and his friars desired was to some extent protected by the itinerancy of their lifestyle: living on alms was quite feasible when one was able to walk the streets and appeal to the wider community in person. Clare's community, however, was entirely reliant on the stability and support of the institutional Church. By her community's very existence, Clare challenged the Church to fulfil its apostolic and pastoral mission to all Christian society, and her determination to live in absolute poverty demonstrated her faith in the Church's ability to do so.[42] In Clare, Armstrong sees not a follower of Francis, but the 'necessary complement and fulfilment' of Francis's vision.[43]

The Privilege of poverty was not, however, without its problems for the Church and the friars: the strain of feeding and caring for an enclosed female community was felt by many other male orders of the period, including the Dominicans and the Cistercians.[44] Francis's own attitude to the issue seems fairly clear – he supported the Poor Ladies' right to absolute poverty, and encouraged them to cling to it, aware of the challenges they would face. Perhaps, as Armstrong suggests, Francis saw Clare and her sisters as a unique and lasting living expression of his ideal, which was both protected and threatened by the enclosed lifestyle.[45] It is also important to note, as Lezlie Knox does, that Francis's support of Clare and her community at San Damiano did not necessarily mean that he supported all Clarissan houses – the Poor Ladies of San Damiano were treated (both in negative and positive senses) by Francis, his friars and successive papacies as a special case.[46]

In 1247 the new pope, Innocent IV, provided the Poor Ladies with a new Rule – a milder form of Ugolino's Rule – which reinstated the Friars Minor as the chaplains of the Poor Ladies, thus conferring on the Friars Minor the pastoral and physical care of the women.[47] The San Damiano community's dislike of Innocent IV's Rule can be deduced from the papal bull of 1250, *Inter personas*, in which he conceded no sister could be forced to accept the Rule.[48] Over the next few years, as her health declined and death approached, Clare composed her own Rule. It was the first Rule written by a female, and gained the official approval of Innocent IV in 1253, shortly before Clare's death, through the papal bull *Solet annuere*.[49] Importantly, the Rule was written for use by the community at San Damiano alone; that the papacy did not wish other female houses to follow Clare's example of corporate, cloistered poverty is clear from the number of bulls issued to prevent other Umbrian Damianite houses from relinquishing property that had been bestowed on them.[50] Clare died at San Damiano on 11 August 1253 (aged 59), the day after receiving the official confirmation of her Rule. The process of canonization began in 1254 and was concluded on 26 September 1255, when she was pronounced a saint by Pope Alexander IV.

In 1263, the Friars Minor (under the direction of Minister General Bonaventure of Bagnoregio) made it abundantly clear to the papacy that they no longer wished to be legally responsible for the Poor Ladies.[51] Pope Urban IV obliged them by putting the Poor Ladies under the guardianship of a separate cardinal protectorate, effectively removing the Poor Ladies from the Franciscan family. Interestingly, he also revised the Rule of St Clare and formally changed the name of her community from 'the Poor Ladies of San Damiano' to 'the Order of St Clare'.[52] Clare was simultaneously recognized and dismissed – her personal wish to maintain Francis's ideal of absolute poverty suffered under Urban IV's revisions, yet her importance as a leader of the community was emphasized. In terms of liturgy, Clare's position seems to reflect the ambiguity with which the Friars Minor viewed her and her community. She is included in the Franciscan liturgy of the selected manuscripts, but in greatly varying forms, and is never acknowledged as a Franciscan.

After Francis's death, some friars like Francis's early companions Leo and Elias had continued to visit the Poor Ladies (even to their own detriment, as in the case of Elias who was eventually excommunicated, in part for persisting with his unauthorized visits to San Damiano).[53] However, not all friars displayed this devotion to the care of the Poor Ladies, and as the thirteenth century wore on the Order as a whole came to reject all responsibility towards Clare's community: as Miles Pattenden notes, by the time of Bonaventure's *Legenda maior*, Clare was not identified by name, nor was her community acknowledged as Franciscan.[54] The physical and economic strain of caring for Clare's community must be considered as an important factor in the almost comic succession of papal bulls and rules in which the Friars Minor were alternately removed and re-instated as the Poor Ladies' protectors, but perhaps more important was the friars' own struggle to construct and maintain their Order's identity after the death of Francis – without a unanimous understanding of their own identity, the friars as a whole were loath to accept responsibility for another complicated (and complicating) group with yet another understanding of Francis's message.

It is highly significant that Clare was intimately associated with Francis's earliest and closest companions, Leo, Rufino and Angelo, and that these friars actively supported the election of John of Parma, a sympathizer of the proto-Spiritualist movement of 'hard-line' friars, to the Minister Generalship in 1247.[55] The successive Minister Generalships of John of Parma (1247–57) and the more moderate Bonaventure (1257–74) demonstrate the divided nature of the Franciscan Order during and immediately after Clare's lifetime, both in terms of its understanding of its own origins and mission, and in its understanding of the role of Clare's community within that mission. Perhaps Bonaventure's obvious wish to exclude Clare and her community from the Franciscan family was as much motivated by a desire to marginalize the proto-Spiritualist movement as it was by the fact of her female gender.

The ongoing conflict of opinion between the papacy and the friars regarding the temporal and pastoral care of the Poor Ladies of San Damiano is but one example of a broader issue within the Church during this period. The increasing urbanization of society resulted in growing numbers of men and women wishing to live in religious communities within an urban setting, rather than along the rural paradigm of preceding centuries. The new mendicant orders such as the Friars Minor and the Order of Preachers were one way that this urban religious life found its expression, and it was to these orders that medieval popes sought to entrust the care of urban women's religious communities.[56] This was not always a welcome duty to the friars; indeed Pattenden suggests that in their rejection of the idea, the Friars Minor 'did no more than follow a trend set by other orders in opposing the incorporation of responsibilities towards female houses into their duties'.[57] In part, the friars' unwillingness to care for the Poor Ladies may have stemmed from an ongoing lack of clarity about many other female religious houses in Italy. Papal efforts to gather these disparate houses together into one 'Damianite' Order were to some extent thwarted by the women themselves: not all houses wanted to follow Clare's Rule nor to identify themselves as Franciscan.[58] Given the lack of unity amongst the women themselves, the friars' hesitation to accept responsibility for all such female houses is less surprising.

When comparing the feasts of Clare with those of Francis and Anthony in the selected manuscripts, the variety of Franciscan liturgical records comes into sharp focus. Francis was unanimously celebrated for all his feasts, as one might expect. Secondary figures, such as Clare and Anthony, underscore the fact that Franciscan liturgy was, in the thirteenth and early fourteenth centuries, not as uniform as Van Dijk and others have suggested. While Anthony's *dies natalis* was more frequently celebrated than Clare's, both saints' *translatio* feasts were infrequently included in the calendars and sanctoral cycles of the selected missals. The concern these five liturgical manuscripts show for identifying Anthony as a member of the Order of Friars Minor may stem from the saint's life story – he was initially a member of the Order of Canons Regular of St Augustine, but in 1220 left this Order to become a Friar Minor, which he remained until his death in 1231. It may also be due to a desire to distinguish him from the other (more famous) Anthony: St Anthony the Hermit (c. 251–356), abbot and one of the founders of the monastic way of life. It is plausible to suggest that while these scribes found it important to emphasize the Franciscan identity and role of Anthony, they found it less easy, or even perhaps less desirable (given the disparity of the friars' opinions on the subject) to clarify Clare's status as a member of the Franciscan movement.

Conclusions

In assessing the liturgical evidence regarding Clare of Assisi drawn from these five manuscripts, we may pose more subtle questions than those exploring potential misogyny on the part of the medieval Franciscan friars. The manuscripts selected present a confused picture of Franciscan liturgical life regarding Clare, not a clear-cut diminution of her status. The texts provide an opportunity to question how the Franciscan liturgy both reflected and shaped the wider problems plaguing the friars during this period, problems which for the most part were more concerned with authority, authenticity and inheritance than gender.

There were many factors affecting the ability and willingness of the friars to provide temporal and spiritual care for the Poor Ladies – not the least of which was their uncertainty over the spiritual character of all the female communities swept together with the Poor Ladies by papacies desirous of a neat solution to the crisis of administering urban religious houses. From the respect paid to Clare by cardinals and popes, and most especially from the papal approval of her Rule, it is clear that Clare was not for the most part a marginalized figure within her lifetime – rather the opposite. Just as the confines of the cloistered life could in fact bring great spiritual freedom, so too the unusual nature of Clare's position brought her respect and power, both spiritual and temporal. She commanded great personal respect from Francis's close companions Leo, Rufino and Angelo as well as from Popes Innocent III, Gregory IX and Alexander IV.

While there were clearly some groups of friars who deliberately ignored Clare and her community, particularly the moderates as led by Bonaventure, the hesitation of the First Order to take on the official responsibility for care of these women does not necessarily condemn the friars as misogynist, but rather underlines the complexity of the Franciscan situation in the thirteenth century, which came to a head in the acrimonious split between the Spiritual and moderate groups in the early fourteenth century. Clare's association with people aligned to the proto-Spiritualist camp, such as Elias, is highly significant and must inform our understanding of the mainstream Order's rejection of her community in the 1260s. In a sense, both Francis and Clare experienced posthumous marginalization by the moderates of the Order. It is testament to the magnetism of their personalities and spiritualities that each of them drew intense devotion in their lifetimes, yet it is also testament to the confronting and challenging nature of their spiritualities that many of Clare and Francis's followers could not live up to these ideals once the two great leaders had died. Clare and Francis were not spiritual moderates in life, but in death they could be shaped by Bonaventure and the later thirteenth-century Order in response to the various religious and political challenges facing the friars.

The First Order's reputation for liturgical uniformity in the thirteenth century derives from the work of modern liturgical historians. Whilst it would be unwise to dismiss this work, it is time to engage in a re-evaluation of the actual liturgical evidence, particularly using previously unstudied manuscripts. In the case of the Order of Friars Minor, engagement with this primary evidence shows a far more complex and irregular situation than has previously been depicted. Assessing the liturgical manuscripts used by Friars Minor reveals an irregular attitude towards Clare's feasts, but this attitude is not a totally negative one. In several of the manuscripts considered in this study, emphasis is placed on Clare as part of a community which maintained a link to the teachings and lifestyle of Francis and his earliest companions, and in those same manuscripts we see that Francis himself receives no special acknowledgement as the founder of the Order.[59] On the other hand, other manuscripts show a special interest in Francis and none in Clare.[60] Anthony of Padua is often explicitly identified as a member of the Franciscan Order, but his *translatio* was not included in the Franciscan liturgy until 1350, more than a century after it actually occurred.

That the friars were not in fact celebrating a uniform liturgical calendar, even within a small section of Umbria (Perugia and Gubbio are within a 20–kilometre radius of Assisi), indicates the difficulty the Order as a whole experienced in establishing a unified liturgy for themselves. Similarly, precisely for which groups of friars these manuscripts were produced remains unknown. It could be speculated that Ms. B, which includes such a specific reference to Clare and her community at San Damiano, may have been used by friars with proto-Spiritualist leanings, and that Ms. C, which excludes all Clare's feasts despite being an unequivocally Franciscan text, may have been used by a group of moderates – but these suggestions remain speculative. The liturgical evidence pertaining to the feasts of Clare underlines the internal divisions and general administrative difficulties experienced by the First Order of Friars Minor, while also confirming the particular difficulties the friars (and the Church) experienced in achieving consensus regarding the spiritual nature of Clare and her community, and their role within the Franciscan movement. It also suggests new avenues of thought regarding current scholarly understandings of both Franciscan liturgical history and historiography.

In the last three decades there has been a much-needed revival of scholarly interest in Clare, particularly in the field of gender theory, as part of a broader revival of interest in medieval women and their spirituality. The rise of gender history as a discipline in its own right and the seminal work of historians such as Caroline Walker Bynum and Jacques Dalarun has led to a significant re-reading of medieval women's lives and works, providing us with a much richer understanding of the role of women and feminine spirituality in medieval society and culture. It has also allowed for a more nuanced reading of male spirituality, and of the liminality of gender itself within Christian spirituality of the period. Catherine Mooney, amongst others, has suggested Clare's gender played a part in her marginalization within Franciscan history more generally, but further research and a more extensive reading of the primary evidence has led to the very different conclusions presented here, which concern historiography and methodology as much as historical data.[61] The work of historians such as Bynum and Dalarun addressing the complex, nuanced world of medieval gender has been embraced to some extent by liturgical historians, as the increased interest in women and liturgy from cultural historians shows.

However liturgical history as a discipline has yet to strike a balance between a valid and necessary critique of so-called '"male-stream" constructions' of liturgical history, and an inclusive reading of the complexities of gender in medieval spirituality and liturgical commemoration.[62] The case of the feasts of Clare of Assisi and their commemoration in the liturgy of the male Franciscan friars, as recorded in these selected manuscripts, suggests that liturgical historians can afford neither to ignore nor to overplay the issue of gender. Gender is not irrelevant to liturgical commemoration and the construction of communal identity, but nor is it the only factor to be considered: one cannot in fact speak of a single, gender-based attitude from the friars towards Clare and her feasts, but rather a multiplicity of attitudes which reflect the fragmented nature of the Order in the late thirteenth and early fourteenth centuries.

Until recently, scholarship regarding Clare of Assisi (in both liturgical and cultural disciplines) had fallen under the spell of Bonaventure, as though other male Franciscan thirteenth-century voices had become inaudible. Clare was represented as the marginalized and rejected figure that Bonaventure's *Legenda Maior* intended her to be. A study of the relationship(s) between Clare and the Friars Minor highlights the necessity of an awareness of our own constructive process regarding the past. With the development of sophisticated interdisciplinary methodologies, liturgical evidence can be subjected to a critical and creative re-reading. The results demonstrate the necessity of looking beyond gender alone as an explanatory factor for perceived anomalies, but also show the depth of understanding which an awareness of gender issues provides for any historian of medieval spirituality. Reading liturgical evidence in this interdisciplinary yet focused light illuminates the complicated relationships between Clare, her community and the friars in the first century of the Franciscan movement.

Notes

1. My thanks to Dr Claire Renkin (Melbourne College of Divinity) and Julian Welch (Random House Australia) for reading drafts of this chapter and providing constructive criticism. Any errors which remain are entirely my own. I gratefully acknowledge Professor Sherry Reames (University of Wisconsin-Madison) for discussion and references regarding the issue of St Anthony of Padua's *translatio* feast.

2. For example: P. Sabatier, *The Life of St Francis of Assisi*, translated by L. Seymour Houghton (London: Hodder & Stoughton, 1894); J. R. H. Moorman, *Richest of Poor Men: The Spirituality of St Francis of Assisi* (London: Darton, Longman and Todd, 1982); M. Robson (OFM Conv.), *St Francis of Assisi: The Legend and the Life* (London: Geoffrey Chapman, 1997); C. Frugoni, *Francis of Assisi: A Life* (London: SCM Press, 1998); J. Dalarun, *The Misadventure of Francis of Assisi: Toward a Historical Use of the Legends*, translated by E. Hagman (OFM Cap.) (New York: The Franciscan Institute, St Bonaventure University, 2002).

3. C. Mooney, '*Imitatio Christi* or *Imitatio Mariae*? Clare of Assisi and Her Interpreters', in C. M. Mooney (ed.), *Gendered Voices: Medieval Saints and Their Interpreters* (Philadelphia: University of Pennsylvania Press, 1999), p. 52. See also R. J. Armstrong, 'Introduction to the Legend of Saint Clare', in R. J. Armstrong (ed.) *Clare of Assisi: Early Documents* (New Jersey: Paulist Press, 1988), p. 184.

4. M. Bartoli, *Clare of Assisi*, translated by Sr Frances Teresa OSC (London: Darton, Longman & Todd, 1993), p. 199.

5. Mooney, '*Imitatio Christi* or *Imitatio Mariae*?', pp. 52–77; Bartoli, *Clare of Assisi*, pp. 199–200.

6. See for example and further references: T. Berger, 'Women in Worship', in G. Wainwright and K. B. Westerfield Tucker (eds), *The Oxford History of Christian Worship* (Oxford: Oxford University Press, 2006), pp. 755–68.

7. This is clear in the case of the missals studied, which would naturally have been used by priests celebrating the Mass. In terms of provenance, there is no indication that any were used in saying mass for female communities. The breviary included in our selection (Ms. E) appears to have been made for use in the Sacro Convento, Assisi, as indicated by the inventories of that friary.

8. Further information regarding this larger group will be included in my doctoral thesis (PhD dissertation, Melbourne College of Divinity, 2010).

9. These manuscripts are currently held in the collections of the Sacro Convento di San Francesco (Assisi), the Capitolo di San Lorenzo (Perugia), the Biblioteca

dell'Accademia (Cortona) and the State Library of Victoria (Melbourne, Australia).

10. The manuscripts have here each been assigned a letter (A to E). This is not deference to a common way of describing these texts (as they have never been studied in this formation before), but merely a device to keep references within the text short and readable. The manuscripts are listed, with as much accuracy as is possible, in chronological order.

11. For further information about this manuscript (including bibliography), see its catalogue entry in *The Medieval Imagination: Illuminated Manuscripts from Cambridge, Australia and New Zealand*, edited by Bronwyn Stocks and Nigel Morgan (Melbourne: Palgrave Macmillan, 2008), pp. 56–7.

12. M. Manion, 'The Codex Sancti Paschalis', *La Trobe Library Journal*, 51–2 (1993), pp. 11–23.

13. For further information about this manuscript (including bibliography), see its catalogue entry in *M. degl'Innocenti Gambuti, I Codici miniati medievali della Biblioteca Comunale e dell'Accademia Etrusca di Cortona* (Firenze: Studio per Edizioni Scelte, 1977), pp. 105–6.

14. It must be noted that there is no office for St Ubaldo in this missal's sanctoral cycle. However, this is a common feature of missals of the time and area; Ms. A includes a similar highlighting of St Herculanus (a patron saint of Perugia) in its calendar whilst not containing an office for the saint in its sanctoral cycle.

15. For more information on this manuscript (including bibliography), see its catalogue entry in G. Mazzatinti, *Inventari dei manoscritti delle biblioteche d'Italia* (Firenze: Leo S. Olschki, 1894), vol. 4, p. 64.

16. For further information about this manuscript (including bibliography), see its catalogue entry in L. Magionami, *I Manoscritti del Capitolo di San Lorenzo di Perugia* (Roma: Jouvence, 2006), pp. 53–5.

17. For further information about this manuscript (including bibliography), see its catalogue entry in Mazzatinti, *Inventari*, p. 64.

18. 'Scriptum est istud breuarium anno domini m. ccc. xxii. Finito libro referamus gratias christo.'

19. 'virginis prime de ordine dominarum'.

20. An in-depth analysis of the differences and similarities between the wording of the actual offices of Clare contained in these liturgical manuscripts is too lengthy to include in this study. For the purposes of this chapter, we will be concentrating only on the state of the offices – as original, as additions or as absent altogether. For further detail on the offices themselves, see G. Boccali (OFM), 'Testi liturgici antichi per la festa si santa Chiara', *Archivum Franciscanum Historicum*, 99: 1–2 (2006), pp. 3–32; 99:3–4 (2006), pp. 417–66; 100:1–2 (2007), pp. 149–220.

21. G. Boccali (OFM), 'Testi liturgici antichi per la festa di santa Chiara' (sec. XIII-XV) in *Archivum Franciscanum Historicum*, 99:3–4 (2006), p. 3.

22. S. J. P. van Dijk (OFM) and J. Hazelden Walker, *The Origins of the Modern Roman Liturgy* (London: Darton, Longman & Todd, 1960). See also: S. J. P. van Dijk (OFM), 'The Liturgical Legislation of the Franciscan Rules', *Franciscan Studies*, 12 (1952), pp. 176–95, 241–62.

23. See, for example, R. B. Brooke, *The Image of Francis: Responses to Sainthood in the Thirteenth Century* (Cambridge: Cambridge University Press, 2006), pp. 242–43; R. Pfaff, *The Liturgy in Medieval England: A History* (Cambridge: Cambridge University Press, 2009), pp. 320–6.

24. For further information see: A. Bartoli Langeli, 'Libraries, Books and Writing in the Orders of Friars Minor', translated by E. Hagman, OFM Cap., *Greyfriars*

Review, 17:2 (2003) pp. 135–159; B. Roest, *A History of Franciscan Education* (c. 1210–1517) (Boston: Brill, 2000); N. Senocak, 'Book Acquisition in the Medieval Franciscan Order', *Journal of Religious History*, 27:1 (2003), pp. 14–28.

25. Roest, *A History of Franciscan Education*, pp. 229–34.
26. *Ibid.*, p. 213, fn 147.
27. *Analecta franciscana sive chronica alique varia documenta*, Tomus III edited by the Patribus Collegii S. Bonaventurae (Quarrachi: Collegii S. Bonaventurae, 1887), pp. 328–9.
28. L. Wadding, *Annales minorum seu Trium Ordinum a S. Francisco instutorum* (Firenze: Ad Claras Aquas (Quarrachi), 1931–1964) (3rd edition), viii (1347–1376), p. 56. See also: V. Leroquais, *Les bréviaires manuscrits des bibliothèques publiques de France* (Paris: Macon, Protat frères, 1934).
29. Leroquais, *Les bréviaires manuscrits*, v. 1, p. 229.
30. I. Petersen (OSF), *Clare of Assisi: A Biographical Study* (Quincy, Ill.: Franciscan Press, 1993), pp. 114–16.
31. 'The Form of Life given by St Francis to St Clare and her Sisters' in Armstrong, *Clare of Assisi: Early Documents*, p. 243.
32. 'Acts of the Process of Canonization', p. 130.
33. Petersen, *Clare of Assisi*, p. 147.
34. P. B. Pixton, 'Councils, Western 1215–1274' in J. R. Strayer (ed.) *Dictionary of the Middle Ages* (New York: Charles Scribner's Sons, 1983), pp. 640–1. For specifics of the Fourth Lateran Council's rulings, see 'Concilium Lateranense IV, 1215. Constitutiones, 13' in Joseph Alberigo (ed.), *Conciliorum oecumenicorum decreta* (Bologna: Instituto per le Scienze Religiose, 1973), p. 242.
35. Petersen, *Clare of Assisi*, p. 321.
36. *Ibid.*, 322.
37. P. Ranft, 'St Clare of Assisi', in W. M. Johnston (ed.), *Encyclopedia of Monasticism* (Chicago: Fitzroy Dearborn Publishers, 2000), Vol 1, p. 302.
38. Petersen, *Clare of Assisi*, p. 326.
39. Armstrong, 'Introduction', p. 23.
40. M. Robson (OFM Conv.), *Francis of Assisi: the Legend and the Life*, pp. 270–8. For a comprehensive treatment of the issues dividing the Order, see D. Nimmo, *Reform and Division in the Franciscan Order: 1226–1538* (Rome: Capuchin Historical Institute, 1987).
41. 'The Rule of St Clare' in Armstrong, *Clare of Assisi: Early Documents*, p. 69.
42. Armstrong, 'Introduction', *Clare of Assisi: Early Documents*, p. 29.
43. *Ibid.*
44. Petersen, *Clare of Assisi*, p. 327.
45. Armstrong, 'Introduction', p. 28.
46. L. Knox, 'Audacious Nuns: Institutionalizing the Franciscan Order of St Clare', *Church History*, 69:1 (2000), pp. 42–4. See also K. Schreiner, 'Pastoral Care in Female Monasteries: Sacramental Services, Spiritual Edification, Ethical Discipline', in Hamburger and Marti (eds), *Crown and Veil*, pp. 225–44, especially pp. 235–8.
47. Armstrong, 'Introduction', p. 23.
48. *Ibid.*
49. *Ibid.*, pp. 23–4.
50. M. Pattenden, 'The Canonisation of Clare of Assisi and Early Franciscan History', *Journal of Ecclesiastical History*, 59:2 (2008), p. 213. Perhaps sometimes the sisters needed no papal persuasion: Werner Rösener suggests the Poor Clare convent at Söflingen, which was founded in 1237 and amassed great property and wealth, was in fact an example of the standard way a Poor Clare convent was administered

('Household and Prayer: Medieval Convents as Economic Entities' in Hamburger and Marti (eds) *Crown and Veil*, pp. 245–58, especially p. 255).

51. Knox, 'Audacious Nuns', p. 41.
52. M. Carney (OSF), 'Franciscans: Female', in W. M. Johnston (ed.) *Encyclopedia of Monasticism* (Chicago: Fitzroy Dearborn Publishers, 2001), Vol. 1, p. 503.
53. Pattenden, 'The Canonisation of Clare of Assisi', pp. 219–20.
54. *Ibid.*, p. 221.
55. Nimmo, *Reform and Division in the Franciscan Order*, p. 80.
56. Pattenden, 'The Canonisation of St Clare of Assisi', p. 211.
57. *Ibid.*, p. 218.
58. *Ibid.*, p. 212.
59. See Mss B and C.
60. See Ms. D.
61. Mooney, 'Imitatio Christi or Imitatio Mariae?', pp. 52–77.
62. Berger, 'Women in Worship', p. 755.

2

Marguerite Porete and the Predicament of her Preaching in Fourteenth-Century France

Rina Lahav

You have communicated the above mentioned book after it was condemned and burnt, to the reverend father lord John, bishop of Chalons, and to certain other persons as if it were good and lawful.[1]

In Paris, under the reign of King Philip the Fair (1285–1314), Marguerite Porete was charged by the **Inquisition** with continuing to communicate her ideas even after they had been censored; for this crime, she was burnt at the stake on 1 June 1310. Her crime was at least in part that she challenged gendered norms. Porete attempted to fuse a masculine medium, the sermon, structured according to well-defined rules, with a well-established feminine strategy of self-authorization, the claim to speak not as a limited human but as an annihilated self which has become the vessel of God's message. This was in itself a challenge to gendered expectations. But she would probably not have been considered heretical had she not used, as she did, the examples of Mary Magdalene and John the Baptist within her sermon. When she attributed to these well-known characters motives which differed from the established orthodoxy, she committed one of the crimes most feared by ecclesiastics: using the Scripture, the source of all revelation, to fit alternative theologies which endangered the orthodoxy, and threatened, in their perception, the unity of the Church. These underlie the negative reactions from Church officials which resulted in Porete's tragic end.

Apart from very brief reports of her trial, such as the chronicle of Guillaume de Nangis (d. 1300), the main sources concerning Marguerite Porete are the book she wrote, *The Mirror of Simple Annihilated Souls*, and the records made of her trial by the royal ministers of Philip the Fair, William of Nogaret and William of Plaisians.[2] *The Mirror* was rediscovered in 1867, and generally attributed to a male author; it was only in 1946 that Italian historian Romana Guarnieri attributed the book to Marguerite Porete.[3] The only surviving copy of the original version of *The Mirror* in Old French was made in the fifteenth century for the **nuns** of the Madeleine Convent at Orleans.[4] All the other medieval translations of the *Mirror* came from a Latin version, translated from the French sometime in the fourteenth century.[5]

Scholarly attention has been divided between the significance of Marguerite Porete's theological contribution and the role played in her execution by the politics of the French court.[6] In 1969, Ernest McDonnell briefly discussed the case of Marguerite Porete in his comprehensive study. He accused her of discrediting the whole female spiritual movement and sharpening the antagonism of ecclesiastical and secular authorities to extra-regular associations in general.[7] In 1972, Robert Lerner claimed that the trial of Marguerite Porete and Guiard de Cressonesart, a self-appointed defender of Marguerite, was closely linked to the suppression of the Templars in 1308. With difficulties and doubts accumulating in the matter of the Templars, Philip the Fair and his officials wished to display their unwavering orthodoxy in a case against a controversial **beguine**.[8] In 1986, Paul Verdeyen maintained that her trial was a part of a political struggle between Philip the Fair and the Papacy. The King, through the Inquisitor, set out to demonstrate to the Papacy that the inquisition maintained tight control over correct doctrine and ecclesiastical discipline in his kingdom. In addition, Verdeyen asserts, the condemnation of Marguerite was 'given' to the mendicant orders in order to obtain their support in the actions taken against the Templars.[9] This chapter will attempt to place Marguerite Porete in the context of the struggle against heresy, which became more crucial as the thirteenth century was approaching its end.

Preaching by women

The legitimization of female teachers and writers for both their actions and their writing was problematic in the later Middle Ages.[10] Two distinct ways in which a person might acquire sacred knowledge were acknowledged during this period: either by their studies or directly from God. The scholastic route of study and textual interpretation was *de facto* reserved for men. Medieval women, who usually were denied access to higher education and excluded from the ecclesiastical hierarchy, could most often only claim knowledge acquired in visions and revelations received directly from God.[11] Those who did occasionally preach were described by their contemporaries as not having received any systematic training in theology and biblical studies. They were perceived as vessels who received their insight from God, who wrote their words, and could instruct and inspire only through prophecy and song.[12] For example, the preaching of Rose of Viterbo (d. 1252) and Umilita of Faenza (d. 1310), who preached in public and in the cloister respectively, was recounted as a miracle of prophecy, and in the twelfth century Hildegard von Bingen (1098–1179) claimed to receive the power of song through prophecy as well.[13]

The Parisian masters of the university and associated schools explicitly excluded women from the teaching of doctrine, even when they accepted that they might have received something in a vision to communicate to others. Thomas Aquinas (1224–1272) insisted both upon the natural weakness of the female sex and on women's intrinsic lack of wisdom. He emphasized the Pauline injunction which condemned women to silence in churches and to subjection in the company of men.[14] Women were, therefore, subordinate to men, and it was not their place to teach men in public, since they lacked both the intellectual and the moral capacities required of a trusted public preacher.[15] Furthermore, Aquinas claimed that women, by their nature, would lead men into sexual desire and thus harm men rather than benefit them. His patriarchal views on female preachers were shared by the Parisian master Henry of Ghent, who lectured between 1276 and 1292. He argued that women were by nature changeable and easily led astray; thus, they were more likely to promote sin than combat it. Moreover, they were physically unsuited to public speaking: on the one hand, they were too weak to endure such strenuous activities, while on the other, they did not enjoy the freedom of movement necessary since they were controlled by men.[16]

Animosity towards female preaching was never uniform, however. The need to convey messages received from the Holy Spirit was widely acknowledged and examples of female preachers from the past became known by the diffusion of hagiography.[17] Moreover, regardless of the resolve of the theologians, there were examples of contemporaneous women preaching. Rose of Viterbo was a very visible and public lay woman, who preached on the streets of Viterbo, in Italy, in the middle of the thirteenth century. She was tolerated if not officially sanctioned.[18] She was, however, not the only such woman. Hundreds of recluses in northern Europe taught and preached even though they were neither ordained nor invested with any institutional power.[19] None, however, wrote in the systemized way of structured preaching, as did the male writers, with the exception of Marguerite Porete who fashioned her *Mirror of Simple Annihilated Souls* in the form of a sermon.

The sermon

A sermon, as the medievalist historian Beverly Mayne Kienzle has claimed, 'is an oral discourse, spoken in the voice of a preacher who addresses an audience to instruct and exhort them on a topic concerned with faith and morals and based on a sacred text'.[20] Although Kienzle includes written as well as spoken addresses of a person to an audience in her definition, the more obvious form of preaching was always oral. When people were depicted reading, they were presented as reading in groups, to which by necessity the text would have been read aloud.[21] Letters and sermons were composed with oral presentation in mind and thus longer and more complex literary works, including biblical **exegesis**, were often composed as expanded letters and sermons and were primarily for oral group presentation.[22] Although private silent reading became more pervasive in the fourteenth and fifteenth centuries, it did not replace oral reading even at the university.[23]

Scholars from a host of disciplines have attempted to reconstruct the actual act of delivering a sermon.[24] One of the difficulties is to determine the relationship between the actual preaching event and the written text, since preachers might have adjusted the written material to the different audiences and occasions.[25] Moreover, although sermons were usually recorded in Latin, either as a manual to the preacher or as minutes taken at the act of preaching, the delivery itself was almost always in the vernacular. Therefore, even when the preacher wanted to deliver a precise version of the written sermon there remained an issue of translation, which would necessarily vary with each performance.[26] Porete's sermon *The Mirror of Simple Souls* was written in Middle French to be read to listeners in the same language, thereby sidestepping the issue of translation. It was not a manual to the preacher on how to create a sermon from the given material, but rather it was a complete text to be delivered *verbatim* to the listeners.

The Mirror of Simple Annihilated Souls was a guide directing the reader or the listener on their journey to God in seven stages. Marguerite Porete described only six stages or steps in her *Mirror*, explaining that the seventh stage was accessible only after death.[27] The soul completing the journey had nothing of its own; it ceased to exist and was fully immersed in God, making this stage very close to natural death.[28] The road to the final destination was the road of contemplation, which Marguerite Porete explained through the rhetorical device of a didactic dialogue. The main characters were Soul, Love and Reason, with Reason pulling the Soul away from the spiritual union with God and towards earthly devotion, while Love was both a representation of God and the means to reach Him.[29] Porete addressed her hearers in *The Mirror* in second person plural and urged them to become more worthy and to reach perfection through the practice of Christian charity, 'which gift *you* will *hear* explained in this book through the Intellect of Love and following the questions of Reason'.[30] This address was vocal and direct, from the preacher to her audience.

Conforming

The Mirror was structured by Porete as a **thematic sermon**, a form that became common towards the end of the thirteenth century. In addition to having a single point of departure in a form of a single *thema* or quotation from Scripture, thematic sermons followed a precise structure based on the *Artes Praedicandi*, or handbooks instructing the clerics how to preach.[31] The thematic method of preaching was closely related to the new methods of intellectual inquiry, which appeared around the end of the twelfth century and developed during the thirteenth as a form of instruction in the universities.[32] Most sermons that have survived in published form from the later Middle Ages show at least some influence of the *Artes*.[33]

We do not know whether Porete had direct access to *Artes Praedicandi*. If, however, some aspects of the guidelines provided in the *Artes* were present in her work, then it was probable that she had heard actual sermons and learned from them, wanting to speak to the clerics in their language if only to encourage them to listen to her ideas. In order to see exactly how *The Mirror* correlates with these concepts of the sermon it can be compared to the directions for a good sermon in the *Summa* of Alan of Lille (1128–1202), fortified by subsequent additions. Although Alan of Lille did not use the words *Artes Praedicandi*, his was the first comprehensive preaching manual.[34]

Alan of Lille began his guide for good preaching by discussing in general the point of departure of a good sermon.[35] Before discussing the themes of the sermon, he first dealt with the preparation of the preacher, which entailed six steps before finally being ready to preach in the seventh. Alan of Lille used the parable of Jacob's ladder to create the sense of climbing to the sky, or striving to reach God in seven stages. The first three stages were between a man and God: confession, prayer and thanksgiving. The next three steps were gained by mastering Scripture. Then in the seventh stage, or rung, the man preached openly what the Scripture had taught him.[36] Learning from Scripture came as the most advanced level of learning: after establishing a basic relationship with God by acknowledging his sins, praying and giving thanks, he learned to reach a further level of perfection through the study of Scripture. The means by which he moved closer to God was a more profound understanding of Scripture. He then reached the highest level of development not only by teaching others what he had learned himself, but by teaching them in public. More precisely, he should preach to others, exhorting them to follow him on the right way to God, which he had discovered in Scripture.

Marguerite Porete, too, embarked on her apostolate in the seventh step of her alternative development. Although her seven steps differed greatly from these of Alan of Lille, the ultimate stage seemed to be identical. In the theology of Marguerite Porete, the initial six steps can be taken while still alive, whereas the seventh stage could only be achieved after death.[37] Nevertheless she claimed to be writing her book after achieving the full journey she described, alleging that God had given her this book after she reached her destination, as evidence of His love. Therefore Marguerite Porete preached in public not what she learned from the Scripture, as Alan of Lille recommended, but what she believed she learned directly from God. Although she did not prescribe preaching as the goal for her followers, she chose to preach herself. Writing and spreading the ideas of *The Mirror of Simple Souls,* was the method Marguerite Porete employed to preach what she believed was given to her directly by her constant connection to God. Therefore, just as Alan of Lille prescribed, Porete set out to preach the fruits of her learning in public.

After expounding the required preparations for preachers Alan of Lille turned to the specifics of sermon writing. A sermon, he said, should develop from a text which enjoyed undisputed theological authority, such as excerpts from the Evangelists, the Psalms, the Epistles of Paul or the book of Solomon.[38] However, if other Holy texts might facilitate the preaching on a particular theme they should be included as well. Porete, too, dealt with authority at the outset of her book. In the prologue she compared herself to a princess who had fallen in love with Alexander the Great and her book to the image the princess created to assuage her longings for him.[39] Although Porete presented this comparison as an *exemplum*, the two parts of her equation were not identical. In both cases the images were created to bring the lover and the object of love closer to each other. But whereas the princess had created the image of her lover according to rumours about him, Marguerite Porete believed that her book had been created by God. The princess created the relationship by herself and within herself, while Porete was convinced that she was given this book as a token of love by the lover himself. The authority Porete proclaimed for her book was, therefore, God himself.

In order for the authority of her book to be recognized, Porete based her elaborate argument on a scriptural quotation. 'One thing is necessary for you to do if you want to be perfect. It is: go and sell all the things which you possess and give them to the poor, and then follow me, and you will have treasure in the heavens' (Matthew 19:21).[40] According to Porete, Jesus exhorted His followers to relinquish not only all material concerns in order to attain to perfection, but also to neutralize themselves completely. The fact that this understanding underlies her choice of a verse is made abundantly clear: 'the one who would have perfect charity must be mortified in the affections of the life of the spirit,' she says.[41] The two beginnings, the comparison with the princess and the verse from Scripture, supported each other even on a **mystical** level. The first beginning enabled Porete to indicate that there was a communication with God, who had given her the book to demonstrate to the world what His divine love could do for a soul. The second hinted at a promise that was given in the Scripture that Porete's treatise came to explain fully and set into action: how one can achieve perfection by emptying oneself.

The next mission of the preacher, according to Alan of Lille, was to capture the good will of the audience.[42] In Alan's case this was accomplished through the humble demeanour of the preacher himself, an explanation of the usefulness of the matter to be discussed and the assumption that the preacher was merely the vehicle for the truth of his sermon. Porete invested much space and effort in her book to explaining the usefulness of her theology, because unlike orthodox preachers, who preached well-known morals using known texts, she needed to propagate something new. The sole purpose of Porete's theology was to benefit her listeners, whose spiritual happiness was at the centre of her attention. Porete argued that, after relinquishing the will to God, the person was no longer capable of willing or doing anything that was not compatible with God's will, because the person could not will anymore, but only God willed in him. Such a person ceased to exist as an independent thinking and acting creature that could choose good or evil. God willed in them. These annihilated souls became empty vessels for God to fill and be goodness through them. Therefore they could not will nor act wrong.

Following on from this, the preacher had to declare to the audience which divisions or dilations were made in order to treat the subject in the sermon. The expansion of a sermon was the most detailed part in most of the *Artes*. The guides were adamant that the topic of the sermon was to be expanded by three divisions which were in turn then subdivided, but apparently the actual texts were not always in keeping with these rigid instructions and usually the divisions blurred towards the end of the sermon.[43] Porete outlines her divisions very distinctly, even enumerating them. While she does not signify which were more important, a combination of three fits exactly with the conventional structure of good sermons. The divisions were:

1. a soul
2. who is saved by faith without works
3. who is only in love

4. who does nothing for God
5. who leaves nothing to do for God
6. to whom nothing can be taught
7. from whom nothing can be taken
8. nor given
9. and who possesses no will.[44]

Porete then develops the first part of her distinction. First she elaborates on the nature of the soul, using a triple subdistinction:

> this Soul, says Love, has six wings like the Seraphim. With two wings she covers her face from Jesus Christ our lord [...] with two other wings she covers her feet [...] with the two others the Soul flies, and dwells in being and rest.[45]

This passage, like so many others throughout *The Mirror*, abounds with a kind of sermon expansion very commonly used in mystical sermons, to the extent that it became a prerequisite of the genre: the four part exegesis on the Scripture. Since the purpose of a mystical sermon was creation of a union between man and God, it usually presented a discourse in which the metaphysical or transcendent realm was made real.[46] Michael D. McGuire and John H. Patton have studied the patterns of the mystical sermons of Meister Eckhart (1260–c. 1328), who may have been influenced by the work of Marguerite Porete.[47] They arrived at the conclusion that there was a certain pattern in mystical sermons, which distinguished them from all the other sermons.

Eckhart greatly magnified the role of amplification by the '*sensus allegoricus*' and '*anagogicus*' in order to bring the divine reality closer to the reader/listener. In essence he opened a new level of reality for the listeners. In medieval exegesis the senses were considered to be multiplied by the four ways of interpretation of Scripture. First, the *sensus historicus* or *literalis*, the literal sense, interpreted the Biblical text only by simple explanation of the words; second, *sensus tropologicus*, the moral sense, which provided the meaning of the text that looked to instruct on the correction of morals. Third, the *sensus allegoricus*, the allegorical sense, which looked for a meaning other than the literal. This interpretation assumed that the Biblical text had an additional mystical meaning that used exemplification by simile. There was also the *sensus anagogicus*, the celestial sense, which was used mystically or openly, to stir and exhort the minds of the listeners to the contemplation of heavenly things. This interpretation to the text involved divine beings and their interactions.[48]

The Mirror overflows not only with *sensus allegoricus* and *anagogicus*, but also with the *sensus tropologicus*, which seems at first glance out of place in a treatise so preoccupied with the abandonment of the virtues. An example is Porete's development of the message found in this small portion of the text: 'Christ was transfigured on Mount Tabor, where there were only three of his disciples. He told them that they must neither speak about it nor say anything about it until His resurrection' (Matthew 17; 1–9).[49] After citing the Scripture Porete divided this small text into three sections. First, she explained why Christ only showed Himself to three disciples.

He did it so that you might know that few folk will see the brightness of His transfiguration, and He shows this only to His special friends [...] this happens in this world when God gives Himself through the ardour of light into the heart of a creature.[50]

All senses were engaged in Porete's explanation of this single part of the Transfiguration. First she explained the passage literally: there were three of His followers so that everybody would know that God will not reveal His true nature to large masses. Then Marguerite Porete moved to the *sensus tropologicus,* or the moral sense. Only His special friends, those ones who engage His special favour by doing something above and beyond Christian duty, will see His true face. The *sensus allegoricus,* or the allegorical meaning, Porete claimed, was that just as God gave the vision of His true self, as light, to His three special disciples, He will give Himself as true ardour of light that will flow into the properly prepared creature who has become special and deserves this. The *sensus anagogicus* was the essence of this discussion; God and the revelation of His true self.

The characters Porete used to progress through the treatise of *The Mirror* served as another set of divisions. *The Mirror of Simple Souls* was designed as a disputation of adversaries on every subject. Porete used the character of Reason to pose the most difficult questions and challenges imaginable. The argument veered occasionally from the main flow, and then rejoined the main argument again just to be divided on the next point in question. Although Peter Dronke has claimed that Porete's deepest inspiration was poetic, and borrowed its literary ideals from *fin amor,* I would point out that it does not contradict the argumentative nature of the characters, or that the same three were pulling the argument forward throughout the treatise.[51]

The predicament

The way to end a sermon was rarely treated in the *Artes.*[52] Alan of Lille was one of the few who did include some sort of ending by concluding his treatment of the subject of the sermon with a recommendation that the preacher 'should also use *exempla* to make his points, because people remember familiar things'.[53] Alan of Lille did not expound on this matter. Humbert of Romans (1194–1277), on the other hand, dealt with the nature of the exemplum in the prologue to his collection of exempla. He enumerated seven considerations for the selection and delivery of the exemplum. The seventh dealt with the matter of authority. No exemplum, he said, should be invented by the preacher, but all should be taken from the various sources of authoritative exempla coming from the Scripture.[54]

Marguerite Porete concluded her teachings with seven considerations. Two of them looked very much like exempla she adopted from Scripture. This was not incidental. As exempla, these two stories were highly effective. Porete managed to convey to her listeners the benefits of her theology using familiar and highly admired characters. Additionally, her unorthodox outlook provided her with the perfect opportunity to legitimize her theology in the eyes of her perceived judges. In the beginning of *The Mirror* she felt compelled to provide Scriptural authority in addition to her claimed divine authority for *The Mirror*. Now, in the conclusion of her book, she used Scriptural authority to provide legitimacy and merit to her theology. It was generally accepted that the significant events recorded in the New Testament had already been prefigured in the Old. It was also believed that events and persons of the New Testament could be seen as foreshadowing the still-hidden mysteries of the kingdom of heaven and also of the life of Christian souls.[55] Porete used this understanding to her benefit: if she could show in the conclusion of her book that her theology was foreseen in the New Testament then it would be seen as legitimate. She used Mary Magdalen and John the Baptist to demonstrate to her readers the happy and serene state a person can achieve after completing the steps she prescribed in her theology.

Mary Magdalen and John the Baptist were presented as free annihilated souls when their actions were seen and recorded in the Holy Scripture. John the Baptist showed Jesus Christ to two of his disciples so that they might follow him but he himself never left the desert to go to see Jesus Christ in his human nature. Moreover, he held a sermon in the presence of Jesus without being distracted. Marguerite Porete argued that these two actions were against the natural inclination of a follower. A person devoted to a teacher would not have elected to stay and direct others to the teacher; he would have followed him wherever he went. Also, she claimed, the knowledge of the nature of Jesus Christ, as the truth itself, should have naturally filled the voice of the sternest of speakers with a tremble. John the Baptist, however, kept his calm and completed the sermon. The explanation Porete gives for this response is that God had filled his soul, becoming solely responsible for his decisions and actions.[56] Mary Magdalen was also portrayed as one of the freed souls.[57] Porete was indicating that Mary accomplished the total annihilation of her human essence and God replaced her being in her soul. Thereupon He acted in the soul of Mary in her stead.

It was not incidental that Marguerite Porete chose the characters of Mary Magdalen and John the Baptist to illustrate her point. Mary Magdalen was considered *Apostolorum Apostola* the apostle of the apostles. She was chosen to announce the resurrection of Christ and featured in every discussion on the preaching of women.[58] Although some clerics tried to diminish the effect of the apostolate of Mary Magdalen, they were never successful in eliminating it completely.[59] Her character was chosen by Marguerite Porete to reinforce the image of a woman carrying the most important messages from God to the people; her authority resonated with the authority Porete claimed and the legitimacy of her theology as the new apostolate to be heard and taken to heart.

The character of John the Baptist allowed Porete to confront the male idea of the right kind of preaching. Although he was a man and did not need to use the female space of receiving and conveying theology he was shown to do it nonetheless. Using the figure of John the Baptist, Porete argued that being a vessel of God's communication to the world was actually the most holy justification for preaching. Therefore although he was a man and could, in theory, claim the right to preach without complete annihilation of self, he was nevertheless shown preaching in an accepted female space, speaking the word of God with no participation of self. He was a mere vehicle for the words of God on their way to the people.

Thus Marguerite Porete's theology, as articulated in *The Mirror*, stood at the border of the male and female spheres. It would seem that Porete naturally chose the female space of an empty vessel filled by God and ordained by Him to spread His ideas from the female authority of a mystical/emotional basis. However, she did it by using the conventional structure of male delivery, by using a thematic sermon as her frame. By mixing the prohibited and allowed she tried to establish her legitimacy in the theological discussion, in two ways. On the one hand she claimed her superiority as a female conduit, on the other as a person who understood the rules and conventions of the male delivery and employed these methods to attract the male interest to her theology.

When a medieval preacher decided to use a story from Scripture for his exemplum he entered the rigid territory of conventional exegesis. A medieval exegete was not free to create new allegorical meanings, or even to substantially extend the ones which were already in use. Both literal and spiritual meanings were considered to be imposed by God. John Hilary Martin has excluded from these constrictions the persons who were given a prophetic insight, but he has indicated that these people were not usually medieval authors.[60]

Marguerite Porete elected to alter the exegesis and create a new meaning for the actions of the protagonists of the stories, adjusting it to exemplify her theology instead of the conventional theology of the Church. Her theology and the presentation of it aimed at blurring the boundary between male and female, and engendering a unique space that should allow both males and females to follow her example. Most of all it aimed at securing continuous readership of her book. Her theology was not only presented from the female space of delivering messages directly, but also delivered without an intermediary. Porete presented her theology as coming from a dehumanized and non-gendered author, speaking in terms of male discourse and producing authoritative exempla accordingly. The combined figures of John the Baptist and Mary Magdalene symbolized an image of a pure preacher, neither male nor female, but a pure conduit to God's voice.

The officials who had heard the ending of her book saw it as proof why women should not preach. In their eyes Marguerite Porete's interpretation of the actions of both Mary Magdalene and John the Baptist demonstrated their perceived fear of sermons created and delivered by women. They were convinced that women would not, or more precisely could not, conform to the rules of interpretation and preaching. In their eyes it proved that women were indeed incompetent, changeable and easily led astray. They lacked the consistency to invest enough effort actually to learn the proper use of the Bible and were fond of every new idea that came along and swept them away. Porete's very success in adapting the sermon to her own ends was a challenge to their claim to exclusive competence in this area.

Furthermore, when discussing the character of a sermon in general, Alan of Lille described two kinds of negative preaching. The first kind was harmful because it was prepared in order to gain the adoration of people. Such sermons may be suspect but they should be tolerated nonetheless, since, according to St Paul every pronunciation of Christ, however insufficient was still profitable. Another type of sermon, altogether more dangerous, was delivered by heretics and was easily identified by the use it made of the Scripture: 'first they propound the truth and then they draw false conclusions from it.'[61] Heretical preaching was especially abhorrent because it made unconventional use of the Scripture, or in other words used the Scripture to prove its points instead of using it in confirmative ways to prove accepted and pre-approved points, as the Church demanded.

Marguerite Porete's attempt at conforming to accepted patterns of clerical male discourse of her time had in fact emphasized her difference in the eyes of her opponents. By the early fourteenth century, these were the errors that were especially abhorrent to the Inquisitors and the canon lawyers. The end of thirteenth century saw the formation of a new group of university-trained clerics, both **secular** and regular, whose wish to homogenize the religious observance overrode their internal differences. With the blessing of the King of France, Philip IV, they systematically persecuted all those elements whose authority challenged their dominance.[62] The very fact that Porete had managed to master the authoritative male medium of delivery made her dangerous. This was why she was accused of attempting to preach, especially to Church officials, and not simply of creating her theology. What the Inquisitors wished to see burnt at the stake was an uncontrollable challenge to clerical dominance: a woman who successfully manipulated the Scripture in order to convey her ideas.

Notes

1. [*Dictum etiam librum post condempnationem et combustionem predictas sicut bonum et licitum communicasti reverendo patri domino Johanni, Cathalaunensi episcopo, et quibusdam personis aliis*], William of Paris in Paul Verdeyen, 'Le Procès d'inquisition contre Marguerite Porete et Guiard de Cressonessart (1309–1310)', *Revue d'histoire ecclésiastique*, 81 (1986), p. 82.
2. M. Porete, *Speculum Simplicium Animarum* in Paul Verdeyen (ed.), *Corpus Christianorum, Continuatio Mediaeualis, LXIX* (Turnhout: Brepols, 1986). This volume holds both the surviving Middle French text of the late fifteenth century (on odd pages) and the Latin version (on even pages) of Porete's *Mirror*. I also used two translations of the texts: M. Porete, *The Mirror of Simple Souls*, translated by E. L. Babinsky (New York: Paulist Press, 1993), and M. Porete, *The Mirror of Simple Souls*, translated by E. Colledge, JC, and J. Grant (Notre Dame: University of Notre Dame Press, 1999).
3. E. Zum Brunn and G. Epiney-Burgard, *Women Mystics in Medieval Europe*, translated by S. Hughes (New York: Paragon, 1989), p. 143.
4. *Ibid.*, p. 150.
5. R. E. Lerner, *The Heresy of the Free Spirit in the Later Middle Ages* (London: University of California Press, 1972), p. 73.
6. B. McGinn, *The Flowering of Mysticism: Men and Women in the New Mysticism (1200–1350)*, Vol. III of *The Presence of God: A History of Western Christian Mystics* (New York: Crossroad, 1998), pp. 246–65; M. Lichtmann, 'Marguerite Porete and Meister Eckhart: The Mirror for Simple Souls Mirrored' (in B. McGinn (ed.), *Meister Eckhart and the Beguine Mystics, Hadewijch of Brabant, Mechthild of Magdeburg and Marguerite Porete* (New York: Crossroad, 1994); A. Hollywood, 'Suffering Transformed: Marguerite Porete, Meister Eckhart and the Problem of Women's Spirituality,' in B. McGinn (ed.), *Meister Eckhart and*

the Beguine Mystics; M. Sells, 'The Pseudo-Woman and the Meister: "Unsaying" and Essentialism' in B. McGinn (ed.), *Meister Eckhart and the Beguine Mystics, Hadewijch of Brabant, Mechthild of Magdeburg and Marguerite Porete*, pp. 65–146; A. Hollywood, *The Soul as Virgin Wife: Mechthild of Magdeburg, Marguerite Porete and Meister Eckhart* (Notre Dame: University of Notre Dame Press, 1995), pp. 87–119; E. L. Babinsky, 'Christological Transformation in the Mirror of Souls by Marguerite Porete', *Theology Today*, 60 (2003), pp. 34–48. See also: M. Lichtmann, 'Marguerite Porete's Mirror for Simple Souls: Inverted Reflection of Self, Society and God', *Studia Mystica*, 16:1 (1995), pp. 4–29; E. Johnston, 'Marguerite Porete: A Post Mortem' and M. Brown, 'Marie D'Oignies, Marguerite Porete and "Authentic" Female Mystic Piety in the Middle Ages', in J. O. Ward and F. C. Bussey (eds), *Worshipping Women: Misogyny and Mysticism in the Middle Ages* (Sydney: University of New South Wales, 1997).

7. E. W. McDonnell, *The Beguines and Beghards in Medieval Culture with Special Emphasis on the Belgian Scene* (New York: Octagon Books, 1969), p. 490.
8. Lerner, *The Heresy of the Free Spirit*, p. 77.
9. Verdeyen, 'Le Procès', p. 85.
10. A. B. Mulder-Bakker (ed.), *Seeing and Knowing: Women and Learning in Medieval Europe 1200–1500* (Turnhout: Brepols, 2004), p. 18.
11. *Ibid.*, p. 3.
12. C. Muessig, 'Prophecy and Song: Teaching and Preaching by Medieval Women', in B. Mayne Kienzle and P. J. Walker (eds), *Women Preachers and Prophets through Two Millennia of Christianity* (Berkeley: University of California Press, 1998), pp. 46–58, 153.
13. *Ibid.*, p. 148.
14. 'St Thomas Aquinas', in R. Potter, OP, trans., *Summa Theologiae*, Vol. 45, 2a2ae, 177, 2, pp. 132–3.
15. *Ibid.*
16. 'Henry of Ghent', *Summa Quaestionum Ordinarium*, Book 1, Article 11, Question 2, reprinted in A. Blamires and C. W. Marx, 'Woman Not to Preach: A Disputation in British Library MS Harley 31', *Journal of Medieval Latin*, 3 (1993), p. 52.
17. A. Blamires, 'Women and Preaching in Medieval Orthodoxy, Heresy, and Saints' Lives', *Viator*, 26 (1995), p. 136.
18. D. Pryds, 'Proclaiming Sanctity through Proscribed Acts: The Case of Rose of Viterbo', in Kienzle and Walker (eds), *Women Preachers and Prophets*, p. 166.
19. A. B. Mulder-Bakker, 'Maria Doctrix: Anchoritic Women, the Mother of God, and the Transmission of Knowledge', in A. B. Mulder-Bakker (ed.), *Seeing and Knowing, Women and Learning in Medieval Europe 1200–1550* (2004), p. 199.
20. B. Mayne Kienzle, *The Sermon* (Turnhout: Brepols, 2000), p. 151.
21. P. Saenger, 'Silent Reading: Its Impact on Late Medieval Script and Society', *Viator*, 13 (1982), p. 379.
22. *Ibid.*, p. 382.
23. *Ibid.*, p. 391.
24. J. W. O'Malley, 'Introduction', in T. L. Amos, E. A. Green, B. Mayne Kienzle (eds), *De Ore Domini: Preacher and World in the Middle Ages* (Kalamazoo: Medieval Institute Publications, 1989), p. 2.
25. Kienzle, *The Sermon*, p. 968.
26. Kienzle, *The Sermon*, pp. 973–4.
27. Porete, *The Mirror* (1993), p. 193.
28. Amy Hollywood cautiously interprets it to mean that all of the creature's human nature – body, spirit and soul – is a burden and must be killed. Seen from this

perspective, the soul in her entirety must be renounced insofar as she is created and other than God. Hollywood, *The Soul as Virgin Wife*, p. 110.

29. Porete, *Speculum*, pp. 320–2.
30. Porete, *Speculum*, p. 15.
31. O'Malley, 'Introduction', *De Ore Domini*, p. 8.
32. M. G. Briscoe, *Artes Praedicandi* (Turnhout: Brepols, 1992), p. 30.
33. O'Malley, 'Introduction', *De Ore Domini*, p. 9.
34. Briscoe, *Artes Praedicandi*, p. 20.
35. A. De Insulis, '*Summa De Arte Praedicatoria*', in J. P. Migne, *Patrologiae Latinae*, PL 210: 52–55, 52 p. 111. Alan of Lille, *The Art of Preaching*, translated by G. R. Evans (Kalamazoo: Cistercian Publications, 1981), p. 15.
36. PL 210: 52, p. 111, 'Septimum gradum ascendit, quando in manifesto praedicat quae ex Scriptura didicit'.
37. Porete, *The Mirror*, summary of the steps are in pp. 189–194.
38. [*ab auctoritate theologica*], Insulis, *Summa De Arte Praedicatoria*, PL 210: 54, p. 113.
39. Porete, *The Mirror*, p. 80.
40. *Ibid.*, p. 82.
41. *Ibid.*, p. 82.
42. [*captare benevolentiam*], Insulis, *Summa De Arte Praedicatoria*, PL 210: 54, p. 113.
43. Briscoe, *Artes Praedicandi*, p. 57.
44. Porete, *Speculum*, pp. 18, 20.
45. Porete, *The Mirror*, p. 83.
46. M. D. McGuire and J. H. Patton, 'Preaching in the Mystic Mode: The Rhetorical Art of Meister Eckhart', *Communication Monographs*, 44:4 (1977), p. 270.
47. Hollywood, *The Soul as Virgin Wife*, p. 121.
48. H. Caplan, 'The Four Senses of Scriptural Interpretation and the Mediaeval Theory of Preaching', *Speculum*, 4:3 (1929), p. 283.
49. Porete, *The Mirror* (1993), p. 149.
50. *Ibid.*
51. P. Dronke, *Women Writers of the Middle Ages, A Critical Study of Texts from Perpetua (+203) to Marguerite Porete (+1310)* (London: Cambridge University Press, 1984), pp. 218–21.
52. Briscoe, *Artes Praedicandi*, p. 57.
53. Insulis, *Summa De Arte Praedicatoria*, PL 210:55, p. 114.
54. S. Tugwell (ed.), *Early Dominicans: Selected Writings* (New York: Paulist Press, 1982), p. 376.
55. J. H. Martin, 'The Four Senses of Scripture: Lessons from the Thirteenth Century', *Pacifica*, 2 (1989), p. 95.
56. Porete, *The Mirror*, p. 206.
57. *Ibid.*, p. 203.
58. Blamires, 'Women and Preaching', p. 138.
59. K. Ludwig Jansen, 'Maria Magdalena: Apostolorum Apostola', in Kienzle and Walker (eds.), *Women Preachers and Prophets*, p. 79.
60. Martin, *The Four Senses of Scripture*, p. 94.
61. Insulis, *Summa De Arte Praedicatoria*, PL 210: 53–4, p. 113.
62. E. Viennot, *Le France, Les Femmes et Le Pouvoir, L'invention de Le Loi Salique (v-xvi siècle)* (Paris: Perin, 2006), p. 293.

3

The Impact of Renaissance Gender-Related Notions on the Female Experience of the Sacred: The Case of Angela Merici's Ursulines

Querciolo Mazzonis

Students of gender history often ponder on how to reconcile the achievements of spiritual women during the Renaissance with the misogynistic culture of the time. Recent studies have shown that mainstream views of the female both limited and fostered women's opportunities within religion.[1] Focusing on the Company of St Ursula founded by Angela Merici (1474–1540), this essay will provide a further illustration of how a certain model of female spirituality was articulated in connection with contemporaneous cultural notions of the female.

Modern historiography has tended to consider Merici's Company as an institute teaching poor girls; yet this image fails to capture the aim of the Company, which offered women an innovative secular form of religious life.[2] The Company fits within a history of penitential and **mystic** spirituality which manifested itself especially between the thirteenth and the sixteenth centuries, a history where women attained forms of authority and creative opportunities which ordinary women normally did not have. Merici's contribution to this history is that she codified some of the most original traits of female spirituality into a religious Rule for women.

This essay will compare Merici's ideal of experience of the sacred and her notion of woman with the cultural notion of the female of the time – whether expressed by theologians, humanists and lawyers or derived from women's social roles, from family and the world of work. This comparison will be established through a cultural perspective, in terms not of direct influence but of thematic consistency, meaningful correspondence and conceptual discrepancy. It emerges that gender norms and customs, on the one hand, shaped Merici's religious ideal both positively and negatively and, on the other, were adapted and surpassed. Indeed, Angela Merici's proposal empowered women, both in their daily life and at an ideological level. Finally, this essay offers a tentative and synthetic cultural evaluation of women's achievements within mystic and penitential religiosity, considered as the product of the combination between a set of gender-related notions and contemporaneous religious models.

Introductory notes on the Company of St Ursula

A Franciscan tertiary from the age of 20, Angela Merici spent her first 40 years between her native village of Desenzano del Garda and the nearby town of Salò. In 1516, she went to Brescia, where she soon attracted the attention of a group of noblemen and merchants, who often visited and hosted her in their houses.[3] In Brescia (and beyond) Angela established her reputation as a spiritual leader by virtue of her devout life, religious knowledge and human qualities. From 1532, she began to share her life with a group of women of mixed social backgrounds with whom, in 1535, she founded the Company of St Ursula.

Historiography has often associated Merici's name and original Institute with religious education and charity. While it is possible that some Ursulines were individually involved in these activities, neither in the Company's writings nor in the early sources and biographies regarding Merici was there any reference to them. Such references emerged in the Rules of the new Companies and in later hagiographies, and found fertile ground in the more recent literature stressing charity as a distinguishing trait of the Catholic Reformation.[4]

The original Company was composed of lay women who lived a life of prayer and penance in their own homes, without **vows** or common habit. However, the Company required a strong religious commitment. The Ursulines, like **nuns**, were called 'brides of Christ'; they had to be virgins, were expected to follow the **evangelical counsels** (obedience, virginity and poverty), and to remain in this status for their entire life. Furthermore, Merici did not propose a common life or specific activities to carry out in the world: rather, the Ursulines were free to follow their personal inspiration and simply met a few times a month – once for communion and occasionally to hear a sermon or to talk about their **spiritual life**. Financially, the Company was self-sufficient: the members could keep their properties, inherit, earn a salary (some of them worked in the houses of the Brescian aristocracy), and offered one another support in times of need. The Company was not subjected to ecclesiastical jurisdiction and was entirely composed of women. It was divided into three tiers: first, there were the ordinary Ursulines; then the 'wiser' Ursulines, called *Colonelle*, who acted as spiritual guides; and finally the 'lady-governors', or *Matrone*, aristocratic Brescian widows, who were not members of the Company but who were elected to administer it and to deal with the Ursulines' everyday problems (such as legal, economic and medical issues). The *Colonelle* visited the Ursulines once every week or fortnight, and then met the *Matrone* to discuss the virgins' needs.

The Company grew rapidly: it began in 1535 with 28 members; two years later it had 75, and in 1540 it reached 150. Although after Merici's death the

Company was criticized, it received papal approbation in 1546 and, from the second half of the sixteenth century, it was founded in several Italian cities by some Counter-Reformation bishops and especially with the support of the Archbishop of Milan, Carlo Borromeo (1538–1584). Hundreds of women joined the new companies, which offered a devout life in the world. The Company's aims, however, were altered and the Ursulines became a pioneering institute for teaching Catholicism in the schools of Christian doctrine and within families, and for organizing women's secular religious life.[5]

The period in which Merici founded her Company was still open to new ideas and different religious trends. Particularly significant for Merici was a medieval and Renaissance tradition of secular penitential and mystic female spirituality (i.e. tertiaries, **beguines** and *bizoche*). In Merici's times, in conjunction with the Italian wars, a conspicuous number of charismatic women (known as 'living saints') were venerated by common people and by the elite in several cities of northern and central Italy.[6] Merici knew or was devoted to some female 'living saints', both in Brescia and in other cities, and her life fitted within this phenomenon. Although she was not famous for prophetic and mystical gifts, she was nonetheless believed by many Brescian people to have a privileged relationship with the divine and she became a point of reference for the community, in which she was asked to provide advice, spiritual protection and informal preaching.[7]

The writings of the Company provide revealing insights into the relationship between the experience of the sacred which Merici proposed to her Ursulines and the main cultural notions of the female at that time.

Identities and behaviour

Merici's writings proposed religious identities which bore similarities with the notion of womanhood as expressed in Renaissance conduct treatises and various sources, such as contracts, wills and other legal documents. Didactic literature classified women and defined their duties around the distinction between virgins, wives and widows, rather than classifying them by age, class and work. Coherent with the theoretical identification of women with familial and sexual roles, women's main social function was in the family (as wives) and the convent (as brides of Christ), while women's occupational identity was weak and remuneration was often conceived as a contribution towards the dowry.[8]

Merici's Company was organized following a sexual or familial classification of women: the members of the Company were virgins and considered to be brides of Christ ('true and virginal spouses of the Son of God'), while the *Matrone* were widows and, like the *Colonelle*, were described as mothers of the virgins, or even 'mothers-in-law of the son of God'. Merici did not propose a feminization of the divine. Indeed, the Ursulines' celestial world was dominated by male figures who held traditional roles: if Christ was the bridegroom, with whom one established a relationship of love, God was the creator of the universe, a judge and, above all, a caring father who would never abandon his daughters: 'Your heavenly Father knows very well' – the Rule states – 'that you have need of all these things [...] He who wants nothing for you but only your good and your joy.'[9] Mary, who did not have familial connotations, in contrast to God and Christ, did not seem to occupy a central place in Merici's spirituality: she was mentioned only four times, against 61 references to God and 26 to Christ.[10]

Following women's social roles and experiences, the Company's female government was understood in terms of maternal love and its main duty was protecting the honour of the daughters: 'And the widows [should be] as mothers, full of concern for the good and welfare of their spiritual sisters and daughters.'[11] The *Matrone* were to administer the Company's possessions 'according to [...] motherly discretion and love'. Merici referred to the role of mothers in aristocratic familial strategies directed to the improvement of the status of the family through the marriage of daughters:

> Now one sees temporal mothers putting a great deal of care and effort into attiring, adorning and embellishing their daughters in many different ways, so that they may please their earthly spouses; and the more important and noble these men are, the more the mothers strive with all diligence to make their daughters more and more attractive [...] for in this way they also hope [...] to have the love and favour of their sons-in-law. How much more must you do this for those heavenly daughters of yours [...] Oh, what a new beauty and dignity to be lady-governors and mothers of the spouses of the King of kings and Lord of lords [...] and thus, by means of the daughters, to win the favour and love of the Most High.[12]

Furthermore, Merici expected from the Ursulines those virtues that moralists and theologians reputed the most appropriate for women: virginity (or chastity), modesty and obedience. She considered virginity the most important status for women, as she required it as a condition for the entry in the Company: 'everyone [...] must be a virgin and have a firm intention to serve God in this way of life.'[13] Merici proposed modest behaviour for her daughters, as they had to wear simple dress, avoid contact with people of doubtful reputation, walk without looking around and with their eyes lowered, and talk, laugh, listen, eat and drink moderately.[14] At the same time she required women to comply with the religious and political establishment: with God's commandments, the Church, the bishop, the **confessor**, the secular state (laws and government), their employers and their families.[15]

Although Merici reiterated a set of traditional values, within her whole programme they carried a new meaning and challenged social expectations concerning the role of women. First, Merici's unenclosed form of life did not fit the traditional notions of female honour, because the daughters' virginity was not protected by convents or by families, but was managed by the daughters themselves, under the supervision of the female governors. As emerges from a letter by the Company's notary, the Brescian elite criticized Merici's choice of leaving virgins in the world:

> What Company is it that each person mocks it? Friars, priests, especially and other wise people [...] And that sister Angela deserves to be vituperated, for having solicited so many virgins to promise virginity, without a thought for where she was leaving them in the dangers of the world [...] to place virgins in the midst of the world, a thing which none of the patriarchs ever dared to do.[16]

Central to Merici's daring choice was her ideal of virginity. Merici did not adhere to the conventional notion of virginity as a 'precious treasure in a fragile vase of glass' (reiterated by many churchmen and in the later editions of the Company's Rule)[17] that needed to be protected and controlled by men, but associated it with independence and empowerment. Thus, Merici required physical virginity because she wanted to free the Ursulines from the links that normally tied married women and widows to the secular world: that is, children and former husbands. Then, Merici's ideal of unsupervised virginity should be explained within the ideological tradition that considered virginity as a powerful female *status vitae* that freed women from male dominance and secular links.[18] In a society which identified women mostly with reproduction and sexuality and exchanged them between families in order to reinforce lineage,[19] the virgin who eschewed matrimonial exchange and did not fulfil women's social roles was a potentially independent woman. By refusing the sexual and reproductive role, the virgin overcame the female identity, represented a middle course between the male and the female – a powerful figure able to mediate between the divine and the human.[20] Finally, Merici did not identify women's worth with their sexual status, because her notion of virginity also referred to moral qualities, that is, inner purity (for example, patience and love) and detachment from worldly values.[21] Thus, as virgin-brides of Christ, the Ursulines were empowered and could subsume virile connotations, embodied by the biblical figure of Judith:

> we are called to so *glorious life* [...] *Come then*, let us all embrace this holy Rule which God in his grace has offered us. And *armed with its sacred precepts, let us behave so bravely*[22] that we too, like holy Judith, having *courageously cut off the head* of Holofernes, that is of the devil, may return *gloriously* to our heavenly home, where, from everyone in heaven and earth, great *glory and triumph will burst for us.*[23]

Merici's choice to associate the Company's government with widowhood expressed the same desire for independence. During the Renaissance, the widow represented another female figure potentially free from male control and more autonomous in the use of money and property. Merici wanted to exploit the widows' freedom and experience in the administration of wealth.[24] Advising the *Matrone* on how they should administer the goods of the Company, she affirmed: 'In this matter I do not want you to seek outside advice; you decide, only among yourselves.'[25] Finally, as I will clarify below, the 'motherly love' required from the widows did not represent a reductive view of female government, because it led to an alternative form of authority.

Contrary to what renaissance moralists advocated, Merici did not impose a form of discipline on women. While the recommendations regarding daily behaviour protected the Ursulines from the dangers of the world, obedience and modesty (as virginity) did not mean passive submission to others, but rather a spiritual disposition suited to freeing the individual from the obstacles, created by the individual and directed towards the world, that obstructed the following of God's will. That Merici was not concerned with the control of the Ursulines emerges from the fact that she let her daughters decide about their daily life: they did not have a daily routine, they chose – without asking permission – where to live, with whom, whether to work or not, when to go out, whom to visit, when to receive visitors, in which church to pray and for how long.[26]

Moreover, Merici's writings evinced no common prejudice on female psychology and manifested a profound respect for human beings. The nucleus of the Ursuline's identity was in her interiority, in her heart and her thoughts. This idea clearly emerges when Merici warned the *Colonelle* not to judge their daughters' choices: 'you do not know what God wants to make of them [...] who can judge the heart and the innermost secret thoughts of any creature? [...] it is not up to you to judge the handmaids of God; he well knows what he wants to make of them.'[27]

Indeed, Merici did not consider women irrational and to be confined to the private sphere, as she accorded them the possibility to exercise their human and intellectual capacities in society.[28] First, the virgins were asked to act as civic peacemakers: 'In speaking, that their words be wise [...] and leading to concord and charity [...] And seek to spread peace and concord where they are.'[29] Merici proposed a role of public utility, either through the exercise of the word (advising and teaching, in a wide sense) or through example: 'let all words, actions and behaviour always be for the instruction and edification of those who have dealings with us';[30] 'tell them that, wherever they are, they should give good example. And be to all good odour of virtue [...] And let all behaviour, their actions and their words be with charity; and let them bear everything with patience.'[31] Merici proposed civic and spiritual public roles that society often recognized for women,[32] and that she herself had exercised. Her friends recounted that Brescian people used to visit her in order to 'pacify discord which had arisen between citizens and other nobles of the city'[33] and that she was known for her theological wisdom and sermons:

> she gave such beautiful, learned, and spiritual sermons, which at times lasted one hour [...] she not only read a quantity of holy books, but many times I have also seen religious men, and in particular preachers and theologians, ask her to expound concerning many passages in the Psalms, the Prophets, the Apocalypse, and all of the New and the Old Testament, and hear from her such expounding that they remained amazed.[34]

As emerges from her writings, Merici also intervened in various issues debated by Catholics and Protestants: she defended free will and confession, she supported Church reform, and criticized the corrupt clergy (the 'wolves') and the Protestant preachers (the 'thieves').[35] It is possible that Merici supported the Catholic belief in the human role in salvation – particularly free will – because she saw human life as intertwined with the divine. It was in connection with this notion that women could establish themselves, through mysticism, as spiritual leaders – an opportunity that Protestantism was less inclined to offer.[36] Thus, by defying traditional prohibitions regarding women's preaching and public roles in her life, it is possible that Merici wanted to offer her 'daughters' the opportunity to do the same.

Finally, although Merici proposed a conventional identity to women (that of the 'bride'), the Company challenged the expectations regarding women's social roles. In a society where women were expected to choose between marriage and the convent, the Ursuline was the prototype of the lay single woman.[37] Once the Church had legitimized and reorganized the Company, the new female figure proposed by Merici, albeit tamed and controlled, was also accepted by Italian society, as is testified by the Company's spread and the entry of aristocrats into it in the late sixteenth century.

Government and relationships

Merici's respect for women as rational individuals also emerged from – and was at the source of – the fact that, unlike other devout organizations that women could join, she entrusted the government of the Company to women without involving men. In this sense Merici went against the traditional exclusion of women from official positions of command such as ecclesiastical, political, legal, military and academic offices. Merici, however, did not really break with a tradition which denied women formal authority, because she displayed an alternative view of 'power' where women were in charge but held no 'powerful' roles. Indeed, in Merici's Rule, hierarchy, the exact definition of positions of command, obedience and the perfect execution of exterior practices – which were emphasized in many Rules contemporaneous to hers[38] – were marginal or even absent. Merici's ideal of female government, instead, valued the individual and her humanity. Several women displayed a similar approach to power.[39]

Merici's government was conceived without complicated hierarchies and in a simple and practical way, with spiritual guides (the *Colonelle*) and a board of administrators (the *Matrone*). It is revealing that in her writings Merici never used the term 'superior' for the members of the government, that she did not justify governmental positions with a universal order established by God, and that initially the Company had no head.[40] The Company was democratic as the Ursulines elected, on the basis of merit, all the positions in the government and the confessor. Even Angela Merici became General Mother by election. Merici established that if one of the *Matrone* was 'unable to fulfill her office or behaved badly, that person should be removed from the government',[41] and that the *Colonelle* had the right to question their authority without due respect: 'And if you see them slow to provide, *be insistent*; and in that case, in my name even be *importunate and troublesome*';[42] 'where you see clearly that the salvation and honour of your daughters are in danger, you must on *no account consent to it, nor tolerate it, nor have any respect*.'[43] Merici's notion of authority thus defied class boundaries: the *Colonelle*, who, in Angela's times, came from the lower or middle strata of society, could contest the authority of aristocratic widows and were responsible for virgins who could be of a higher social background.

Furthermore, Merici's view of authority lacked the 'obligation' to carry out the observances of religious life, which was replaced with the Ursulines' humanity, and in particular with their will. Merici explained this to the *Matrone*: 'be on your guard not to want to get anything done by force; because God has given free will to everyone, and wants to force no one, but only proposes, invites and counsels.'[44] Coherently, the Rule did not threaten the virgins with penalties. Merici expected the Ursulines to be actively willing to follow the Rule's precepts and it was for this reason that, when she prescribed something, she used the word *volere* (want, wish, desire) instead of the word *dovere* (must, ought). Respect for the Ursulines' individuality and inclusion of their personhood in religious life was also reflected in the instructions – given to the *Colonelle* and the *Matrone* – on how to deal with the Ursulines. Rather than establishing a specific common practice, Merici proposed strategies *ad personam*: 'If you see one faint-hearted and timid and inclined to despondency, comfort her, encourage her [...] And on the contrary, if you see another presumptuous, and who has a lax conscience and little fear of anything, into this one instill some fear.'[45] Merici's idea of authority was founded on the concept of love. The guiding principle for directing the Ursulines consisted in the affective participation to the daughters' character. If the *Colonelle* and the *Matrone* loved their 'daughters' their decisions would necessarily be respectful of their personalities, and consequently, the most appropriate: 'For the more you esteem them, the more you will love them; the more you love them, the more you will care for and watch over them[46] [...] charity [...] moves the heart to be, according to place and time, now gentle and now severe, and little or much as there is need.'[47]

Finally, Merici's depiction of **sisterhood** emphasized, together with reciprocal charity, the importance of human values and friendship: 'Live in harmony, united together, all of one heart and one will. Be bound to one another by the bond of charity, esteeming each other, helping each other, bearing with each other [...] And believe firmly that then, especially, *you will recognize me to be your faithful friend.*'[48]

Imitatio Christi

If we consider more specifically how Merici conceived the Ursulines' experience of the sacred, we find that this was not mediated or represented by institutional and exterior structures and that it had at its centre a mystical relationship with God. These aspects of Merici's spirituality – which were common with many spiritual women before and during Merici's times – can be viewed in continuity with two broad aspects of women's condition within culture, which were logically linked: women's supposed natural incompatibility with expressions of institutionalized worship and their 'openness' to the transcendent. However, as in the case of many mystic women, Merici's elaboration of these cultural notions gave way to an original and alternative ideal of religious experience, which differed from male depictions of female spirituality and which offered women new opportunities for self-expression.

This can be first illustrated through the analysis of Merici's view of religious consecration. As I have just argued, Merici's concept of female government and relationships within the Company – based on individual worth, will and humanity – was consistent with women's exclusion from secular official forms of power. Similarly, I would argue that Merici's ideal of female consecration was compatible with women's exclusion from the institutional sharing and managing of the sacred: women, for example, could not be ordained, administer sacraments or the word of God or, with few exceptions, write religious **Rules**. This was based on the perception of the female as weak, irrational, impure and not made in the divine image.[49] Such exclusion may have led Merici and her followers to develop an experience of the sacred which was not lived through institutional aspects of devotion, but rather through their individual humanity and interiority. It has been observed that such an 'a-institutional' approach to the sacred was shared by several spiritual women.[50]

Thus, Merici's Rule did not associate institutional and ritual elements, such as the ceremony of acceptance, to the condition of the Bride of Christ.[51] Moreover, the Ursuline's consecration was sanctioned not by the **profession** of vows but by her will, a human element which depends only on the individual: 'Each one should also preserve sacred virginity, *not making a vow on account of any human persuasion, but voluntarily* making to God the sacrifice of her own heart.'[52] Furthermore, Merici presented a view of religious consecration that did not require an exterior sacred space within which to live the relationship with God – the convent – or a visible sign of the religious status – the common habit.[53] Merici substituted physical separation and distinction with an 'existential transformation', consisting of an inner detachment from secular values, elaborated through the concepts of 'virginity' and 'poverty.'[54] Finally, the lack of daily routine and common life indicates that Merici subordinated institutional and exterior forms of devotion to the respect of personal spiritual choices.

Second, Merici's mystic ideal of relationship with the sacred may be connected to the cultural perception of femininity as naturally close to the realm of the supernatural. Although female mysticism elicited mixed reactions from churchmen (especially after the mid-fourteenth century, when growing suspicion spread among theologians), as several studies on the medieval and the early modern period have pointed out, theologians and hagiographers tended to consider spiritual women as having a special connection with the divine, predisposed to the visionary experience, and mediators with the supernatural.[55] Such a view of spiritual women should be connected with the cultural perception of the female as lacking a stable identity, changeable, subjected to external influences, open to the other world, mysterious, made of an impressionable soft and humid nature, socially and symbolically liminal and charged with 'alterity'.[56] Furthermore, women were considered as more apt to identify with Christ's humanity and suffering because late medieval culture tended to invest the body with a spiritual significance and established a connection between 'woman' and corporality.[57] Within this cultural framework, hagiographers tended to depict women's religiosity as primarily mystical, bodily and sexual, and women's mysticism as passive, private and in need of male supervision.

How did Merici's ideal of the relationship with God relate to these cultural associations? On the one hand Merici depicted the Ursuline in close connection with the divine, but on the other she differed significantly from male representations of female religiosity and notions of womanhood. First, in the chapter 'On Obedience', she put women in direct contact with the divine but, unlike theologians and later reformers of her Company, she did not believe that the confessor was necessary to act as mediator: 'above all: to obey the counsels and inspirations which the Holy Spirit unceasingly sends into our hearts.'[58] The official recognition of a personal and unmediated relationship with God shows Merici's trust in women's capacity to discern God's inspirations and consequently offered women the possibility to decide about their spiritual and material life.[59]

Furthermore, if the highest moment of religious experience was mystical union, this was not described as a private and passive experience lived by an 'empty vessel'. In Merici's spirituality, the Ursuline was asked to establish a dynamic relationship with the divine which gave her an active public role. Active and **contemplative** life, charity and prayer, were considered together, all in the imitation of Christ's redemptive role. Merici exemplified the daughters' spiritual elevation in the chapter 'On prayer'. Here she offered a model of **mental prayer**, consisting of three steps: self-abasement, personal identification with Christ's salvific role and union with God.[60] At the beginning there was the inner experience of emptiness and humility, which led to despair, restless imploration and penance:

> My Lord, light up the darkness of my heart [...] I deserve to be devoured alive in hell, seeing in myself so many errors, so much ugliness and vileness [...] Therefore I am compelled, day and night, moving, staying still, acting, thinking, to call out and to cry to heaven, and to beg for mercy and time for penance.

Subsequently, the Ursuline was encouraged to seek identification with the Christ-man on the cross, by engaging in redemptive sufferance both for her own sins and for those of the world:

> Alas! Until now I have never shed even the smallest drop of blood for love of you [...] Lord, in place of those poor creatures who do not know you, and do not care to be partakers in your most sacred Passion, my heart breaks, and willingly (if I could) I would shed my own blood to open the blind eyes of their minds.

The Ursuline's *Imitatio Christi* sanctified the penitent who could eventually reach the mystic fusion of the heart and passions with divine love: 'My Lord, my only life and hope, I pray that you deign to receive this most vile and impure heart of mine, and to burn its affection and passion in the fiery furnace of your divine love.'

This type of mysticism allowed women to express themselves beyond the sphere of the private. Indeed, by identifying with Christ's saving role, the Ursulines were given an active role within the community. Such a role was further exemplified in the chapter 'On Fasting', where Merici proposed that her daughters abstained from food and practised intercessory prayer to obtain forgiveness for people's sins:

> They should fast [...] to subdue the senses and the appetites and sensual desires which then, especially, seem to lord over the world, and also to implore mercy [...] for the many dissolute actions committed by Christians [...] they should fast [...] to implore divine help for the Christian people.[61]

Thus, the perception of women in close connection to the divine led Merici to offer the Ursulines the opportunity to carry out a social function that she and other women had.[62] However, Angela did not conceive women's participation in social life solely through the experience of the divine: she gave the Ursulines active roles which were exercised through their intellectual and human capacities, such as advice, peacekeeping and informal preaching.

A final point to be discussed in Merici's mysticism concerns the significance she accorded to the body – an important religious symbol to female religiosity, given the cultural association between femaleness and corporality. Although Merici gave physical penance religious significance, divine union was not realized and lived primarily through the body, but in the Ursulines' interiority and humanity: 'reduce and diminish these fasts, as they see that to be needed, because to afflict one's body indiscreetly [...] would be to offer in sacrifice something stolen.'[63] Furthermore, in relation to fasting as a means of self-purification, Merici moved the focus from the body to inner life. She clarified that food abstinence was instrumental to the achievement of an inner and spiritual condition, that is, separation from worldly values: 'Embrace bodily fasting as something necessary, and as a means and way to true spiritual fasting through which all the vices and errors are cut away from the mind.'

Finally, Merici depicted the Ursuline's experience of God as lived through her whole person, and primarily through her interiority: 'And strengthen my *affections* and *senses* [...] I pray you that you deign to receive this most vile and impure *heart* of mine... receive my *free will*, every act of my own *will* [...] Receive my every *thought*, *word* and *deed*, everything that is mine finally, both *interior* and *exterior*.'[64] Merici's case supports the argument that the importance of body for women's spirituality was particularly emphasized by male hagiographers, who often interpreted female inner experiences as bodily phenomena.[65] It is also possible that Merici's attitude testified a decline in the importance of the body for some sixteenth-century spiritual women, which can be put in relation to the influence of the spirituality of the *devotio moderna*, which stressed inner virtue instead of physical penance.

Conclusions

Within the context of penitential and mystic spirituality, Angela Merici established a dynamic relationship of adoption, rejection and innovation of medieval and renaissance attitudes towards femininity. On the one hand, she proposed for the Ursulines a religious identity, codes of behaviour, forms of government and spiritual life which were largely consistent with mainstream cultural notions linking the female with family and sexuality, with the supernatural, corporality and sacrifice, and considered women incompatible with institutional roles and forms of power.

At the same time, however, Merici's Bride of Christ did not fit within traditional social and religious expectations of women. Merici proposed an improved type of life for women, by adapting some of these notions, developing inherent possibilities, and rejecting some of their premises and consequences. Indeed, she used the ambivalent meanings of virginity and widowhood to cut the social ties that bound women to male familial strategies, offering female members independence and a new female identity. She rejected the notion that women were irrational and weak, that they should be confined to the private and submissive to men, as she encouraged them to express their rational capacities publicly. She capitalized on female privileged access and likeness to the divine, on female bodyliness and sacrifice, and on the social opportunities they offered to promote an unofficial manner of relationship with God (personal, unmediated, interior and based on the identification with Christ's redemptive role), and to affirm women's authority within the community. Moreover, women's exclusion from the managing of institutional forms of power led Merici to develop an alternative model of religious life which valued humanity more. Indeed, the Company's organization – its government, guidance and bonds among members – was based on human worth, love and friendship, instead of hierarchy and obligation. Similarly, the Company proposed an experience of the sacred that was lived without the mediation of exterior, collective and institutional means (such as convent, habit, vows, ceremonies and common life), but through an individual and spiritual detachment from worldly values and inner union with God. By developing such spirituality, Merici allowed women to have a profound experience of their selves in the religious sphere. In all aspects of her life, the Ursuline was considered, and could live, as a unique individual, responsible for her own deeds, inwardly complex, a full human being with intellect, thoughts, feelings and will.[66]

Merici's writings – which presented many points in common with several medieval and renaissance spiritual women – therefore offer an example of how some of the women who followed a mystic and penitential spirituality dealt with attitudes towards the female and provides a way of reconciling misogyny with the prestige of spiritual women.[67] Merici's case indicates that these women's achievements should be explained through – rather than despite of – contemporaneous cultural notions of the female.[68] This was possible because the latter were compatible with certain characteristics of penitential and mystic spirituality. Within a late medieval religious model that prized the supernatural contact between the individual and God, gender-related notions deemed women more apt than men to pursue it. Furthermore, it was a religiosity that – like the cultural notion of 'womanhood' – figured as bridal, affective, maternal, bodily, self-sacrificial, a-institutional, liminal and mediatory. Within this spiritual context it was possible for women to gain positions of spiritual leadership and thus to tackle and adapt mainstream perceptions of femininity, and to overcome some of the limits that society imposed on them. Through these views of the female, women – obviously not all women and not only women – could also contribute to religious history, by promoting alternative forms of the experience of the sacred, which deemed powerful institutions as marginal and gave greater importance to the individual and her humanity.

Despite these achievements, this model of female spirituality had some limitations when viewed from the perspective of the history of women. Angela Merici, and other women like her, did not radically challenge those mainstream gender attitudes that led women to restrictive roles within religion and within society at large. Women's privileged spiritual position was not an indication of female superiority because it was based on negative stereotypes regarding femininity, and women's important active and public religious roles were probably accepted by society because female authority came from God and thus did not challenge the hierarchy of genders. Women like Merici did not advocate equality before religious (or civic) institutions, but rather promoted an alternative experience of the sacred which relied on a social context that prized the personal relationship with God.

If many aspects of this type of female religiosity continued to exist in the late sixteenth and in the seventeenth centuries,[69] spiritual women – in conjunction with an increasingly secularized society and a reorganized Church – gradually lost much of their social influence, became more controlled, and were often accused of false sanctity or demonic possession. Spiritual women became active in education, charity and missions, but in these domains they overall had fewer opportunities for social prestige and autonomy.[70] Nevertheless, one lasting effect of female spirituality on women's history was that it contributed to the idea that women could live in the secular world without marriage – as the successful development of the figure of the Ursuline shows.

Notes

1. C. W. Bynum, *Holy Feast and Holy Fast: The Religious Significance of Food to Medieval Women* (London: University of California Press, 1987); C. W. Bynum, *Fragmentation and Redemption: Essays on Gender and the Human Body in Medieval Religion* (New York: Zone Books, 1991); J. Coakley, 'Introduction: Women's Creativity in Religious Context', in E. A. Matter and J. Coakley, *Creative Women in Medieval and Early Modern Italy: A Religious and Artistic Renaissance* (Philadelphia: University of Pennsylvania Press, 1994), pp. 1–16; B. Newman, *From Virile Woman to WomanChrist: Studies in Medieval Religion and Literature* (Philadelphia: University of Pennsylvania Press, 1995); A. Hollywood, *The Soul as Virgin Wife* (Notre Dame: University of Notre Dame, 1995); C. Mooney (ed.), *Gendered Voices: Medieval Saints and Their Interpreters* (Philadelphia: University of Pennsylvania Press, 1999); N. Caciola, *Discerning Spirits: Divine and Demonic Possession in the Middle Ages* (London: Cornell University Press, 2003); D. Elliott, *Proving Woman: Female Spirituality and Inquisitorial Culture in the Later Middle Ages* (Oxford: Princeton University Press, 2004); M. Sluhowsky, *Believe not Every Spirit: Possession, Mysticism, and Discernment in Early Modern Catholicism* (Chicago: The University of Chicago Press).

2. The Company's writings, composed in the vernacular, consist of the rule (*Regula della Compagnia de Santa Orsola*) and two sets of advice manuals for the government: the counsels (*Arricordi che vanno alli Colonelli*) and the 'testament' (*Testamento della Madre suor Angela lassato alle Matrone*). Merici, who apparently could not write, dictated the Company's writings to Gabriele Cozzano, a Brescian notary who became her follower and the Company's notary. Merici's authorship is discussed in Q. Mazzonis, *Spirituality, Gender and the Self in Renaissance Italy: Angela Merici and the Company of St. Ursula (1474–1540)* (Washington, DC: Catholic University of America Press, 2007), pp. 87–94. The writings are published in L. Mariani, E. Tarolli and M. Seynaeve, *Angela Merici: Contributo per una biografia* (Milan: Ancora, 1986), respectively at pp. 436–58, 507–12, 512–17. The English translation of Merici's writings comes from *Saint Angela Merici, Writings: Rule, Counsels, Testament* (Rome: Ursulines of the Roman Union, 1995). From now on I will refer to the rule as *Reg*, to the counsels as *Ric* and to the testament as *Tes*.

3. The sources regarding Merici's life mainly consist of a recollection of testimonies given by four friends 28 years after her death, with a view to promoting her

canonization process: *Le Justificationi della Vita della Reverenda Madre Suor Angela Terzebita* (known as *Processo Nazari*, hereafter *PN*). It is published in Mariani et al., *Angela Merici*, pp. 533–40.

4. Particularly influential was J. Hugues Quarré, *La vie de la Bienheureuse Mère Angèle* (1648). More recently, see T. Ledòchowska, *Angèle Merici et la Compagnie de Ste-Ursule à la lumière des documents* (Rome–Milan: Ancora, 1968).

5. As stated in the introductions of several new rules. In this form the Company also developed in France, where it eventually became an enclosed religious order. For the French Ursulines see L. Lux-Sterritt, *Redefining Female Religious Life: French Ursulines and English Ladies in Seventeenth-Century Catholicism* (Aldershot: Ashgate, 2005).

6. For an overview of the phenomenon see G. Zarri, 'Living Saints: A Typology of Female Sanctity in the Early Sixteenth Century', in D. Bornstein and R. Rusconi (eds), *Women and Religion in Medieval and Renaissance Italy* (London: The University of Chicago Press, 1996), pp. 219–303; and T. Herzig, *Savonarola's Women: Visions and Reform in Renaissance Italy* (London: The University of Chicago Press, 2008).

7. Furthermore, Merici's spirituality bore aspects in common with an interior and moral spirituality (based on the ideas of the *devotio moderna*), characteristic of groups such as the Theatines, the Barnabites, the Angelics and the Jesuits. For the spirituality of the period see H. Outram Evenett, *The Spirit of the Counter-Reformation: The Birkbeck Lectures in Ecclesiastical History Given in the University of Cambridge in May 1951,* edited by J. Bossy (Cambridge: Cambridge University Press, 1968).

8. See, for example, G. Zarri (ed.), *Donna, disciplina, creanza cristiana dal XV al XVII secolo: Studi e testi a stampa* (Rome: Edizioni Storia e Letteratura, 1996); M. Wiesner, *Women and Gender in Early Modern Europe* (Cambridge: Cambridge University Press, 2000).

9. *Reg*, X.

10. Several other spiritual women showed a similar attitude to Merici. See Bynum, *Holy Feast*, p. 269. However, women such as Hildegard of Bingen and Bridget of Sweden gave an important role to Mary: K. E. Børresen, *From Patristics to Matristics: Selected Articles on Christian Gender Models* (Rome: Herder, 2002).

11. *Reg*, XI.

12. *Tes*, 4.

13. *Reg*, I.

14. *Reg*, II, III, X, *Ric*, 5.

15. *Reg*, VIII.

16. G. Cozzano, *Risposta contro quelli che persuadono la clausura alle Vergini di Sant'Orsola*, Brescia, f. 15r. Brescia, Biblioteca Queriniana, MS. D.VII.8.

17. C. Atkinson, '"Precious Balsam in a Fragile Glass": The Ideology of Virginity in the Later Middle-Ages', *Journal of Family History*, 8:2 (1983), pp. 131–43.

18. Newman, *From Virile Woman*, pp. 31–4. For men, chastity was less significant because sexuality was only one aspect of male connection with the world. Renunciation to the world was more complex for men and more emphasized in hagiographical accounts regarding their lives.

19. C. Klapisch-Zuber, *Women, Family and Ritual in Renaissance Italy* (Chicago: The University of Chicago Press, 1985).

20. A. Blok, 'Notes on the concept of Virginity in the Mediterranean societies', in E. Schulte Van Kessel (ed.), *Women and Men in Spiritual Culture (XIV–XVII Centuries): A Meeting of South and North* (The Hague: Netherlands Government Publishing Office, 1986), pp. 27–33.

21. *Reg*, IX.
22. 'Virilmente' in the Italian original.
23. *Reg, Prologue*. In all quotations the italics are mine. In Borromeo's rule the word 'virilmente' was dropped and instead of cutting off the head of the devil the virgins 'cut off the *deceits* of the devil' (*Regola della Compagnia di S. Orsola di nuovo revista corretta e confirmata da Monsignor illustrissimo Carlo Cardinale di S. Prassede, Arcivescovo di Milano e Visitatore Apostolico*, In Brescia (appresso Pietro Maria Marchetti), 1582, *Prologue*). From now on '*Reg*, 1582'.
24. During the sixteenth and seventeenth centuries rich widows often sponsored female religious groups. See C. Valone, 'Roman Matrons as Patrons: Various Views of the Cloister Wall', in C. Monson (ed.), *The Crannied Wall: Women, Religion, and the Arts in Early Modern Europe* (Ann Arbor: The University of Michigan Press, 1992), pp. 49–72.
25. *Tes*, 9.
26. In the new Companies, by contrast, the Ursulines underwent new restrictions.
27. *Ric*, 8.
28. Some women like Hildegard of Bingen and Teresa of Avila, did adopt the notion of the 'weak woman' chosen by God to puzzle proud men. They did it, however, in order to justify their preaching, writing, teaching and founding monasteries, without subverting male supremacy. See A. Weber, *Teresa of Avila and the Rhetoric of Femininity* (Princeton: Princeton University Press, 1990).
29. *Ric*, 5.
30. *Reg*, IX.
31. *Ric*, 5.
32. Spiritual women sometimes even held a political role, as in the case of Catherine of Siena, Bridget of Sweden, and several charismatic women who – during Merici's times – were at the centre of political and religious circles (Zarri, 'Living saints'). One famous woman geographically and temporally close to Merici was Paola Antonia Negri, who, in the 1540s, was revered as the charismatic leader of the Barnabites and the Angelics.
33. *PN*, ff. 938r.
34. *PN*, ff. 941r, 944r-v. Merici's religious knowledge also emerges in her writings for the Company, which abound with references to the Bible and to church fathers.
35. *Reg, Prologue* and VII; *Ric*, 7.
36. On 'free will' Merici may have also been influenced by Brescian circles (which included some of Merici's friends) supporting the ideas of Erasmus of Rotterdam. For a discussion of women's response to the Protestant Reformation see A. Leonard, 'Female Religious Orders' in R. Po-chia Hsia (ed.) *A Companion to the Reformation World* (Malden, MA: Blackwell, 2006), pp. 237–54.
37. By contrast, contemporary institutes protecting female honour reinserted women in society either as wives or nuns: see S. Cohen, *The Evolution of Women's Asylums since 1500* (Oxford and New York: Oxford University Press, 1992). **Third Orders**, which allowed women to live on their own, were mainly conceived for married and widowed layfolk.
38. Such as those of the Company of Divine Love, the Company of Christian Doctrine and the Jesuits.
39. The rule of Clare of Assisi (1193–1253), for example, envisaged very little hierarchy and many exemptions from usual restrictions such as enclosure and perpetual silence (unlike that by Cardinal Hugolino). See E. A. Petroff, 'A Medieval Woman's Utopian Vision: The Rule of St. Clare of Assisi' in E. A. Petroff (ed.) *Body and Soul: Essays on Medieval Women and Mysticism* (New York and Oxford: Oxford University Press,

1994), pp. 66–79. According to Catherine Vigri of Bologna (1413–1463) blind obedience to the abbess was a temptation caused by the devil and government was service rather than authority (C. Foletti (ed.), *Sette Armi spirituali* (Padua: Editrice Antenore, 1985), pp. 125–6, 132).

40. In 1537 Merici became 'Principal Mother' in order to inherit some money left to the Company.

41. *Reg*, XI.

42. *Ric*, 4.

43. *Ric*, 3.

44. *Tes*, 3.

45. *Ric*, 2.

46. *Ric, Prologue*.

47. *Ric*, 2.

48. *Ric, Last*.

49. These were the reasons given for women's exclusion from priesthood: see A. Valerio, 'Il vero sacerdote: trasfigurazioni e assimilazioni nel pensiero e nelle pratiche di Domenica da Paradiso', in D. Corsi (ed.), *Donne cristiane e sacerdozio. Dalle origini all'età contemporanea* (Rome: Viella, 2004), pp. 87–9.

50. Bynum, *Fragmentation and Redemption*, pp. 63–5. Kieckhefer has shown that exterior and ritual devotions were more important in male saints: R. Kieckhefer, 'Holiness and the Culture of Devotion: Remarks on Some Late Medieval Male Saints', in R. Blumenfeld-Kosinski and T. Szell (eds) *Images of Sainthood in Medieval Europe* (London: Cornell University Press, 1991), pp. 288–305.

51. The ceremony of acceptance was introduced in the Brescian Company in 1572.

52. *Reg*, IX.

53. Absence of common habit held a great significance to Merici and the Ursulines: soon after Merici died, the Company split into two groups (1545–59) because some of the *Matrone* introduced a black leather cincture as a distinctive exterior sign.

54. *Reg*, IX, X.

55. C. Mooney, 'Voice, Gender, and the Portrayal of Sanctity', in C. Mooney (ed.) *Gendered Voices*, pp. 1–15; J. W. Coakley, *Women, Men and Spiritual Power: Female Saints and Their Male Collaborators* (New York: Columbia University Press, 2006), pp. 7–24; J. Bilinkoff, *Related Lives: Confessors and Their Female Penitents* (New York: Cornell University Press, 2005).

56. Caciola, *Discerning Spirits*, pp. 140–58, Elliott, *Proving Woman*, pp. 204–11, and Sluhowsky, *Believe not Every Spirit*, have shown how the same ideas could justify belief in both women's divine and diabolical possession.

57. Bynum, *Fragmentation and Redemption*, pp. 181–238.

58. *Reg*, VIII. In Borromeo's rule we read: 'And also to obey the inner inspirations, which, with the *judgment and approbation of the confessor*, will be recognised to be coming from the Holy Spirit' (*Reg*, 1582, 8).

59. Indeed, Merici simply gave a sacramental role to the confessor. Furthermore, she was a rather 'independent' saint. For example, she rejected invitations, made by Pope Clement VII, the Duke of Milan Francesco Sforza and some Venetian noblemen, to move to their cities.

60. This type of union with God was characteristic of beguines' spirituality (Hollywood, *The Soul*, pp. 54–86). We also find it in Italian women's writings, such as Catherine of Siena's *Dialogo della divina provvidenza* (G. Cavallini (ed.), Rome: Edizioni Cateriniane, 1980, pp. 45–48).

61. *Reg*, IIII.

62. 'Many came to her from the city of Brescia [asking] for her most devout prayers to obtain a grace from the Lord' (*PN*, f. 937v). On this type of female spirituality see Newman, *From Virile Woman*, pp. 108–36.

63. *Reg*, IV. Although Merici's *vitae* do emphasize her penitential life, this does not appear as severe as in other women's biographies.

64. *Reg*, V.

65. See, for example, A. Hollywood, 'Inside Out: Beatrice of Nazareth and Her Hagiographer', in C. Mooney (ed.) *Gendered Voices*, pp. 78–98. In the auto-biographical text by Genoese mystic, Catherine of Genoa (1447–1510), *Spiritual Dialogue Between Soul and Body*, bodily religious phenomena were predominant in the sections written by her male disciples.

66. Merici's views of the Ursuline's selfhood in the religious experience can be analysed in connection with renaissance notions of the 'self': see Mazzonis, *Spirituality*, pp. 178–88. A recent discussion of the notion of the 'self' in the Renaissance is in J. J. Martin, *Myths of Renaissance Individualism* (New York: Palgrave Macmillan, 2004).

67. Obviously not all women followed this spirituality: P. Galloway, 'Neither Miraculous nor Astonishing: The Devotional Practice of Beguine Communities in French Flanders', in J. Dor, L. Johnson, and J. Wogan-Brown (eds) *New Trends in Feminine Spirituality: The Holy Women of Liège and Their Impact* (Turnhout: Brepols, 1999), pp. 107–27.

68. This may also be true, at least to a certain extent, of those women such as Hildegard of Bingen, Bridget of Sweden and Julian of Norwich, who proposed a more radical feminization of the divine – because this was achieved by following the cultural perception of the female, that is by exalting virginity, procreation, maternity, nurturing, suffering and love.

69. See Marit Monteiro's essay in this volume on the case of the Dutch 'spiritual virgins' and of Agnes van Heilsbach and Joanna van Randenraed. On female mysticism in France during the wars of religion see B. Diefendorf, *From Penitence to Charity: Pious Women and the Catholic Reformation in Paris* (New York: Oxford University Press, 2004). On the connection between female spirituality and Quietism see Sluhowsky, *Believe Not Every Spirit*.

70. See for example, the hostility of the Church to Mary Ward's religious project, discussed by Lux-Sterritt in this volume.

4
Teresa de Jesús's *Book* and the Reform of the Religious Man in Sixteenth-Century Spain

Elizabeth Rhodes

'Let me so read thy life, that I
Unto all life of mine may die.'

Richard Crashaw (?1613–1649), 'The Flaming Heart, Upon the Book of the Seraphical Saint Teresa'

Seeking the unexpected, even the apparently paradoxical, is a postmodern intellectual exercise of surprising benefit in early modern texts. It seems unlikely that a **spiritual life story** such as Teresa de Jesús's *Book* (often called the *Book of her Life*) would contain a prescription for the perfect religious man, yet there it is.[1]

St Teresa, renowned author, reformer and **foundress** of the Discalced **Carmelites**, lived from 1515 to 1582, was canonized in 1622 and made a Doctor of the Church in 1970. By the time she died at age 67, she had written four long prose works, poetry, **accounts of conscience**, instructions for monastic administrators, monastic constitutions and personal recollections, and left some 468 extant letters.[2] During her lifetime, she also personally founded 15 convents for women and directed four other foundations, two of which were Discalced Carmelite houses for men.

The initial question: 'what are you doing?'

The first full text Teresa completed was her spiritual life story, which she referred to as her *Book*, and which she wrote because one of her superiors asked her to describe her experiences of God.[3] This written response legitimized her in the eyes of the religious community, and her activity in the world increased as she aged. Teresa became one of the greatest success stories of Catholicism, a defender of the faith who managed to sustain an intense **mystical** life, write about it in a compelling fashion, and live an active **apostolate**. In the history of women's Catholicism, she is unique.

The manuscript we now know as Teresa de Jesús's *Book* is the culmination of many documents she composed about her life with God. It focuses on the years she was negotiating her direct experience of the divinity with her **confessors'** determination to control that experience, but includes events from her childhood through the foundation of her first convent in 1561. It was probably in the text's last draft, and perhaps in the penultimate one of 1562, that the future saint modelled ideal behaviour for religious men, originally her superiors and her manuscript's only official readers. Teresa literally wrote her *Book* for them, although other readers enthusiastically picked up the manuscript as soon as it began to circulate after 1565.[4]

Remarkably, the same text is also one in which a woman used a document about herself to establish a model for religious men guiding religious women, thereby promoting the most beneficial relationship possible for female seekers of God and those supervising them. Hypothesizing the *Book*'s progressive layers reveals the evolution of her superiors' question to her from 'What are you doing?' to 'How do you do that?' Those superiors' ultimate interest in and support of Teresa de Jesús's spiritual praxis is one reason why her reform succeeded where the efforts of other women failed. History makes it clear – as do most of the essays in this volume – that without the support of the appropriate men, religious women of reformist ambitions get only trouble.[5]

This reading differs from interpretations of the 40-chapter *Book* in which scholars (myself included) have read Teresa as intimidated by the task given her, which was 'to write about the favors and the kind of prayer the Lord has granted me'.[6] There is no denying that she was in danger of being silenced during the years she was trying to establish her spiritual authority.[7] Known inquiries into her prayer life date from 1554, when she was 39,[8] and in her *Book* she records having been required to write reports for her superiors several times. Even though she insists that she herself originally sought out the advice about her extraordinary prayer experiences that led to requests for written documentation, Teresa's exasperation over the process is also manifest. Prominent are recollections of her advisors' persistent attempts to tamp God down by controlling her, efforts that culminate in her description of the moment when they were preparing to have her exorcised.[9] Until the end of Chapter 29, she regularly relates the difficulties she had convincing religious authorities, and herself, that she knew what she was doing in her prayer practice.[10]

However, by the time she put the final flourishes on the extant version of her spiritual life story, between 1563 and 1565, Teresa's career as a foundress had been launched and she had considerable – if still problematic – religious and social capital. The tide of religious politics in Ávila had not yet turned from reformism to retrenchment, and Teresa was still riding the wave of cautious support for interior piety; her encounters with the **Inquisition**, unrelated to Ávila's history, would not begin until 1574.[11] After her foundation of the first Discalced Carmelite convent in 1562, her advisors knew that she had been under close ecclesiastical supervision for at least eight years and by then they were perhaps no more worried about Teresa than they were curious about her method of prayer and desirous to imitate it. It was clearly working well for their middle-aged charge, whose authoritative, direct experience of God and power to work in the world only intensified as she aged.

The final question: 'how do you do that?'

The notion that Teresa's *Book* was initially a response to a potentially threatening inquiry into her prayer life, and later a request for description of what that prayer experience felt like, requires evidence of a shift in the balance of power between Teresa and her male advisors from subordinate/superiors to a partnership. The fundamentals of this evidence are well established and are based on the text's complicated history.

Kieran Kavanaugh describes this history, from its presumed origins in Teresa's underlining passages in Laredo's *Ascent of Mount Sion* to give her confessors an idea of what she was experiencing, which she did in 1554–55, through her *Book*'s various written renditions.[12] Although scholars postulate that Teresa composed multiple earlier versions of her *Book*, all of these early versions have been lost, except for her **spiritual testimonies** (*cuentas de conciencia*) dated 1560–63, which contain material also in the *Book*.[13] To complicate matters, portions of the lost drafts probably remain in the extant draft, such as the author's historical account of her life that is now Chapters 1–9.[14] Dámaso Chicarro, following Enrique Llamas, proposes that there were no less than ten successive documents, the first of which she wrote in 1554, that led to the 1565 draft of her *Book* whose manuscript was recalled and impounded by the Inquisition until after her death. Weber identifies seven drafts, and indicates that between 1580 and 1582, the year of Teresa's death, her text, supposedly still sequestered by the Inquisition, was nevertheless being copied and distributed.[15]

One piece of the *Book*'s history is key in tracing its progression from a defensive description to a proud pedagogy. In the early part of 1562, Teresa's close spiritual friend and sometime confessor, the Dominican Diego García de Toledo, requested that she detail her prayer experience for him in writing, for reasons unknown.[16] She complied, passing him the manuscript in June of that year, and he consulted with colleagues about its content. By the next year, he had asked its author to provide fuller information about her method of prayer and details about the foundation of San José, which had taken place in 1562. By asking for details about an important event in the history of female convents, an event sanctioned by the proper authorities and already carried out, García de Toledo was clearly seeking documentation for posterity, which indicates high esteem for Teresa.

The future saint responded to this request with the text we now know as her *Book*, although exactly what she may have removed, altered and added to the previous version in the process is unknown. New sections appear to include the treatise on prayer based on the metaphor of the four waters, now Chapters 11–22. As requested, she added information about her first foundation, now Chapters 32–36. It was perhaps her own idea to include the last four chapters, which recount some of her visions in a matter-of-fact, self-confident tone similar to the voice she used to recount the same kind of material in Chapters 27 and 29–31. These 21 new chapters not only (apparently) more than doubled the length of the previous draft, but also gave voice to an authoritative Teresa who would brook no challenge to her credibility, a voice rhetorically obedient and simultaneously defiant.[17]

Teresa's *Book* tells the story of its author's slow and painful empowerment, of the years of tribulations she underwent at the hands of a litany of advisors and confessors who, on the one hand, were trying to discern the spirit at work in her and, on the other, were educating and exercising her in purgation, the first stage of the mystical way that requires focus and discipline of intention, thought and deed. She used her need to establish God's presence in her life to record her difficulties with God's ministers, thereby implicating those ministers in any problems they might find in her piety: if they were directing her, then she was not the only one responsible for any unorthodoxy in her experience. Had she failed to insist on her ongoing problems with her confessors, the spotlight of the interrogation would have shone exclusively on her.

The text represents the culmination of the antagonism between the author and her advisors when five or six men together insisted it was the devil at work in her and not God. In Chapter 25, after describing their verdict, she recounts the locution, 'Do not fear, daughter, for I am, and I will not abandon you; do not fear,' after which she recalls, 'I saw my soul become another [...] I was another person.'[18] Never again did she did record extreme doubt in herself or in her relationship with God.

The experience of God's explicit support enabled Teresa not only to live her mission, but also to write the final version of her story with a confidence she did not have before. In the additions she made to her text for García de Toledo, it is likely that she altered the hues of her self-portrait from those of a self-doubting woman under the thumbs of her male superiors to a self-confident companion of the divinity who had something to tell those same men that they wanted to hear. It is with that palette that she completed her *Book*, and there are brush strokes throughout the text in the same hues, passages that appear to have been inserted by a very experienced mystic and writer into an otherwise tentative text.

Not surprisingly, the extant version of the narrative hides multiple palimpsests, some of which are partially visible.[19] The most significant story the text tells is how its author learned rigorous discipline in the practice of **mental prayer**, leading to unshakable faith in God and herself, which in turn enabled her to do God's work in the world. Throughout this narrative runs the author's prescription for a spiritual master, never the subject but never far from it.

Teresa's negative answer: 'do not do this'

In Chapters 4–10 and 23–25, Teresa represents her troubles with confessors with special vehemence. Together, these criticisms of male ineptitude and failure invert correct standards of religious behaviour for men, providing a negative example; with them, the author uses the wrong things they did to imply what should have happened. Before analysing these passages, it is worth pointing out that her initial difficulties with her advisors are not at all surprising: she was woman with no official education whatsoever in the practice of mental prayer, who claimed she had gone straight from reading Francisco de Osuna's *Tercer abecedario espiritual* (Third Spiritual Alphabet) not only to the prayer of quiet (advanced prayer) but that of union (mystical prayer), all in nine months (4.7).[20] Along the way, and while seriously ill, she confessed and converted a corrupt priest from sin to virtue (Chapter 5).

One can imagine the dismay of a man like the pious layman Francisco de Salcedo, whose advice about her extraordinary experience Teresa sought first, when he learned of her do-it-yourself mysticism and unorthodox confessional praxis. Salcedo had been practising prayer 'for some forty years and had diligently followed the course in theology at the College of St Thomas for twenty'.[21] The contrast between what Teresa accomplished with ease and the men around her longed for – direct experience of God – is clear from the *Book*'s beginning. Salcedo consulted with Gaspar Daza, an ascetic and a priest, but, as Kavanagh indicates, 'Neither Salcedo nor Daza were prepared to deal with anything of this kind and depth.'[22] They called in the cavalry, the **Jesuits** and then the Dominicans got involved, and by that time Teresa had collected an arsenal of experience in bad spiritual advisement.

As Jodi Bilinkoff has indicated, historically the role of the spiritual advisor has been crucial to holy women, because it offered them an emotional intimacy otherwise unavailable to them: 'Unlike fathers, husbands, or civic authorities, then, **spiritual directors** were obliged to truly listen and talk to women.'[23] For an advanced and enthusiastic conversationalist like Teresa, this would have been particularly important. A self-declared avid learner, she surely would have appreciated the opportunity to be educated and corrected by wise advisors, and was disposed to bring something to the table for them; as we shall see, she represents them as benefiting greatly from their exchanges with her.[24] Teresa was clearly a deeply devout woman who had many extraordinary experiences that left her in need of support and guidance. Problems with her spiritual advisors when she sought that support and guidance completely disrupted her relationship with God, and she repeatedly defines that relationship as the foundation of her entire life.

And problems she had. The apparent abundance of Teresa's negative experiences with confessors explains why the most obvious features of her prescription for the ideal priest are rhetorically negative. Criticism of spiritual advisors in the *Book* has two major themes: first, their inability to guide her prayer and her soul due to their lack of learning and/or lack of experience in mental prayer; and second, their frustration over not being able to experience God directly, as Teresa did. As regards the former, as early as Chapter 4 Teresa launches one of her *Book*'s prominent complaints, her inability to find a spiritual director with anything close to the insight necessary to advise her instead of scare her. This suggests the need for priests to be much better and more uniformly educated and prayerful than they were:

> For during the twenty years after this period of which I am speaking [1537–57], I did not find a master, I mean a confessor, who understood me, even though I looked for one. This hurt me so much that I often turned back and was even completely lost, for a master would have helped me flee from the occasions of offending God.[25]

Such negative observations punctuate her entire narrative. In Section 9 of the same Chapter she adds, 'I think that with God's help it would have been so [she would have been in no danger with her prayer] if I had had a master or person who would have counseled me about fleeing occasions at the beginning and made me turn away quickly when coming upon them.'[26] By the moment in her text where such critiques are a regular topic, she generalizes about the problem to say, 'For I believe that all men must be more friendly toward women whom they see are inclined toward virtue [than they were to me]. And this is the means whereby women ought to gain more [than I did] of what they are seeking from men, as I shall say later.'[27]

After she recalls reviving from the four-day coma into which she fell after a serious illness in 1539, the author speculates that had she died then, the state of her soul would have been in jeopardy, 'since on the one hand my confessors were so poorly educated'.[28] Immediately after beginning to recover from her paralysis, she says she attempted to make a definitive break from human attachments that were keeping her from God, but later concluded about that period of her life:

> The whole trouble lay in not getting at the root of the occasions and with my confessors who were of little help. For had they told me of the danger I was in and that I had the obligation to avoid those friendships, without a doubt I believe I would have remedied the matter. I have understood that to be the case.[29]

Whether the inability to break with human friendships constitutes a mortal sin or not, Teresa puts on record the failure of Catholic priests not only to save her soul, but even to realize it was in danger, and why. Time and time again, she catches her confessors doing an imperfect job:

> Since my confessors saw my good desire and my devotion to prayer, they thought I was doing a great deal. [...] I consider it now a pity that so much happened and so little help was found anywhere, except in God, and that they [her confessors] gave it [her weakness for human friendships] a great pretext for its pastimes and satisfactions by saying that these were licit.[30]

Well-educated men who fail to meet the foundress's high standards of apostolic authenticity meet with no better fate than the unlettered. Remembering how hard it was to found the convent of San José without income, Teresa says, 'I did nothing else but dispute with learned men,' and when Pedro Ibáñez sent her a theological disquisition in favour of accepting income, she recalls retorting, 'I didn't want to benefit from theology if it wasn't conducive to my following my vocation, my **vow** of poverty, and the counsels of Christ with total perfection.'[31] Such incidents accumulate, communicating a need for priestly reform, in keeping with the objectives of the reformists whose proponents had taught Teresa how to pray in silence: education in and the practice of Christian perfection, meaning living in consonance with religious vows and ancient Christian ideals.

Teresa reveals that a particularly egregious fault her confessors practised was not safeguarding the confidentiality of her problematic experiences, although they were bound to do so for ecclesiastical reasons, as they were confessional matters, or morally, as private information she did not want circulated. (In her essay in this volume, Marit Monteiro observes that Dutch **spiritual virgins** encountered the same problem, which makes one wonder how pervasive such indiscretion was in early modern Catholicism.) Moving indeed is Teresa's description of feeling a great need for help and getting only humiliation from her superiors, when they failed to protect her secrets. She paid the price for their lack of discretion:

> [Spiritual advisors] should be counseled on the importance of keeping things secret; this secrecy is fitting. In this respect I am speaking as one who is suffering a bitter trial because some persons with whom I have discussed my prayer are not keeping it secret, but in consulting this one and that other, they have truly done me great harm. They have spread things that should have remained very secret – these matters are not for everybody – and it seemed that I was the one who published them abroad [...]. it seemed to me they should have kept quiet. Nonetheless, I never dared to conceal anything from these persons.[32]

As a female confessant, Teresa was obliged to seek the guidance of men who were violating the private nature of her relationship with God. Since she could not stop doing this, the only solution was for them to rectify their behaviour.

This problem intensified, and she recalls the measures to which they subjected her, only to mock her:

> I had for many days given up receiving Communion and given up solitude, which was my whole consolation, since I had no one with whom to speak. They were all against me; some, it seemed, made fun of me when I spoke of the matter, as though I were inventing it; others advised my confessor to be careful of me; others said that my experience was clearly from the devil.[33]

Her advisors' indiscretions continue as a topic that Teresa addresses less pointedly, but just as tellingly. Late in her *Book*, she recalls coming upon García de Toledo unexpectedly and specifically notes that he 'came to speak with me *in the confessional*.'[34] Therein, she records admitting to him that she was going through some difficulties. 'He strongly urged me to tell him what the trials were,' she wrote.[35] When she refused, he reminded her that he could get the information whether she told him or not, by asking her confessor: 'He said that since the Dominican Father I mentioned [Pedro Ibañez] – who was a great friend of his – knew about them he would find out from him and that I shouldn't worry about it.'[36] Exposés such as these implicitly prove the importance of professionalism in male religious, and the tendency of the same men to disregard their professional obligations. Clearly the **nuns** were not the only ones in need of reform.

The second large smirch on Teresa's portrait of the male spiritual advisor is a subset of the first, and points to the lack of humility explicit in those men's failure to accept God's will. Teresa was blunt in her critique of religious men who got upset because they did not enjoy God's favours of the type she received in abundance, which she calls 'devotion':

> [W]hen I see servants of God, men of prominence, learning, and high intelligence make so much fuss because God doesn't give them devotion, it annoys

me to hear them [...] when they don't have devotion, they shouldn't weary themselves. *They should* understand that since His Majesty doesn't give it, it isn't necessary; and they should be masters of themselves. *They should* believe that their desire for consolation is a fault. [...] When the intellect ceases to work, they cannot bear it. [...] *We should* think that the Lord is not concerned about these inabilities.[37]

This overt instruction of her superiors, all with more book learning than she had, privileges vital experience over intellectual experience as the key to advancement in one's relationship with God. She later astutely explains a fundamental feature of human psychology: 'It frightens those whose intellects are not occupied with things of the earth that they have no intellect by which they can understand divine truths.'[38] In order to be a mystic, one must ultimately surrender the control of knowing and identity.

Teresa reveals that surrender, however, posed special challenges to religious men because of the arresting effects that learning can have on piety, prayer and turning everything over to God:

So it is very important that the master have prudence – I mean that he have good judgment – and experience; if besides these he has learning, so much the better. But if one cannot find these three qualifications together, the first two are more important since men with a background in studies can be sought out and consulted when there is a need. [...] I say that if these learned men do not practice prayer their learning is of little help to beginners. [...] I've always been a friend of men of learning. For though some don't have experience, they don't despise the Spirit nor do they ignore it, because in Sacred Scripture, which they study, they always find the truth of the good spirit.[39]

This contradiction, in which the author claims that experience in prayer is more important than learning in a confessor and then proceeds to exalt the learned man, exemplifies how Teresa negotiated the double bind that Weber has analysed in the *Book*, which presents a speaker with multiple demands that can only be resolved by addressing both, producing rhetorical conflict.[40] The double bind ironically allowed Teresa to articulate her recipe for the ideal spiritual director, the man who has learning *and* experience in mental prayer and the favours of God.

The sympathy Teresa expressed for men whose obligations relentlessly kept them struggling in the world articulates her sensitivity to the burdens of masculinity, burdens that might have made a life of prayer in removal from the world as tantalizing to men as it was hard for them to realize: 'I often marvel thinking about learned men, religious especially. [...] I see these men subject to the hardships of religious life which are great, with its penances and bad food, subject to obedience [...] everything a trial, everything a cross.'[41] Reflections such as this allowed her to hypothesize the reconciliatory position of working together, as she concluded, 'In the midst of tempests as fierce as those the Church now endures, what would we be without them? If some have gone bad, the good ones shine more brilliantly.'[42]

Teresa's positive example: 'do this'

By revealing her trying experiences with her many advisors, Teresa de Jesús defines the ideal spiritual director as a learned man experienced in mental prayer who would work with women rather than against them, would accept whatever God gave him in humility, and would reject worldly honours. As if to assure her readers that such a spiritual man is possible, she represents three individuals who lived this delicate balance, all of whom intervened directly on her behalf. All of them, interestingly, became saints: the holy man and preacher Pedro de Alcántara, OFM (1499–1562); reformer, pedagogue and author Juan de Avila (1500–1569); and nobleman-turned-religious Francisco de Borja, SJ (1510–1572). Teresa's standards for spiritual direction were high indeed, and it is no wonder that all the other men in her life story fall short of their mark.[43]

The spiritually advanced religious man was key to Teresa's reform of female convent life, in which women could not avoid their reliance on men for the sacraments and supervision, on the one hand, and would also be practising the very kind of prayer that Teresa describes in her *Book*, on the other.[44] She had to ensure their sanction of her experience to assure the future of her Carmelite reform, and one way to do so was to include accounts of her superiors' turning to mental prayer and its mystical consequences as part of her own story. Not surprisingly, her *Book* recounts such conversions, on the parts of men less impressive than the future saints, but more attainable as models for men at large.

Her case studies of these men intensify in sophistication as the *Book* progresses, developing from a straightforward rejection of obvious and serious sin to increasingly complex relationships with God, of the type Teresa herself enjoyed. First to appear is Pedro Hernández, the corrupt priest of Becedas who confessed to Teresa – when she was but 23 years old and a novice mystic – that he had lived with a concubine for seven years, then followed her advice to break free of sin, and died 'a very good death' a year later.[45] The incident with Hernández, which reads like a Virgin miracle, is remarkable indeed for the manifest role inversion explicit in it: a needy, corrupt priest finds salvation thanks to the guidance of a young woman wise beyond her years. Her second recruit, her father, accepted her instruction in prayer and became advanced in it, to the extent that he was preternaturally aware of his impending demise.[46] Recalling these modest male conversions justifies Teresa's subsequent undertakings to improve men of a more complex nature: educated confessors.

Early in the treatise on prayer she inserted into her *Book*, Teresa records the transformative power of mental prayer saying:

> For in my opinion a background of studies is like a treasure to aid in this practice if the studies are accompanied by humility. Some days ago I saw the truth of this statement in the case of a few learned men. They began only a short time ago, and they have advanced very far. This makes me most anxious that many learned men would becomes spiritual men, as I shall say afterwards.[47]

The cross-reference is to Pedro Ibáñez (Professor of Theology at St Thomas in Ávila) and Diego García de Toledo (a confessor to whom Teresa sent the first complete draft of her *Book*), both Dominicans, both of whose stories she tells at the end of the text. She represents Ibañez as having retired to a life of contemplation after hearing her account of her visions and manner of prayer ('I begged him to consider my prayer very carefully [...] and, in my opinion it benefited him,' 33.5). This leads to a summary of how 'previously he assured me and consoled me only by his learning, but now he did so also through his spiritual experience, for he was receiving a number of supernatural experiences.'[48] Ibáñez thus becomes an ideal male advisor to a religious woman, an ideal not at all surprising in a text by a female religious reformer who emphasizes the primacy of experience over all other forms of knowledge.

It was García de Toledo who had asked Teresa to write what eventually became the treatise on prayer in which she refers to him. His success at prayer moved her to exclaim, 'I considered the wonderful talents and gifts he had for doing much good, were he to give himself totally to God.'[49] She claims that God 'sent him [García de Toledo] some truths by means of me [...]. Consequently [...] he turned to God so completely that every time he speaks to me, I'm stupefied.'[50] For those men frustrated by God's failure to regale them with mystical gifts, Teresa provides Pedro Ibáñez and García de Toledo as evidence that in fact it can happen, ironically enough, were they to heed the recommendations of the very woman they were supposed to be evaluating and advising.

Teresa embedded the presence of García de Toledo in her text on several levels, as an addressée, a superior, a reader and editor, and a spiritual son. By describing his role in her life in this rich and varied way, she provides evidence of her commitment to introducing the priesthood to the virtues and benefits of a personal relationship with God, which scholars have identified as a fundamental piece of her life objective. As Bilinkoff has stated, Teresa 'adopted as her particular mission ministry to the ministers of the Church' and 'continued throughout her life to counsel, comfort and offer prayer for "troubled priests"'.[51] It is likely that any priest who did not have a personal and intimate relationship with God would be qualified as 'troubled' by the energetic reformer, troubled at least by the confessional challenges posed by women such as Teresa.

Why it matters: Teresa's inheritance

What was at stake in Teresa's quest for a helpful confessor or spiritual director only became fully apparent after she died and was canonized in 1622, in record-breaking time: the safeguarding for posterity of the most important female Catholic mystic of all time. Had Teresa failed to persist, using God to override her male advisors, she would have gone the way of the 'heretic' women to whom she was often compared. Her insistent complaints about priestly and advisory incompetence in her *Book*, combined with her subsequent success, necessarily required her male readers to admit that indeed, things should have gone otherwise, that she became a saint in spite of them more than because of them. The fact that Teresa never identified the teaching of this lesson as her text's objective surely mitigated its impact on religious authorities who read it.

Teresa and those men were well aware of the long tradition of Catholic holy women who had men at the helm of their futures, men who were promoting them and who directly intervened in the production of their *vitae* and the preservation of their writings: Catherine of Siena's confessor/hagiographer Raymond of Capua and Angela of Foligno's Brother A were the most well known in Spain, and Teresa was familiar with the roles of both.[52] In contrast to this tradition of male support, Teresa wrote alone, having met with incapacity, resistance and doubt.[53] Whereas one can rest assured that most if not all holy women from the Middle Ages forward had to defend themselves from ecclesiastical suspicion of their piety, Teresa's wrangling with those men is not only inscribed in, but is a major theme of, her first written work. To the religious males reading her *Book* after her death, and certainly after her canonization, it was crystal clear that something had gone awry with her confessors, in contradistinction to established tradition.

Recent research in masculinities and religious biography contextualizes Teresa's prescription for the ideal spiritual director by providing long-standing evidence of Catholic men's admiration for and interest in women's piety, which they perceived of as different from and complementary to their own. In his seminal study of medieval religious women and their mendicant friar counterparts, John Coakley maintains that those friars were keen on women's intimacies with the divine: "[I]t seems to have been exactly that prospect of encountering something legitimately beyond them that made holy women figures of fascination for clerical men," and it was through their female charges that they witnessed the limits of earthly authority and explored what lay beyond it.[54] Writing of five confessors who wrote biographies of their female penitents in Avila between 1500 and 1650, Bilinkoff asserts that, 'Far from occupying positions of unqualified control, male confessors were strongly attracted to the idea of directing spiritually advanced woman and, in turn, became deeply influenced by them, identified with them, and even became dependent upon them.'[55]

Teresa's *Book* provides evidence of this give and take between spiritual women and their advisors, even though it is highly unusual as a first-person narrative of an early modern woman's spiritual experience unmediated by a male voice (if vetted by multiple male superiors). Its exclusive employment of the author's own voice, and the conciliatory rhetoric in which she encased some of her critiques of her male advisors, may explain why those critiques were never edited out of her manuscript. Recognition of the need for clerical reform on the part of the men who oversaw her text's production, survival and publication surely played an equally important role, for any number of them could have edited those comments out, had they chosen to do so.

The early modern model of masculinity

The fact that they did not, and that Teresa's *Book* still holds out a model for the ideal male religious, is testimony of something larger than Teresa and the Carmelite reform. In her analysis of why the **Society of Jesus** was as successful as it was during the sixteenth and seventeenth centuries, Ulrike Strasser points to the great appeal it had to early modern men. That appeal, she says, derived from the way in which Ignatius of Loyola (1491–1556) and his immediate followers re-defined the medieval model of masculinity, based on competition and aggression, to a post-Renaissance variety characterized by support, intimate friendship and shared ideals. In the narrative about his life that Ignatius dictated, the male hero also appropriates established practices of medieval female piety, such as suffering, fasting, emotiveness (particularly weeping), scrupulousness and Eucharistic fervour, to arrive at what Strasser calls a 'volatility of affect' that was highly appealing to the early modern male.[56] The coterie of men buzzing around Teresa, inside her *Book* and out, suggests not only a desire to control her but also, in tandem with the changing nature and functions of religious male behaviour and evolving models of masculinity itself, a desire to experience, directly or indirectly, the intimacy she enjoyed with God and the courage with which she defied the world to make God the centre of her life.

The information in Teresa's *Book* about religious men, positive and negative, not only served the men who read it as a cautionary tale and inspiration, but also the nuns living Teresa's legacy. The management of masculinity is a prominent theme in all of the foundress's writing, both the management of fortitude that she recommends for women (to which her age referred as *varonil*, or manly) and the management of the specific men under whose wings her nuns negotiated their lives.[57] In one of the last chapters of her *Book*, Teresa insists that her text be passed along to her spiritual daughters:

> And when I'm dead, give it [what is written here] to the **Sisters** who live here that when those who are to come see the many things His Majesty arranged for its establishment by means of so wretched and dreadful a thing as myself, they might be greatly encouraged to serve God and strive that what has been begun may not collapse but always flourish.[58]

Among the things to 'always flourish' was Teresa's dream of Catholic men who did not fear women's intimacy with God, men who would be spiritually, emotionally and intellectually enlightened.

Notes

1. Out of respect, I use the name Teresa de Jesús took upon her religious profession; on the other options, see E. Carrera, *Teresa of Ávila's Autobiography: Authority, Power and the Self in Mid-Sixteenth-Century Spain* (Oxford: Legenda, 2005), p. 1. I cite Kieran Kavanaugh's English translation of Teresa's works and follow the standard practice of citing her writings by chapter and section: Teresa de Jesús, 'The Book of Her Life', in *Saint Teresa of Ávila: Collected Works*, translated and edited by K. Kavanaugh (Washington: ICS Publications, 1987), pp. 53–365. Other translations are mine.

2. Using Teresa's own comments about her letters, which she wrote every night, Alison Weber calculates that she likely composed between 10,000 and 22,000 in total; see her study, '"Dear Daughter": Reform and Persuasion in St. Teresa's Letters to Her Prioresses', in J. Couchman and A. Crabb (eds) *Women's Letters Across Europe, 1400–1700* (Aldershot: Ashgate, 2005), pp. 241–61.

3. Teresa and her contemporaries called it simply her 'book.' On the inaccuracy of labelling this text Teresa's *Life* an autobiography, see E. Rhodes, '"What's in a Name": On Teresa of Ávila's *Book*', in R. Boenig (ed.) *The Mystical Gesture: Essays on*

Medieval and Early Modern Spiritual Culture in Honor of Mary E. Giles (Burlington VT: Ashgate Press, 2000), pp. 79–106; A. Weber, *Teresa of Ávila and the Rhetoric of Femininity* (Princeton: Princeton University Press, 1990), pp. 41–42.

4. Weber identifies the men for whom the various known versions of the manuscript were written: 'The Three Lives of the Vida: The Uses of Convent Autobiography', in M. V. Vicente and L. R. Corteguera (eds) *Women, Texts and Authority in the Early Modern Spanish World* (Burlington, VT: Ashgate, 2003), p. 110.

5. For case studies in the Spanish Empire, see *Women in the Inquisition: Spain and the New World* edited by M. E. Giles (Baltimore: Johns Hopkins University Press, 1999).

6. Teresa was unafraid of the Inquisition. Her recorded response to the warning of 'some persons' that she might be reported to the Holy Office is well known: 'This amused me,' she writes and then adds, 'if I did have something to fear I'd go myself to seek out the Inquisitors' (*Book* 33.5). All evidence indicates that what worried her was the possibility that she was unorthodox in any fashion. The fact that her life encompasses the end of reformist Spanish Catholicism through a conservative period in the 1550s, then into a less rigid conservative phase means that what constituted orthodoxy was in flux throughout her lifetime; see E. Rhodes, 'Mysticism and History: The Case of Spain's Golden Age', in A. Weber (ed.) *Teresa of Avila and Spanish Mysticism* (New York: MLA, 2009), pp. 47–56.

7. The question of whether Teresa wanted to write, and whether she wanted to write the text she was ordered to compose, remains unsolved. Jodi Billinkoff says it was established practice in the Middle Ages and Early Modern periods that male superiors, 'anxious to gauge the orthodoxy and authenticity of their spiritual daughters' would request just such documents (J. Bilinkoff, *Related Lives: Confessors and Their Female Penitents, 1450–1750* (Ithaca, NY: Cornell University Press, 2005), pp. 27–28.

8. E. Llamas Martínez, 'Libro de la vida', in A. Barrientos (ed.) *Introducción a la lectura de Santa Teresa.* (Madrid: Editorial de la espiritualidad, 1978), pp. 211–16.

9. *Book* 29.4.

10. See Gillian Ahlgren's analysis of the religious conflicts that conditioned Teresa's writing, *Teresa of Avila and the Politics of Sanctity* (Ithaca, NY: Cornell University Press, 1996). The most complete resource remains Efrén de la Madre de Dios and Otger Steggink, *Tiempo y vida de Santa Teresa*, 2nd edition (Madrid: Editorial Católica, 1972).

11. Jodi Bilinkoff studies Ávila's transition from support of the Catholic reform to hostility toward it (*The Avila of St. Teresa: Religious Reform in a Sixteenth-Century City* (Ithaca, NY: Cornell University Press, 1989)). Enrique Llamas Martínez (OCD) offers the most complete study of Teresa's interactions with the Inquisition (*Santa Teresa de Jesús y la Inquisición española* (Madrid: Consejo Superior de Investigaciones Científicas, 1972)).

12. K. Kavanaugh (OCD), 'Introduction', in *Saint Teresa of Ávila: Collected Works* (Washington D.C.: ICS Publications, 1987), pp. 35–37.

13. These spiritual testimonies are in *Collected Works* I: pp. 372–85.

14. Cf. Father Pedro Báñez's testimony that she wrote 'her life and the way of prayer along which God had brought her. She had this book written already when I began to deal with her' (S. de Santa Teresa, 'Introdución' in *Vida de Santa Teresa de Jesús*, cxii–cxx (Burgos: Monte Carmelo, 1934–35), p. cxvii).

15. *Ibid.* 66–68. Weber, 'Three Lives,' pp. 110, 117.

16. Victoria Lincoln suggests that García de Toledo was the man for whom Teresa felt excessive friendship while at the convent of the Encarnación (*Teresa: A Woman. A Biography of Teresa of Avila* in E. Rivers and A. T. de Nicolás (eds) (Albany,

NY: State University of New York Press, 1984), p. 24). Cathleen Medwick attributes the *Book*'s 'warmth and accessibility' in part to the fact that Teresa wrote it at his request (*Teresa of Avila, The Progress of a Soul* (New York: Doubleday, 1999), p. 79).

17. On Teresa's rhetorical strategies, see Rossi ('Teresa de Jesús: La mujer y la palabra', *Mientras tanto*, 15 (1983), pp. 29–45), Weber (*Teresa*), and Ahlgren (*Teresa*, pp. 67–84).
18. *Book* 25.18–19.
19. James Fernández calls the text a palimpsest that hides the successive voices of its author; see 'La *Vida* de Teresa y la salvación del discurso', *MLN* 105.2 (1990), p. 285. Inquisitorial authorities were not among the addressées for whom Teresa wrote her *Book*, although it was eventually examined and exempted by the Inquisition (the Holy Office) after the headstrong and jealous Princess of Eboli denounced it as heretical. Teresa finished the extant draft nine years before the Inquisition had it examined.
20. As baroque poet Francisco de Quevedo pointed out long ago, there were many books from which Teresa could have learned how to practise what was then called mystical theology (Carrera cites the Quevedo text, *Teresa*, p. 46).
21. Kavanaugh, 'Introduction', p. 32. The first detail comes from the biography of Teresa by Julián de Ávila, a secular priest from Avila; the second is from testimony by doña Mencía del Aguilla, a member of Teresa's extended family; see Efrén and Steggink for the Spanish sources, (*Tiempo y vida*, I, p. 190).
22. Kavanaugh, 'Introduction', p. 35.
23. *Related* 18.
24. Her declaration of how much she liked to learn is set in a critique of unlearned confessors: 'I began to confess to him for I was always fond of learning. Half-learned confessors have done my soul great harm when I have been unable to find a confessor with as much learning as I like' (5.3).
25. *Book* 4.7.
26. *Ibid.*, 4.9.
27. *Ibid.*, 5.6.
28. *Ibid.*, 5.10.
29. *Ibid.*, 6.4.
30. *Ibid.*, 8.11.
31. *Ibid.*, 35.4.
32. *Ibid.*, 23.14.
33. *Ibid.*, 25.15.
34. *Ibid.*, 34.6; my emphasis.
35. *Ibid.*, 34.6.
36. *Ibid.*, 34.6; this meeting was in 1562.
37. *Ibid.*, 11.14–15; my emphasis.
38. *Ibid.*, 18.3.
39. *Ibid.*, 13.16–17.
40. Weber analyses these conflicts in her chapter on Teresa's *Book* (*Teresa*, pp. 42–76).
41. *Book*, 14.20.
42. *Ibid.*
43. On Pedro de Alcántara see 30.4, 35.5, 36.20 and 40.8; on Juan de Avila, the Epilogue; on Francisco de Borja, 24.3.
44. Nonetheless, Teresa invested her Mother Superiors with particular power to circumvent male authority, see Alison Weber, 'Spiritual Administration: Gender and Discernment in the Carmelite Reform', *Sixteenth Century Journal*, 31.1 (2000), pp. 123–46.

45. *Book*, 5.6.
46. *Ibid.*, 7.14–16.
47. *Ibid.*, 12.4.
48. *Ibid.*, 33.5.
49. *Ibid.*, 34.7.
50. *Ibid.*, 34.11.
51. J. Bilinkoff, 'Woman with a Mission: Teresa of Avila and the Apostolic Model', in G. Barone, Marina Caffiero and Francesco Scorza Barcellona (eds), *Modelli di Santità e modelli di comportamento: Constrasti, intersezioni complementària* (Turin: Rosenberg & Sellier, 1994), p. 299.
52. On the texts by Catherine of Siena and Angela of Foligno in Spain, see E. Rhodes, 'What's in a Name'. Catherine Mooney analyses the role of Brother A in Angela's dictations to him in 'The Authorial Role of Brother A. in the Composition of Angela of Foligno's Revelations', in A. Matter and J. Coakley (eds), *Creative Women in Medieval and Early Modern Italy* (Philadelphia: University of Pennsylvania Press, 1994), pp. 34–63, and Coakley emphasizes collaborative efforts between penitent and biographer/editor in his chapters on Angela and Catherine (*Women, Men and Spiritual Power: Female Saints and Their Male Collaborators* (New York: Columbia University Press, 2006), pp. 111–48; pp. 170–92).
53. Logically, Teresa is not included in Bilinkoff's book about the mutually supportive relationships between female penitents and their confessors (*Related Lives*).
54. Coakley, *Women, Men and Spiritual Power*, p. 214, p. 215.
55. J. Bilinkoff, 'Confessors, Penitents, and the Construction of Identities in Early Modern Avila' in B. Diefendorf and C. Hesse (eds), *Culture and Identity in Early Modern Europe (1500–1800): Essays in Honor of Natalie Zemon Davis* (Ann Arbor: University of Michigan Press, 1994), p. 84.
56. U. Strasser, 'The First Form and Grace' in S. H. Hendrix and S. C. Karant-Nunn (eds), *Ignatius of Loyola and the Reformation of Masculinity*, pp. 45–70; *Masculinity in the Reformation Era* (Kirksville, MO: Truman State University Press, 2008), p. 58. The conservative wing of the Catholic establishment reacted negatively to the Jesuits' embrace of affect. The Dominican theologian Melchor Cano, for example, categorized their practices as effeminate: 'One of the causes that moves me to be discontented with these Theatine [Jesuit] fathers is that rather than make lions of the gentlemen they take up, they make them hens, and if they make them hens they make them chickens; and if the Turks had sent men to Spain with the idea of removing the nerve and power from the country and turning our soldiers into women and our gentlemen into merchants, they couldn't send anyone better for the job' (cited in E. y Steggink, *Tiempo y vida* I: 204). According to the *Diccionario de la Real Academia*, 'Theatine' was a common confusion for 'Jesuit.'
57. María de San José, one of Teresa's protégées and the first prioress of the Discalced Carmelite convent in Seville, was put in solitary confinement for her fearless critiques of the convent's confessor as ignorant and inexperienced. Ana de Jesús, another of Teresa's immediate spiritual daughters, was similarly critical. See M. E. Perry, 'Subversion and Seduction: Perceptions of the Body in Writings of Religious Women in Counter-Reformation Spain', in A. Saint-Saëns (ed.), *Religion, Body and Gender in Early Modern Spain* (San Francisco: Mellen Research University Press, 1991), pp. 67–78.
58. *Book* 36.29.

5

Mary Ward's English Institute and Prescribed Female Roles in the Early Modern Church[1]

Laurence Lux-Sterritt

Introduction

Protestantism gained much ground in late sixteenth and early seventeenth-century Europe, prompting the Catholic Church to embark upon a worldwide catechizing endeavour. The reforming Council of Trent (1545–63) sought to respond to the challenges of the rapidly changing religious picture, giving increased importance to missionary vocations amongst the clergy. However, it made no provision for **women religious** to become part of this common effort; on the contrary, in 1563, it reasserted that the only acceptable form of religious life for women was cloistered contemplation. Yet before and after Trent, many unenclosed female movements emerged which sought to complement male **apostolic** movements. Earlier in this volume, Querciolo Mazzonis evoked the vocation of the Italian Angela Merici (1474–1540), whose Company of Saint Ursula combined contemplation and care of one's neighbour. Marit Monteiro's essay also shows that, in the Netherlands, **spiritual virgins**, or '**beguines**', found it difficult to match the usefulness of their active endeavours with the authorities' reticence towards females who escaped traditional status definitions. In France, the Congrégation de Notre-Dame (1597), François de Sales's Visitation (1610–16) or the Filles de la Charité (1634) all shared the same apostolic essence.[2] Their main vocation was not the observance of a monastic way of life but rather an evangelical brief which implied constant interaction with others. For England, the main representative of this female apostolic movement was Mary Ward.

Born at Mulwith near Ripon, in Yorkshire, Mary Ward (1585–1645) became acquainted, from an early age, with missionary activities in **recusant** networks. She felt called to serve God and, in 1606, she left England to become a Poor Clare in St Omer. Yet taking the veil did not bring her spiritual peace; between 1607 and 1611, she received what she later described as a series of revelations through which God called her to serve Him in a different way.

Initially, she could not envisage any religious life outside the convent; in 1607, she left her Flemish convent to found a house of Poor Clares specifically for English women. Finally, in 1611, she received what she described as the divine command to 'Take the Same of the Society' (that is, to imitate the Ignatians as faithfully as possible): this epiphany prompted her to found a congregation modelled upon the **Society of Jesus** 'both in matter and manner'.[3] Within a few years, houses were opened across the Continent, in Liège (1616), in Cologne and Trier (1620–21), in Rome (1622), in Naples and Perugia (1623), in Munich and Vienna (1627) and finally in Bratislava and Prague (1628). In parallel, small clandestine houses also operated in England.

When Mary Ward created her Institute of English Ladies[4], her purpose was to provide a female counterpart to the male missionaries in England and on the Continent. Yet her dedication to the creation of an independent Society of Jesus for women, combined with the canonical transgressions this entailed, triggered a violent clerical reaction against her proposal. In 1621, the **secular clergy** wrote a Memorial against the English Ladies; *Propaganda Fide* began enquiries into their orthodoxy in 1624.[5] Finally, in 1631, Pope Urban VIII suppressed them with the bull *Pastoralis Romani Pontificis*, condemning their vocation and their way of life.[6] Defeated by clerical opposition, Ward returned to England, where she died in January 1645.[7]

Until recently, most publications on Mary Ward came either from members of her Institute or from supportive clerics. The authoritative biography written by M. C. E. Chambers is a mine of detailed information, but has a marked tendency towards hagiography. Similarly, remarkable studies such as those undertaken by Josef Grisar, SJ, Immolata Wetter, IBVM, or Henriette Peters, IBVM, were written in the cause for Mary Ward's canonization.[8] Because of their nature, these highly valuable sources sometimes neglect the general context which influenced Ward's fate. Yet the most recent publications indicate that this trend may be coming to an end: both Ursula Dirmeier, CJ, and Christina Kenworthy-Browne, CJ, have taken exciting steps to make the Institute's primary sources available in print, thereby ushering a phase in which Mary Ward's historiography may quickly take new directions.[9]

This chapter seeks to examine the difficulties which led to the suppression of Mary Ward's Institute. Rather than dealing with the Institute's merits or shortcomings *per se*, it will examine the extent to which Mary Ward's congregation diverged from clerically imposed norms by comparing her own definition of her vocation (which she gave in her 1622 Plan known as the *Institutum*[10]) with male-filtered expressions of what was acceptable. Indeed, plans for the approbation of the Institute were written both before and after Ward's own *Institutum*. The earliest document was drafted by her **spiritual director**, Roger Lee, SJ (1568–1615), and the Institute he described in his 1612 *Schola Beatae Mariae* was far removed from Ward's missionary project, offering a more traditional female religious Order.[11] The same can be said of the 81 **Rules** which were finally approved after Frances Bedingfield (1616–1704), once a follower of Mary Ward, took it upon herself to initiate a new phase in the history of the English Ladies. When she purchased houses to be used as centres for priests and elementary schools in Hammersmith (1669) and York (1686), a new Institute was born from the ashes of the old one; yet, in order to seek papal approval, it kept its heritage from Mary Ward carefully hidden.[12] Its Rules – actively supported by Bishop John Leyburn, **Vicar Apostolic** of the London District (1685–1702) – were presented in 1699 by the then Chief Superior Mary Anne Babthorpe (d. 1711), and gained Clement XI's approbation on 13 June 1703.[13]

What were the elements which made both Lee's *Schola* and Babthorpe's Rules more likely to gain papal approval than Mary Ward's own *Institutum*? This chapter will show that the reasons for the Church's coSndemnation of Mary Ward's vocation stemmed from the missionary nature of that vocation, but also from the institutional form which Ward gave her Institute. Underpinning both, however, was the thorny issue of gender and the prescribed female roles in the early modern Church.

Mary Ward's vocation: unenclosed and missionary

In her 1622 *Institutum*, Mary Ward emphasized her desire to assist her fellow Catholics and to support her Church. Some aspects of this apostolate remained in keeping with roles deemed acceptable for women, such as catechizing and educating girls 'in day and boarding schools'.[14] Although opening the doors to day pupils and catechizing adults were both relatively new briefs for women religious, such a way of life had been sanctioned by Pope Paul V for the Ursulines of Paris in 1612.[15] As the example of the so-called 'teaching **nuns**' was adopted by others, it became part of a movement which witnessed the rapid development of teaching female Orders.[16] This aspect of Mary Ward's vocation therefore remained within the tolerated sphere of female religious activity.

Nevertheless, the duties of the English Ladies exceeded this traditional brief; in England, they would facilitate the work of missionaries by preparing lay folk for the sacraments and providing spiritual assistance in the absence of priests. They would serve prisoners and attend to the sick; more controversially still, they would 'seek women of doubtful lives' and work for the conversion of those 'estranged from the Church', a role normally recognized as perilous for women.[17] Mary Ward never envisaged a typical conventual life in her 1622 *Institutum*; on the contrary, she openly presented her Institute as missionary. Inspired by the **Jesuit** *Formula Instituti* and using the same martial vocabulary, she presented her Ladies as crusaders:

> Whoever wishes to serve *beneath the banner of the cross as a soldier of God* in our Society [...] is a member of a Society founded primarily [...] *to strive for the defence and propagation of the faith* and for the progress of souls in Christian life and doctrine, leading them back from heresy and evil ways to the faith.[18]

Moreover, the Ladies' mission was to operate on a worldwide level, 'among the Turks or any other infidels, even those who live in the region called the Indies, or among any heretics whatever, or schismatics, or any of the faithful'.[19] Implicitly, of course, they also hoped to work in the English mission, reconquering their native land.

Such a missionary vocation violated the laws of **enclosure** which had been strictly enforced upon women since the Council of Trent's 1563 decree endorsing Boniface VIII's medieval bull *Periculoso*.[20] In seventeenth-century Europe, the

English Ladies were not the only women to denounce the limitations of such a definition of female religious life. Beguines, Ursulines and Visitandines all claimed to play an active part in the ongoing mission of Catholic recovery. The Spanish Luisa de Carvajal even claimed a missionary vocation very similar to Mary Ward's, and took an active part in the Catholic mission in England.[21]

Yet although Mary Ward's Institute was part of a broader female movement challenging Tridentine decrees, it was also unique. Luisa de Carvajal acted as a rogue individual, and her actions remained localized in London. The spiritual virgins and widows of the Low Countries, on the contrary, were legion, and highly visible in their local *milieus*.[22] But like Carvajal, they functioned outside religious status; although their endeavours served the Church, they did not claim to be officially part of it. Unlike Mary Ward, they neither founded multiple branches throughout Europe, not sought papal recognition for an entirely novel female missionary Order. The Ursulines did gain official religious status, but this came at the price of their original active vocation, as they gradually moved away from Angela Merici's initially broad apostolic brief and accepted *clausura* as a teaching religious Order for girls. Mary Ward, on the other hand, refused all compromise, but rather hoped to change the Church's views on women's roles as active militants of the Catholic Reformation.

As mentioned earlier, the secular clergy responded to Mary Ward's *Institutum* with a Memorial addressed to the Pope, in which they denounced the Institute as 'directly contrary to the decrees of the Sacred Council of Trent'. Although the authors recognized the Ladies' teaching work as worthy of praise, they insisted that these teachers could not be considered religious if they remained unenclosed.[23] Later, in October 1622, the English secular priest John Colleton[24] (1548–1635) wrote:

> If [the Institute] abode within its cells and walls, after the example of other religious communities, [it] would perhaps deserve much praise, but when it claims the duties of the apostolic office, wanders unrestrainedly about hither and thither [...] and in spite of this insists on being numbered amongst the religious communities, [it] is certainly exposed to the censures and reproaches of many pious people.[25]

The Ladies' geographical mobility was interpreted as symptomatic of their rebelliousness. In the same year, Fr. John Bennet (d. 1623), the agent for the English secular clergy in Rome, summarized the situation: 'Briefly closure they must embrace, and some Order already approved, or else dissolve. But of closure they will not hear.'[26] Pope and clergy alike perceived Mary Ward's missionary vocation as a threat to Catholic institutions, since it openly advocated an alternative to the only female religious life heretofore recognized.

Mediated expressions of Mary Ward's vocation: an enclosed teaching Order

If Mary Ward's own expression of her vocation was controversial, the texts written before and after the *Institutum* under (male) clerical guidance left more room for compromise. Before the **foundress** wrote her own plans, her spiritual director Roger Lee, SJ, had cast a first draft in 1612, the *Schola Beatae Mariae*. Long after

Mary Ward's death in 1645, when the 'second Institute' developed by Ward's friend and follower, Frances Bedingfield, sought approval of its Rules, it presented a profile which was closer to Lee's *Schola* than to Ward's missionary Order. Both documents downplayed the women's agency and emphasized their compliance with Tridentine decrees. They described Institutes which focused primarily upon the spiritual welfare of their own members through contemplation and prayer, and whose only active brief was the teaching and catechizing of girls and women.

As Roger Lee strove to ensure a positive reception for the Institute, he presented its vocation with the vocabulary of modesty and deference suited to all religious, and to women in particular; he described the aim of the Institute as follows: 'Firstly, that [...] we may make timely provision for our own salvation by a complete renunciation of the world: Then *in accordance with the capacity of our own sex* we may devote ourselves to the Christian education of maidens and girls whether outside or inside England.'[27] Lee chose to comply with conventual tradition: like other women religious, his Ladies sought the advancement of their own souls through detachment from the world and dedication to God. Gendered roles were respected also, since the Ladies' teaching brief was limited to their 'own sex', never venturing into the sphere of male activities and responsibilities. To all intents and purposes, his proposed Institute resembled the French Ursulines, who, by then, had become an enclosed Order of teaching and catechizing nuns. In fact, throughout the years of controversy in the 1620s, various clerics recommended that the Institute should adopt the Ursuline rules; yet Mary Ward refused to compromise the global missionary nature of her vocation and found such suggestions unpalatable, answering: 'If God give health, we shall find another way to serve him than of becoming Ursulines.'[28]

When comparing Lee's *Schola* to Ward's *Institutum*, it appears that the cleric negotiated the politics of religion more subtly than his penitent. He knew that women's place in the Church was defined by the male hierarchy which determined standards of acceptable female behaviour. Tellingly, Lee utilized the trope of female humility in a way which is reminiscent of Teresa of Àvila's rhetoric. Alison Weber showed how Teresa's recognition in the Church owed much to her 'pragmatic stylistic', which seemingly endorsed the patriarchal definition of female abilities, the better to gain the trust of clerical sceptics.[29] Echoing Teresa's strategy, Roger Lee's prose constantly highlighted the 'littleness' of the English Ladies; the Plan was presented as a plea in which they 'begged' to be allowed to 'render services'. Their vocation, described in an almost apologetic fashion, was shown as a mere 'pious desire' to help the Church. The opening paragraph set the tone by suggesting, in the meekest of terms, that the Catholic crisis in England and in Europe called for a reassessment of female involvement, arguing that 'it seem[ed] right that, *according to their condition*, women also should and c[ould] provide something more than ordinary in the face of this common spiritual need.'[30] It was not by chance that Roger Lee chose to conclude this paragraph on typically female virtues likely to meet with the clergy's approval: 'But let them specially strive to be outstanding in humility and meekness.'[31] In his *Schola*, not unlike Teresa of Àvila in the *Book of Her Life*, he utilized gendered clichés the better to achieve his goals; such pragmatic compromise was, however, entirely absent in Mary Ward's own *Institutum*.

In contrast to Mary Ward, Roger Lee also realized that female enclosure was not a condition which could be breached. The Continental houses of the Institute were to be cloistered, while in Protestant England, where houses could not function openly as convents, monastic enclosure would be relaxed only to avoid detection. Yet Lee worded this request carefully:

> And although this Institute, of its nature, does not allow of the strict cloister in the present condition of England, still, far from having the house open to all, *we desire rather to have cloister so strictly observed that no access is to be allowed* to any extern whatsoever in the chapel and schools [...]. But necessary and serious conversations will be referred to *the grille* destined for that purpose, and no one shall go without permission of the Superior who shall be present at the conversation.[32]

Even as the *Schola* proposed a Catholic Order of women which would function both on the Continent and in Protestant England, it remained tentative in its attitude to enclosure or the evocation of an active apostolate.

The similarity between Roger Lee's 1612 *Schola Beatae Mariae* and the 81 Rules which obtained papal approval in 1703 is most striking. It is as though the new Institute had used Lee's *Schola* rather than Ward's *Institutum* as its model, highlighting contemplation, prayer and the spiritual salvation of its own members, while mentioning the education of girls only in second place: 'The end of this Rule is to enable us to work out, with the grace of God, our own perfection and salvation, and aided by the same Divine grace, to labour for the perfection and salvation of our neighbour, by means of the education of children of our own sex.'[33] Quite contrary to Mary Ward's explicit wish, but in keeping with Lee's proposal, the new Institute's active vocation was limited to the instruction of girls, to the exclusion of any missionary ambition. The 81 Rules also echo the *Schola* on the issue of enclosure: contacts with the outside were to be limited and supervised at the grille, all letters were checked, and correspondence should not be smuggled in or out by externs. Private conversations with day pupils were also to be punished.[34] The same provisions were made to observe in England a *modus vivendi* which was as close to cloistered life as possible.

Yet as the Congregation of the Council of Trent examined Mary Anne Babthorpe's petition for the approval of the new Institute, they noted that it breached strict monastic enclosure, since it undertook the education of both boarders and externs and also functioned in England, where *clausura* was impossible. Its slight adaptation of enclosure therefore denied the new Institute any official religious status. This objection was overcome only when the Ladies argued that they did not request approbation as a religious Order in the Church, but merely as a devout congregation of pious women, whose work carried papal endorsement.[35] Although it was a clear departure from Mary Ward's intentions, such a compromise represented a first step towards official recognition.

Moreover, Mary Anne Babthorpe recognized that women's spiritual endeavours could succeed only with clerical support, and she had gained strong clerical allies. Bishop John Leyburn, Vicar Apostolic of the London District (1685–1702) supported her appeal in a letter addressed to the Pope, in which he underlined the orthodoxy of those 'noble virgins'.[36] By presenting an unassuming profile, complying with male-defined female religious roles and publicizing its acceptance of episcopal guidance, the new Institute secured the approbation of its 81 Rules in less than four years.[37]

Thus, the 1612 *Schola* and the 1703 Rules presented only a few differences from female religious orthodoxy and proposed an Order which was more likely to obtain papal assent than that presented by Mary Ward in her 1622 *Institutum*. Indeed, both depicted a congregation which was strikingly similar to that of the French Ursulines, who had reconciled teaching and enclosure in a teaching Order officially confirmed in Paris in 1612.[38] It is possible that, aware of the developments in religious and apostolic life in Europe, Lee and Babthorpe had decided to propose an Institute which, though not entirely faithful to the missionary ideal of Mary Ward, might be better attuned to the definition of female roles in the post-Tridentine Church.

Yet it was not only Mary Ward's active vocation which had been at the core of the virulent debate leading to the Institute's suppression in 1631; her proposed unenclosed mission was novel in itself, but it became all the more dangerous in the context of the dispute between Jesuits and secular clergy, and particularly in the English context where secular priests and Jesuit missionaries were in open conflict. Thus, the fact that Mary Ward chose to model her congregation on the Society of Jesus played a crucial part in the condemnation of her Institute.

Institutional issues: Mary Ward's female Society of Jesus

Mary Ward claimed that her definition of the Institute was not a personal choice, but rather an act of self-surrender to God's commandment to 'Take the Same of the Society'. She therefore adopted both the vocation and the hierarchical structure used by the Society of Jesus, which gave unprecedented levels of autonomy to her English Ladies. Internally, all the branches of the Institute were coordinated by one central figure, the Mother Superior General, who fostered a unity of rule and governance between all the houses across Europe and England.[39] This organization in a generalate departed radically from the norm of female religious Orders and was highly controversial, especially since the Superior General's authority was second only to that of the Pope.

Indeed, the foundress requested that the Institute should bypass all clerical authority, and make a vow of direct obedience to the Pope.[40] In her Memorial addressed to Pope Gregory XV in December 1621, she explained why her Institute, unlike traditional female Orders, should not be subject to clerical supervision: '[religious life under episcopal control], though holy in itself and helpful to other religious communities [is] not only contrary to the Institute allotted unto us, but would moreover [...] much molest and hinder us [in] the service we are to perform towards our neighbours'.[41] Despite the formulaic lip-service paid to the tradition of episcopal control, Mary Ward associated submission to bishops with a hindrance, an impediment which would interfere with the Institute's functioning and violated its vocation. The English Ladies requested self-government and wished (in addition to the customary three **vows**) to take a fourth vow of direct obedience, recognizing the pope as their only authority outside the Institute's Mother Superior General.

Clerics were incensed by what they perceived as a woman's presumption to dispense with male jurisdiction altogether. In the controversy which escalated in the 1620s, the English Ladies were repeatedly accused of usurping male privileges; more specifically, Mary Ward was accused of founding a female Society of Jesus. In their 1621 memorial, the secular clergy referred to the Ladies as '**Jesuitesses**', a term which showed that they misconstrued the Institute's imitation of the Society of Jesus as some sort of assimilation into the Ignatian **fraternity**.[42] Although they may well have objected to unenclosed female Orders, these clerics were also taking a political stand when they condemned Mary Ward's imitation of the Society of Jesus.

Mary Ward's battle for papal recognition was caught in the cross-fire of the bitter internal fight which opposed the secular clergy to the Jesuits; her handling of this issue demonstrates that she had not fully comprehended the seriousness of the dispute which was tearing the fabric of the Church asunder. Far from realizing that her vindication of the Jesuit model was probably her most hazardous argument, she saw in this spiritual affiliation a convincing model. In her correspondence with the Curia, she argued that the Society of Jesus had created a favourable precedent when it was recognized by Paul III in 1540. At a time when the Church needed every advantage it could summon, a congregation of women working to catechize the female half of the population would represent a formidable asset. Mary Ward knew that the Society was not allowed to take the direction of a female Order, but did not consider this as a difficulty since her own Society was to be fully autonomous. Her Ladies' independence was a point upon which she insisted in her 1621 memorial to Gregory XV: she described her Institute as modelled on the Constitutions of the Jesuits, yet 'altogether independent, nevertheless, of the said Fathers'.[43] In this memorial, Mary Ward attempted to clarify her Institute's independence from the Society of Jesus, thereby denying that it was an unlawful branch of the Society. Her Ladies would be faithfully *like* Jesuits, yet not a part of Ignatius Loyola's Society of Jesus.

Despite opposition to her project, she was unwilling to compromise on the terms of her mission; the vision she claimed to have received in 1611 had called for a female counterpart to the Society of Jesus and she had no intention of departing from this in any way.[44] She therefore also demanded that her Institute be named after Jesus: 'Whoever wishes to serve beneath the banner of the cross as a soldier of God in our Society, *which we desire to be designated by the name of Jesus.*'[45] By using the terms 'Society' and requesting the name of Jesus, Mary Ward proposed nothing less than her own Society of Jesus, adapted for women. This, of course, greatly contributed to the erroneous but nevertheless widespread amalgamation of the English Ladies with the Jesuits. In the context of the bitter dispute which opposed seculars and Jesuits, this was to throw countless difficulties in the path of the Institute.

If the English Ladies faced the opposition of the secular clergy, they also provoked reactions within the Society of Jesus itself.[46] From the very beginnings in 1612, the General of the Jesuits, Claudius Aquaviva (1543–1615), had received warnings from alarmed brethren concerned that their Society would be accused of protecting a female branch, in breach of their founder's recommendations. The General had ordered the Jesuits of St Omer to hand over the direction of the Institute to the secular clergy; their only contact with the Ladies of St Omer should be in church, to hear the confessions of those who asked for a Jesuit **confessor**, in the same way as was customary with any other women.

In the context of the English mission, Mary Ward's enthusiastic imitation and support of the Jesuits was a source of deep embarrassment for the Society, and exacerbated the secular clergy's animosity. As a consequence, most Jesuits detached themselves publicly from the female congregation. The stigma endured and, in 1623, the Provincial Richard Blount (1565–1638) addressed his brethren thus:

> [you should] not meddle with any thing belonging to the temporals of Mrs Mary Ward, or any of her company [...] and make the world know that the Society has no more to do with them than with all other penitents who resort unto them, whereby I hope in, a short time, the manifold calumniations, which for their cause and proceedings are laid upon us, will have an end.[47]

Above all, the Fathers should make it quite clear that their Order had no more particular link with these women than they did with other penitents. The few priests who had supported the Ladies, such as Roger Lee himself, but also John Gerard (1564–1637) or Edward Burton (d. 1624), incurred reprimands from their superiors. Slander had thus left a deep scar in the relationship between English Ladies and the Society they so admired, as Jesuits were anxious to dissociate themselves from the so-called 'galloping girls'.[48]

An institutional compromise: a Marian congregation for women

In this context, Roger Lee's early defence of Mary Ward's unenclosed female Order had been risky. His *Schola Beatae Mariae* demonstrates his political acumen, as he attempted to distance Loyola's Society of Jesus from the Ladies' Institute while remaining steadfast in his support to Mary Ward:

> Among those Orders [the English Ladies] should specially look to those which most resemble the Institute amongst which not the last is the Society of Jesus [...]. And although *from its Institute it cannot undertake the direction of women, it is, however, lawful for all the faithful to be present at their sermons, to confess to them and to profit by their excellent advice.*[49]

In this passage, Roger Lee openly recognized that Ignatius Loyola had excluded women from his Society, and that no female branch of the Society of Jesus could be envisaged; having acknowledged this key principle, he emphasized the informal nature of the relationship between Jesuits and Ladies. Although he evoked some links of affinity between the two congregations, he downplayed any special relationship. As a further argument in his favour, he evoked the pragmatic reality of work on the Continent, where the English Ladies found few opportunities to have contact with English-speaking priests, and would therefore naturally attend the services of English Jesuits. As he argued for a continued collaboration between the English Ladies and Jesuits, he chose to overlook their shared Rules or ideology, and brushed aside any political connivance in order to highlight harmless practicalities.

Moreover, as Roger Lee portrayed a congregation which did not present a profile modelled on the Society of Jesus, he silenced Mary Ward's unabashed claims for female authority in the form of a generalate and her refusal of episcopal authority, which he replaced with a more traditional subjection to male authority. The Institute was to be placed under episcopal control, and its members' willing obedience was emphasized throughout: '[they] make the three Solemn Vows in the hands of the Bishop, who shall be their Ordinary, to whom they shall with a complete self-oblation bind themselves by vow to the service of God in the education of maidens and girls.'[50] The issue of name was also circumvented. Lee proposed a simple 'School' of virgins placed under the protection of the 'Blessed Virgin Mary', and called after her; Mary Ward's desire for a 'Society' named after 'Jesus' was not expressed, thereby avoiding any misapprehension of the English Ladies as 'Jesuitesses'.

Lee's version of female obedience and organization eventually proved more fruitful than Mary Ward's: it was echoed in the 1703 new Institute's willing submission to episcopal authority. As mentioned earlier, Mary Anne Babthorpe's petition was aided greatly by Bishop Leyburn, who in turn mentioned the support of other bishops in his address to Clement XI: 'One thing only, most Holy Father, seems in the eyes of not a few, to be wanting to the perfection of this pious work, namely that the said Institute, so lauded by several Bishops, and welcomed into their dioceses, should by your Holiness be deemed worthy of approbation and confirmation.'[51] Validation from local ecclesiastical authorities weighed heavily in favour of the petitioners. This proved that the new Institute was in keeping with male definitions of female religious roles; but equally importantly, it also showed that, politically, the new Institute had no suspicious affiliations with the Society of Jesus. Where Lee's *Schola* merely recognized the authority of bishops (while being championed by a Jesuit), the new Institute also boasted influential episcopal patronage; thus, it left the perilous waters of political controversy and came back to the fold of religious orthodoxy.

Although neither the 1612 *Schola Beatae Mariae* nor the 1703 Rules were true expressions of Mary Ward's vocation to 'Take the Same of the Society', there remained a point which they would uphold: both preserved her desire for unity. In 1612, as the idea of multiple foundations was raised, the office of 'Principal', acting as overseer and co-ordinator of all the houses, was evoked. In the *Schola*, this was perhaps the only element which was not typical of contemporaneous female Orders and gave the virgins an unusual degree of authority. Aware of the bold nature of this innovation, Roger Lee made no mention of a Superior General, whose title was not deemed acceptable for female Orders and remained the preserve of male congregations. In his proposal, the Mother in charge of the global overseeing of the Institute was to be called simply 'Principal', and her role was akin to that of a mother.

Dominating this rather informal, maternal authority, the Ordinary embodied official Church supervision; he was the representative of male clerical hierarchy, whose approval was to be sought before the 'Principal' could undertake her duties. Roger Lee may have realized that the office of Superior General could only hinder the Institute's approval and therefore toned down his request; he diffused the potentially offensive novelty of the post of 'Principal' by not calling it 'Superior General' and by placing it under the supervision of an accepted male authority figure.

The very same issue arose again during the examination of the Rules of the new Institute in the eighteenth century, and it was resolved in a similar manner: the petitioners highlighted the fact that each house was under the control of the local bishop, and argued that their own 'Chief Superior' enjoyed a power which was purely maternal, since she simply acted as the Mother of her scattered religious family. Their emphasis upon male authority and their denial of any female empowerment within the hierarchy of the new Institute played a part in the successful approbation of the 1703 Rules, even if like Roger Lee's 1612 *Schola*, they represented a significant departure from the original spirit of Mary Ward's foundation.

It would be dismissive to claim that Mary Ward was unaware of the difficulties she faced when proposing a missionary Society of Jesus for women which operated as a generalate, made a direct vow of obedience to the Pope and bypassed bishops' authority; as a Catholic in early-modern England, she was aware of the female religious standards of her time, and she knew also about the controversy which opposed Jesuits to seculars. In 1617, she exhorted her **sisters** to show the fortitude of pioneers when she declared: 'men you know look diversely upon you as new beginners of a course never thought of before, marvelling what you intend and what will be the end of you.'[52] Yet she ignored these obstacles and strove to see her vocation approved as she believed God intended; it is in this refusal to compromise that the major difference between her *Institutum* and the mediated plans which were the 1612 *Schola* and the 1703 Rules is to be found.

In the seventeenth century, Mary Ward had refused to walk the tightrope of gendered acceptability. Her vindication of female worth in the Catholic mission not only came as a blow to the Church hierarchy but presented a challenge to the received traditional order. Responding to a Jesuit who, in 1617, doubted the constancy of the religious fervour of those he called 'but women', Mary Ward wrote: 'There is no such difference between men and women, that women may not do great matters, as we have seen by the example of many Saints who have done great things, and I hope in God it will be seen that women in time to come will do much.'[53] As the next passage demonstrates even further, Mary Ward did not share the patriarchal views of the early modern Church:

> What think you of this word, 'but women'? If we were in all things inferior to some other creature, which I suppose to be men, which I care be bold to say is a lie then, with respect to the good Father, I may say: it is an error. [...] I would to God that all men would understand this verity: that women, if they will, may be perfect, and if they would not make us believe we can do nothing, and that we are but women, we might do great matters.[54]

By asserting that 'women, *if they will*, may be perfect,' Ward rejected her contemporaries' conceptions of gender and claimed that, when they were inspired by God and dedicated to Him entirely, women were as capable as men of serving the Church. Mary Ward was not the only foundress to reject the patriarchal beliefs which marked women as spiritually inept; before her, Teresa of Àvila had argued that, when filled with God's grace, women were spiritually as worthy, perhaps even more so, than men. Yet there was one major difference between Mary Ward's and Teresa of Àvila's vindication of female religious worth: Teresa expressed her unorthodox ideas through the very orthodox rhetoric of female subjection and inferiority, as a 'little woman' whose ignorance allowed her the better to be filled by the holy spirit.[55] In doing so, she complied with a medieval exalted definition of women as 'empty vessels', elevated above themselves by God's light.[56] Mary Ward, on the contrary, remained assertive through her actions and her prose: where Teresa used gender prejudices subtly, she rejected them openly. To her, divisions of gender were not relevant to spiritual life and served only to hinder the efforts of the Catholic Reformation.[57] Her failure to see the relevance of gender boundaries was going to prevent Mary Ward from enjoying the same degree of success as Teresa of Àvila.

Conclusions

For its opponents, Mary Ward's Order was unacceptable: it claimed religious status but chose to follow a male apostolic life, whose missionary activities flouted every Tridentine decree concerning women religious. Faced with such a novel and androgynous enterprise, clerical authorities acted to restore order and reassert their definition of female acceptability in the Church. Urban VIII's bull *Pastoralis Romani Pontificis* ordered the English Ladies to disband, since their work was 'most unsuited to the weakness of their sex' and represented a danger for the reputation, the organization and the sound doctrine of the Catholic Church. The Pope condemned this 'sect' which mimicked 'the customary religious life' despite flouting the laws of enclosure. The Ladies' work was 'by no means suiting the weakness of their sex, intellect, womanly modesty and above all virginal purity'. Finally, they were labelled 'Jesuitesses'. A canonical aberration which could not be suffered to endure, the Institute was especially abhorrent in the context of the English mission since, through its imitation of the Society of Jesus and its open irreverence towards the secular clergy, it served as a reminder that the Catholic Church was politically divided.

The Institute was condemned to 'perpetual abolition'.[58] Mary Ward's non-conformity with traditional female role definitions had been a crucial bone of contention between the foundress and the Church she aimed to serve, and it had led to the suppression of her work. Of course, the Institute was condemned both on religious and political grounds, yet above all it was suppressed because it was the gendered expression of a *female* free agent who chose to disregard the criteria of a male-defined orthodoxy. Despite the suppression, Ward's mission was kept alive, though her followers usually opted for a less confrontational stance. Compliance with clerically defined female roles was indeed the key to Pope Clement XI's 1703 approbation of the 81 Rules of the second Institute which, like Roger Lee's 1612 *Schola*, closely imitated traditional female religious life. Compliance with gendered norms was, in the end, the only way to gain the approbation of male Church authorities. By respecting some enclosure, accepting episcopal authority, and limiting its activities to the teaching of boarders and externs, this community was in conformity with the clerically accepted roles for women in the Church; moreover, it showed no particular link with the Society of Jesus and therefore was no longer an element of political controversy. Thus, when the Institute of the Blessed Virgin Mary (IBVM) was confirmed in April 1749, by Benedict XIV's Constitution *Quamvis Justo*, it bore, on paper, no relation to Mary Ward's earlier foundation.

The history of the Institute remained a complex one through subsequent centuries, and lies beyond the scope of this brief essay; yet some outcomes can be highlighted here, which show the extent to which Mary Ward's vocation to 'Take the same of the Society' had been ahead of its time. Indeed, it was only in the twentieth and twenty-first centuries, after decades of efforts by members and supporters of the Institute, that it became gradually accepted as the true spirit of the IBVM: the initial breakthrough came when, in 1909, Pope Pius X rehabilitated Mary Ward as the original foundress of the IBVM and recognized the value of her militant work. Later, from 1953 onwards, Immolata Wetter and Edelburga Eibl, IBVM, worked indefatigably alongside Josef Grisar, SJ, for the cause of the canonization of Mary Ward, researching the Institute's history and gaining unprecedented access to the archives of the **Inquisition**. It was only in June 2003, after continued efforts from the IBVM sisters, that the Roman branch of the IBVM[59] was allowed to adopt Ignatian Constitutions, the text of which was feminized, omitting nothing except passages referring specifically to priestly ministries. After nearly four hundred years, members of the IBVM were finally given the right officially to be called the Congregation of Jesus (CJ) and to adapt, in a way which Mary Ward would have recognized as faithful to her original vocation, the rules of the Society of Jesus for the use of women.

Notes

1. I would like to thank Claire Cross, Michael Questier, Carmen M. Mangion and Glyn Redworth for their insights and valuable comments on the early drafts of this essay.
2. See E. Rapley, *The Dévotes: Women and Church in Seventeenth-century France* (Kingston, Ont.: McGill, Queen's University Press 1990) and R. Liebowitz, 'Virgins in the Service of Christ: The Dispute over an Active Apostolate for Women during the Counter-Reformation', in R. Radford Ruether (ed.), *Women of Spirit* (New York: Simon and Schuster, 1979), pp. 131–52.
3. Mary Ward described this episode retrospectively in a letter to Mgr Albergati, reproduced in 'Mary Ward to Nuncio Antonio Mgr Albergati, 1621', in U. Dirmeier, CJ (ed.), *Mary Ward und ihre Gründung: Die Quellentexte bis 1645* (Münster: Aschendorff Verlag, 2007), Vol. 1, pp. 536–42.
4. Since during Mary Ward's lifetime her Ignatian Institute was not given an official name; she and her followers were simply known as 'the English Ladies'.
5. Founded in 1622 by Gregory XV, the purpose of *Propaganda Fide* was both to supervise missions to non-Christian regions and to check the spread of heresy. When Mary Ward's endeavours were perceived as unorthodox, possibly even heretical, *Propaganda Fide* was naturally in charge of the investigations. See M. I. Wetter, *Mary Ward: Under the Shadow of the Inquisition 1630–1637* translated by M. B. Ganne and M. P. Harriss (Oxford: Way Books, 2006), pp. 54–64.

6. L. Lux-Sterritt, 'An Analysis of the Controversy Caused by Mary Ward's Institute in the 1620s', *Recusant History*, 25:4 (2001), pp. 636–47.

7. See M. G. Kirkus, 'The Presence of the Mary Ward Institute in Yorkshire 1642–1648', *Recusant History*, 25:3 (2001), pp. 434–48.

8. The two reference works available in English about Mary Ward's life and work are M. C. E. Chambers, *The Life of Mary Ward, 1585–1645*, 2 vols (London: Burns and Oates, 1882–1885) and H. Peters, *Mary Ward: A World in Contemplation*, translated by H. Butterworth (Leominster: Gracewing Books, 1994). In German, J. Grisar, *Die Ersten Anklagen in Rom Gegen das Institut Maria Wards* (Roma: Pontificia Universita Gregoriana, 1959).

9. The Institute's primary sources are to be found *in extenso* for the first time in Dirmeier, *Mary Ward*; see also the work by C. Kenworthy-Browne, CJ (ed.), *Mary Ward, 1585–1645: A Briefe Relation with Autobiographical Fragments and a Selection of Letters* (Woodbridge: Boydell, 2008).

10. In 1616, Mary Ward had written her first Plan for the Institute, known as the *Ratio Instituti*; yet it is her subsequent 1622 *Institutum* which is recognised as encapsulating most clearly the religious vocation she had received in the 1611 revelation to 'Take the same of the Society'. For that reason, this study will focus upon that version rather than its earlier draft.

11. Peters, *Mary Ward*, pp. 129–31.

12. H. J. Coleridge (ed.), *St Mary's Convent, Micklegate Bar, York, 1686–1887* (London: Burns and Oates, 1887). The Bar Convent is the oldest operating convent to date in England.

13. A manuscript of the 1703 Rules is kept in the Bar Convent Archives (hereafter BCA), file J2: *Letters Apostolic by which Clement PP. XI, June 13th, 1703, approved and confirmed the Rules of the Institute of the Blessed Virgin Mary.*

14. BCA: B18, *Institutum*, item 2. For this essay, I shall use the English translation, kept at the Bar Convent, of the Latin original reproduced in Dirmeier, *Mary Ward*, Vol. 1, pp. 625–30.

15. As Ursuline congregations spread in France and sought papal approval, they adopted conventual enclosure, although they were allowed to receive externs within their walls for their daily lessons. See my *Redefining Female Religious Life: French Ursulines and English Ladies in Seventeenth-Century Catholicism* (Aldershot: Ashgate, 2005).

16. Rapley, *The Dévotes*, pp. 42–73.

17. BCA: B18, *Institutum*, item 2.

18. *Ibid*, item 1, my italics.

19. *Ibid*, f. 22.

20. Session 25, 3–4 December 1563, in N. Tanner, *Decrees of the Ecumenical Councils*, 2 vols (London: Sheed and Ward, 1990), Vol. 2, p. 778.

21. See Rapley, *The Dévotes*; E. Rhodes, *This Tight Embrace: Luisa de Carvajal y Mendoza (1566–1614)* (Milwaukee: Marquette University Press, 2000), and 'Luisa de Carvajal's Counter-Reformation Journey to Selfhood (1566–1614)', *Renaissance Quarterly*, 51:3 (1998), pp. 887–911; also G. Redworth, *The She-Apostle: The Extraordinary Life and Death of Luisa de Carvajal* (Oxford: Oxford University Press, 2008). The difficulties of reconciling action and contemplation and to serve the Church whilst not fully complying with its precepts on female religious life continued to encumber the efforts of nineteenth-century active women religious, as Carmen M. Mangion shows later in this volume.

22. See Marit Monteiro's chapter in this collection.

23. Westminster Diocesan Archives (henceafter WDA), Vol. 16, f. 206.

24. John Colleton formed the Association of the Clergy of England, an independent body in charge of regulating the affairs of the secular clergy. He was later suspended for aggravating the schism between the seculars and the Society of Jesus. See E. Taunton, *The History of the Jesuits in England, 1580–1773* (London: Methuen, 1901), pp. 256–57.
25. BCA: C1, *Translation of Documents re. Jesuitesses*, J3.
26. *John Bennett to Edward Bennett,* in Dirmeier, *Mary Ward*, Vol. 1, p. 659.
27. BCA: B18, *Schola Beatae Mariae*, item 5, italics mine. For this essay, I shall use the English translation, kept in the Bar Convent, of the original Latin document reproduced in Dirmeier, *Mary Ward*, Vol. 1, pp. 171–84.
28. Mary Ward to Elizabeth Cotton and Mary Poyntz, 18 February 1631. In Dirmeier, *Mary Ward*, Vol. 3, p. 165.
29. A. Weber, *Teresa of Avila and the Rhetoric of Femininity* (Princeton, NJ.: Princeton University Press, 1990) and 'Little Women: Counter-Reformation Misogyny', in D. Luebke (ed.), *The Counter-Reformation: The Essential Readings* (Oxford: Blackwell, 1999), pp. 143–62.
30. BCA: B18, *Schola*, item 1.
31. *Ibid*, item 46, italics mine.
32. *Ibid*, *Schola*, item 14, my italics.
33. BCA: J2, *Letters apostolic, f.* 12, item 1.
34. BCA: J2, *Rules*, p. 28–9, items 43–7.
35. Coleridge, *St Mary's Convent*, pp. 106–7.
36. London, 16 October 1699; letter reproduced in Coleridge, *St Mary's Convent*, p. 106.
37. Mary Anne Babthorpe had begun petitioning in Rome in 1699.
38. For a more detailed comparison of Mary Ward's Institute with the Order of the Ursulines, see my *Redefining Female Religious Life,* and A. Conrad, *Zwischen Kloster und Welt: Ursulinen und Jesuitinnen in der katholischen Reformbewegung des XVI-XVII. Jahrhunderts* (Mainz: Von Zabern 1991).
39. BCA: B18, *Institutum*, item 4.
40. *Ibid*, item 7.
41. *Memorial to Gregory XV*, in Dirmeier, *Mary Ward*, Vol. 1, pp. 597–600.
42. WDA: Vol. 16, ff. 201–07.
43. *Memorial to Gregory XV*, in Dirmeier, *Mary Ward*, Vol. 1, pp. 597–600.
44. Mary Ward to Nuncio Antonio Mgr Albergati, 1621, in Dirmeier, *Mary Ward*, Vol. 1, pp. 536–42.
45. BCA: B18, *Institutum*, item 1. Italics mine.
46. Peters, *Mary Ward*, p. 123. See also comments in Wadsworth, James, *English Spanish Pilgrim* (London: Michael Sparke, 1629), p. 30: '[The Jesuits] are grown to a faction about the Jesuitrices or Wandering Nuns, some allowing them, some disliking them utterly.'
47. Provincial Richard Blount SJ to the English Province, 19 July 1623, in Dirmeier, *Mary Ward*, Vol. 2, pp. 3–4.
48. WDA: Vol. 16, f. 207.
49. BCA: B18, *Schola*, item 48–9.
50. BCA: B18, *Schola*, item 8.
51. Coleridge, *St Mary's Convent*, p. 106.
52. *Three speeches of our Reverend Mother Chief Superior made at St Omer having been long absent*, third speech, in Dirmeier, *Mary Ward*, Vol. 1, pp. 362–6.
53. *Ibid*, first speech, in Dirmeier, *Mary Ward*, Vol. 1, p. 358.
54. *Ibid*, p. 359.

55. Weber, *Teresa of Àvila*, p. 37.

56. C. Atkinson, '"Precious Balsam in a Fragile Glass": The Ideology of Virginity in the Later Middle Ages', *Journal of Family History*, 8:2 (1983), pp. 131–43.

57. P. Ellis, '"They are but women": Mary Ward, 1585–1645', in S. M. Brown (ed.), *Women, Gender and Radical Religion in Early Modern Europe* (Leiden: Brill, 2007), pp. 243–64.

58. Wetter, *Mary Ward*, pp. 213–14.

59. Since the mission of the sisters expanded worldwide, the IBVM was divided into three (Roman, Irish, and North American) branches. In 2003, the North American and Irish Branches united to form the Loretto Branch, which is currently transforming, like the Roman Branch, into a female Congregation of Jesus.

6
An English Nun's Authority: Early Modern Spiritual Controversy and the Manuscripts of Barbara Constable[1]

Jenna Lay

In the early seventeenth century, Catholic women who left their homes in England to enter convents in France and the Low Countries were often forced to confront a difficult question: to whom does an English **nun** owe her obedience? As exiles from their country and often from their families, these women entered an ecclesiastical hierarchy that was at once foreign and familiar. The English Reformation had unsettled the relationship between spiritual and temporal authority, casting obedience to the monarch – expressed through oaths and signified by regular attendance at church services – as the primary duty of an English subject.[2] At the same time, the spread of Protestantism led to the disruption of traditional religious hierarchies; in this new religion, priests, popes and saints were no longer necessary intermediaries between an individual and God. The historiography covering early modern English Catholicism has grappled with these issues in the **recusant** context and revealed the internal divisions of the Catholic community regarding religious and political loyalty.[3] But Catholic Englishwomen **enclosed** in monasteries on the Continent have only recently begun to receive the attention of historians and literary critics interested in how authority, loyalty and obedience functioned both within religious Orders and in the world outside the convent's walls.[4] Previous generations of scholars who sought to identify the political investments of Englishmen and women situated within the post-Tridentine Catholic Church have typically looked to the **secular priests** and **Jesuits** who engaged in active work on the English mission. English nuns, who 'secured the calm and peaceful life of the cloister' according to one early chronicler of English Benedictines, were contrasted with 'their brothers ... who were toiling and suffering in their beloved England'.[5] The following essay will engage this frequently invoked – and frequently gendered – dichotomy between the contemplative and active lives of early modern monastics through an analysis of the manuscripts of a nun whose life in the cloister provided the material and methods to question ecclesiastical structures and policies in the English Catholic community.

The manuscripts of Dame Barbara Constable reveal the process by which the English Benedictine nuns of Cambrai came to regard obedience and authority as contingent categories, dependent not only upon community hierarchies but also upon the individual's experience of the divine.[6] Constable is known primarily for her work as a scribe: she penned the Upholland fragment of Julian of Norwich's *Shewings*, one of the few surviving manuscript witnesses to the writings of the English anchoress and mystic, and was also the compiler of numerous unsigned collections and a prolific transcriber of the manuscripts of Augustine Baker (1575–1641), Cambrai's formative **spiritual director**.[7] These authorial activities – writing, collecting and editing manuscripts for the use of her **sisters** in the convent – were essential to the survival of Baker's teachings and to the revival of medieval contemplative practices. But Constable was also an author in a more conventional sense: she wrote and published a series of signed manuscripts, many of which are still extant. Three of the manuscripts, entitled *Advises: For Confessors and Spirituall Directors, Speculum Superiorum*, and *Considerations for Preests*, form a unique trilogy of instructions written by a single nun for her religious superiors.[8] Constable's dynamic understanding of obedience is evident in both the form and the content of her manuscripts: she claims that her books are straightforward collections out of other authors, and yet her quotations of religious authorities are often reduced to brief extracts framed by her own extensive commentary. Constable shares her opinions on a range of topics, from the minutiae of the relationship between a **confessor** and his charges to the political and religious import of a priest's participation in the English mission. By reading Constable's manuscripts as part of Cambrai's more general engagement with Baker's teachings, I will reveal the conditional nature of authority in this early modern convent, where obedience encompassed a shifting set of allegiances and responsibilities within the context of multiple communities.

Baker's books

The English Benedictine nuns of Cambrai and its daughter house in Paris were prolific writers: in the seventeenth century, they created manuscript copies of medieval devotional texts, collected extracts from the works of famed theologians and contemplatives, and preserved the instructions of Father Augustine Baker. These 'Baker manuscripts' have made the nuns' scribal activities known to generations of historians and theologians, but Baker's prolific writings on early modern spirituality have also overshadowed the nuns' contributions to the theory and practice of contemplative life. Baker served the Cambrai convent, which was founded in 1623, in an unofficial capacity: he was its spiritual director and took the role of confessor or **chaplain** only when those positions were vacant.[9] The nuns nonetheless looked to him for guidance, and when Father Francis Hull

(d. 1645) arrived as the convent's new chaplain in 1629, many nuns continued to think of Baker as their primary religious advisor. Baker was a proponent of **contemplative prayer** for enclosed monastics: he believed 'that Contemplation or (which is all one) Spirituall praier, and the perfection of it, is the ende of our Rule and profession, who are of St Benets order'.[10] Contemplative prayer, if perfected, could ultimately lead to **mysticism**, or the union of the soul with God; it was an affective rather than intellectual experience and, as such, it bypassed Jesuit exercises of meditation on an image or idea.

Baker is the most well-known seventeenth-century proponent of the mystical tradition that emphasized contemplative prayer over lengthy **meditative** or discursive prayer. This emphasis led him to recommend books for the nuns of Cambrai 'as are most helpinge towards contemplation',[11] particularly those 'good olde English bookes that are never to be printed againe'.[12] The dominant strain of post-Reformation monastic instruction, however, was based on the Ignatian model of discursive prayer. Baker attempted to mediate between medieval mysticism, especially as it was practised in England, and post-Tridentine continental spirituality, but 'methodical, discursive meditation was the order of the day'.[13] Numerous convents, including the English Benedictine foundation at Brussels, turned to Jesuit spiritual directors and, in some cases, the differences that arose over questions of religious instruction led to significant internal divisions.[14] At Cambrai, Hull ultimately accused Baker of promoting an anti-authoritarian mode of prayer and the nuns of practising it.[15] Hull took his concerns to the General Chapter of the English Benedictine Congregation in 1633 and, while Baker's teachings were approved, both men were forced to leave the convent in the aftermath of the controversy.

Baker's influence on Cambrai has been well documented, and recent editions of the Baker manuscripts have allowed scholars to gain a better understanding of both Baker's practice of contemplative prayer and his sometimes contentious role in the English Benedictine Congregation. To facilitate the nuns' prayer, Baker wrote and compiled a number of books during his time at Cambrai – books which served both as spiritual instructions and as models for the nuns' own collections. As Mark Barrett points out in an insightful study of Baker's reading practices, 'if there is one dominant self-image of Augustine Baker in the books he wrote in Cambrai, that image is of Baker the reader of spiritual texts, a reader whose pedagogic purpose in writing is the mediation of these texts to less experienced readers'.[16] Baker peppered his own writings with quotations and paraphrastic instructions from a wide range of theologians, contemplatives and mystics, including Francis de Sales, Walter Hilton and Hildegard of Bingen. He made lists of books 'most helping toward contemplation' and described the process by which reading might lead to prayer in his biography of Gertrude More, a founding member of Cambrai and the great-great granddaughter of Sir Thomas More.[17] As a part of her contemplative practice, More

> selected out of St Augustin's Confessions and Meditations and out of the workes of other such like affective Praier-men, great store of amorous actuations of soule, which wonderfully fitted her foresaid Propension. And thereby she camme (commonly) to have a verie efficacious Praier, and that of much Recollection and internall sight of herself.[18]

The excerpts and quotations that filled Baker's manuscript collections were, in other words, essential materials for the spiritual practice that he taught.

For centuries, however, the Baker manuscripts were not accessible to a wide scholarly audience. Serenus Cressy (1605–1674), a Benedictine monk and briefly the chaplain at the English Benedictine convent in Paris, printed his edition of Baker's teachings, *Sancta Sophia*, in 1657, and it became the primary source for studies of Baker's contemplative practice and instruction. But Cressy's project was necessarily limited by the overwhelming amount of manuscript material, and his book's title page acknowledged as much: the 'directions for the prayer of contemplation' included therein were 'extracted out of more then XL Treatises' and 'Methodically digested' by Cressy.[19] More than 30 years ago, David Lunn called attention to the limitations of scholarship that depended solely on Cressy's book and, in the decades since, many of Baker's original manuscripts have been published. The crucial work of manuscript recovery has galvanized Baker scholarship in the last decade, due in large part to John P. H. Clark's numerous editions for the *Analecta Cartusiana* series, which allow readers to discover for themselves that 'anyone who reads the Baker MSS. will be struck by the basic differences between them and the text of *Sancta Sophia*.'[20] Many of these manuscripts were produced by the nuns at Cambrai – very few autograph Baker manuscripts survive – but a project of similar scope has yet to be undertaken on behalf of the nuns themselves, most of whom wrote primarily or exclusively in manuscript.[21] Critical examinations of manuscript culture at Cambrai and Paris have thus been dominated by scholars of Baker who, in their eagerness to recover his manuscript writings, have often characterized the convents' nuns as little more than scribes or 'copyists'.[22] The scribal activities of transcription and collection that Baker's female supporters undertook on his behalf and in his defence have thus obscured their original contributions to the seventeenth-century practice and literature of contemplative prayer.

Recent scholarship by Claire Walker and Heather Wolfe has begun to reveal that the 'transmission of "Bakerism" did not rely solely upon the monk's ideas and writings. Many Cambrai sisters wrote pious works of their own which aimed to explicate the religiosity.'[23] Yet the historiographical emphasis of Walker's book – an account of the seventeenth-century English contemplative communities – does not allow for close readings of the many manuscripts produced by members of the convent. Her article on the Cambrai manuscripts as property deftly establishes the nuns' participation in the development of Baker's spiritual instructions, but her focus on the attempted censorship of autograph Baker materials in the 1650s necessarily foregrounds his writings.[24] In two exceptional articles on book culture at Cambrai, Wolfe has provided a solid bibliographical foundation for work on the nuns' manuscript collections. Her descriptive study of the manuscripts written and compiled by Barbara Constable reveals the breadth of nuns' engagements with contemporary religious discourse, but Wolfe too readily describes Constable 'following in Baker's footsteps'.[25] While I agree with Wolfe's contention that 'Baker's contribution to the spiritual welfare of the nuns of Cambrai and Paris' should not be underestimated, I believe that it has too often been overestimated.[26]

Constable's manuscripts must necessarily be contextualized within the tradition of contemplative prayer fostered by Baker at Cambrai, but readings that characterize the nuns' writings as works that 'echo' Baker's arguments or as records and reflections of 'personal struggle' diminish the depth and complexity of the extant manuscripts.[27]

The internal disruptions weathered by Cambrai in its early years – especially those that revolved around the relationships between the spiritual and the material and between prayer and politics – forced the nuns to look outside their community, to the external factors that influenced monastic life. Thus, even when writing devotional texts, the nuns kept a wary eye and pen fixed on the 'obligations and externall obediences' demanded of them as Catholics and contemplatives, Englishwomen and exiles. Gertrude More's *The Spiritual Exercises*, the most well-known book written by a Cambrai nun, includes an extensive 'Advertisement to the Reader', which outlines the controversy at Cambrai over Baker's spiritual teachings and distinguishes 'true Obedience' from the 'pretence of Obedience' or 'blinde Obedience'.[28] More's theory of obedience frames and contextualizes the spiritual confessions advertised on the book's title page, thereby transforming her account of contemplative prayer into a polemical tract that intervenes in a number of contemporary debates regarding spiritual direction and religious faith. This printed edition of More's manuscripts, published more than two decades after Baker's departure from Cambrai and her death in 1633, was a deliberate intervention into the renewed controversy surrounding Baker's instruction in the 1650s, when the nuns were ordered to surrender their autograph Baker manuscripts.[29] Because of its existence in print, *The Spiritual Exercises* could easily be read outside the convent's walls by members of the English Benedictine Congregation, by other nuns living in exile on the continent, and even by Catholics (or Protestants) living in England. But what of the more extensive manuscript materials held at Cambrai and Paris? As the remainder of this essay will demonstrate, the manuscripts written by Barbara Constable were no less relevant to external political and religious affairs than More's printed book or Baker's manuscripts, though they have long been inaccessible to all but a handful of scholars.

Collecting authority

In her three advice volumes – *Advises: For Confessors and Spirituall Directors*, *Speculum Superiorum*, and *Considerations for Preests* – Constable theorizes religious authority through the collection and interpretation of scriptural, theological and contemplative quotations. Reading this trilogy of instructional manuscripts alongside Constable's explication of the *Rule* of St Benedict reveals her deliberately ambiguous conception of obedience, which radicalizes and makes explicit the political and religious critique of post-Tridentine Catholicism implied by Gertrude More's *The Spiritual Exercises*. While Constable's thinking and reading were influenced by Baker's treatises – both authors address contemporary religious issues such as the English mission, and they cite many of the same spiritual authorities – her manuscripts were not simply imitations or reiterations of his. Constable's intimate knowledge of Baker's writings, gained through her prodigious labours as an 'industrious scribe', left traces in her own work but did not constrain it.[30] Perhaps because Constable entered the convent in 1638, five years after More's death and Baker's departure, her books were not marked as defences of Baker's spiritual instruction or his writings, even when both were subject to increased scrutiny in the 1650s. Her relationship with Baker was solely textual: though she followed the course of contemplative prayer that he advised, he was never her immediate spiritual director. Instead, his writings provided the catalyst for her own innovations and elaborations.

Constable transcribed many of Baker's manuscripts in the 1640s and 1650s, probably in anticipation of the spiritual needs of Cambrai's newly established daughter house in Paris. Archival evidence seems to reveal a shift in Constable's scribal activities in the early 1650s: of the 17 extant Baker transcriptions produced by Constable, 12 were completed in 1653 or earlier and four were not dated.[31] At the same time, Constable turned more intently to her own collections: eight of her 11 'original works' were completed after 1652.[32] It is difficult to speculate based on an incomplete archival record – many of Constable's books were probably lost when Cambrai faced the upheaval of the French Revolution – but the existing evidence is suggestive. After completing the scribal production necessary to equip the foundation at Paris, did Constable turn primarily to her own writings? Did she begin collecting and framing religious texts in order to fill a vacuum of spiritual authority in the years after Baker's death? Baker continued to write after he left Cambrai, but his death in 1641 and his obligatory participation in the English mission in the preceding years put an end to Cambrai's supply of new Baker manuscripts. Other nuns created collections, but they were often unsigned and did not include the commentary and analysis that Constable made an integral part of her books of advice. Constable's experience as a reader and transcriber of Baker's collections gave her a thorough knowledge of the form and enabled her to assume a role analogous to Baker's, as Cambrai's primary interpreter of contemplative authorities and an authority in her own right on contemporary religious politics.

Constable's collections are a type of *florilegium*. These relatives of the commonplace books that flourished in the sixteenth and seventeenth centuries focused primarily on a spiritual, rather than scholastic, course of reading and instruction. As Jean Leclercq has explained,

> the monastic *florilegium* [...] grew out of spiritual reading. The monk would copy out texts he had enjoyed so as to savour them at leisure and use them anew as subjects for private meditation. The monastic *florilegium* not only originated in the monk's spiritual reading but always remained closely associated with it.[33]

Leclercq's elegant description of the relationship between author and authority in 'the "little prayer books" by John of Fécamp' establishes the long tradition to which Constable's collections belong: 'it is difficult to detect what is original and what comes from the **Fathers**. The truth is that everything is his and, at one and the same time, everything is the Fathers'.[34] So, too, may we say of Constable, but with a difference: everything is hers and, at one and the same time, everything is the convent's. In her earliest extant treatise, *Gemitus Pecatorum, Or the complaints of sinners*, Constable attributes her knowledge of God to a communal process of learning, example and instruction: 'having brought me to this heavenly paradise, where thou hadst so many true servants whose virtues gave so sweet odours, thou didst not (I say) cease by them & others to teach me the true way of loveing & serving thee, & of attaining to true union with thee.'[35] Constable learns from the example of her sisters and then, in turn, creates manuals of advice and commentary to assist in the spiritual instruction of her religious peers and superiors.

Constable's books are enmeshed in the spiritual community of which she was a part, in the tradition of collection and contemplation fostered by Baker, and in the **rules** and regulations of Benedictine monasticism. Yet they are also designed for readers outside of the convent, some of whom were not monastics. *Advises* and *Speculum Superiorum* were dedicated to Father Benedict Stapleton, her confessor at Cambrai, and Dame Catherine Gascoigne, the convent's abbess, respectively, but each volume also includes a 'Preface to the Reader' that expands the text's potential audience. *Considerations* was intended primarily for an external readership; dedicated to Constable's brother Thomas (Augustine), who was preparing for the priesthood, it included advice 'to Preachers' and 'for missioners'.[36] Within the collections themselves, Constable repeatedly references her other works, thereby implying that she expects a stable cohort of readers with access to her manuscripts. In *Advises*, a manuscript completed in 1650, she looks ahead and promises her readers 'wordes I shall produce in my treatise of prayer'.[37] She also refuses to repeat herself, instead directing readers to her other volumes: 'but I will say no more of these things heere because they more properlie belonge to the Mirrour of Superiours which I have composed of some collections', and 'because I have in other treatises (& perhaps shall in this) said much I will now passe over this subject'.[38] Because Constable's books did not all remain at Cambrai – some were sent to her family in England – these self-reflexive moments raise the possibility that she may have produced multiple copies of some tracts. *Gemitus Pecatorum*, for example, is extant in two copies: one at Stanbrook Abbey and the other at Downside Abbey.[39] In all of her books, Constable wrote with readers in mind: her pages are marked by careful layouts – titles centred and in red ink – and she employs **rubrication** for emphasis throughout her manuscripts, especially when quoting Latin or the aphorisms of men such as Thomas à Kempis and Sir Thomas More. Based on the internal evidence of the manuscripts, including prefaces that point to external readers and self-reflexive references to her previous and future writings, Constable's books were composed for both comparative reading and circulation outside her convent. In other words, in the very decade when the writings of Augustine Baker and Gertrude More were edited for print publication, Constable became the source for unmediated scribal publications that expressed Cambrai's engagement in contemporary religious politics and spiritual controversies.

Cambrai provided Constable with a source of authority and authorization. In her books of advice, she cites her experience of the convent as evidence to support her arguments, particularly those concerning the relative authority of abbesses and confessors. 'Indeed,' she explains, 'I have sufficientlie experienced the sad effects of the Confessors haveinge too much power, & could & would say much of this subject were it not to make my treatise tedious & ungratefull.'[40] She withholds information – the details of these 'sad effects' – from her reader at the same time that she purports to reveal the lived experience of monastic life. The convent is thus simultaneously a source of authority and an unknowable space for unenclosed readers, and the authorization Constable takes from her position as a nun is ultimately more transcendent than immediately experiential. She is one of the 'religious women who are the prime spouses of Jesus Christ', a status which enables her to comment both on life in the convent and on the religious landscape of the post-Tridentine Catholic Church.[41] In her *Considerations or Reflexions upon the Rule of the most glorious father St Benedict*, Constable exploits the tension between spiritual calling and imperfect lived experience, dedicating the *Reflexions* to St Benedict himself while critiquing her own failings as a contemplative. This self-abnegating dedication to the founder of her Order seems at first to indicate Constable's desire to turn inward and examine her 'spiritual difficulties'.[42] But the body of her treatise suggests otherwise: she cites her acknowledged shortcomings in order to condemn the 'tepid lazie negligent & disobedient lives which religious for the most part now adayes live', in contrast to 'our holy father' and calls upon her fellow religious to arise from their metaphorical slumber.[43] Constable silently dismisses contemporary religious authorities – the superiors of the English Benedictine Congregation, for example – in favour of dedicating her *Reflexions* to St Benedict, a pre-Reformation monastic leader in comparison to whom the contemplative practice of 'now adayes' is necessarily found lacking. She also brings her implicit general critique of contemporary monasticism to bear on the specific issues relevant to seventeenth-century English Catholics, arguing that 'everie indifferent Bishop is not capable of beinge a good Missioner in the circumstances that our missioners in England are'.[44] Constable provides advice and commentary on circumstances about which she could have little direct knowledge, dismissing those 'indifferent' clerics who have some claim to temporal authority and appealing instead to a long-dead saint for authorization.[45]

Constable presented her readers with a more elaborate comparison of contemporary priests and 'great saints' just a few years earlier, in the preface to *Considerations for Preests*:

> I have often thought that if Preests were as great saints & as holy as they should be the world would be more holy & fuller of saints then it is, but be it how it will for my thought these followinge Collections taken out of such worthy Authors will sufficientlie let Preests see what they should be & what they are not: I wish that the custome of the Primitive church were now renewed againe that Preests might be fewer & holier as they then were, & then the world would not be so much scandalised as it is to be feared now adaies it is by too many ill Preests that are crept in to the multitude that is now adaies.

This stark distinction between the 'ill Preests' of 'now adaies' and the 'great saints' of the 'Primitive church' is striking, particularly in comparison to Gertrude More's hopeful vision of a primitive Church renewed. In *The Spiritual Exercises*, the religious and political divides occasioned by the Reformation – not only between Catholics and Protestants but also within the various religious Orders of the Catholic Church – are the fault lines running beneath More's explication of the Cambrai controversy over spiritual direction and contemplative prayer. 'When shal it be said', More asks, 'that the multitude of beleivers are of one hart and soul? When shal al be united in the bonds of true *peace*?'[46] More hopes that the Protestant Reformation and its effects may be reversed, but in order to imagine 'the *primitive Church*' renewed, she presents her reader with a conditional:

> if S. Benets, S. Augustin, S. Francis, S. Ignatius Children were al (as perfectly as this life would permit) united together, and did with one hart, and consent seek and labour to advance *thy* honour, and praise, as our Founders do wish in heaven, then would the *spirit* of the *primitive Church* florish, and *thy* torne, and mangled members of *thy Church* be healed.

She envisions a future reunification of the Christian world predicated on the unification of the Catholic contemplative and **apostolic** orders. 'Then sinners, and hereticks would easily be converted by them to thee. [...] Then they by prayer conversing in a familiar, and tender maner with *thee* would speak so that none would be able to resist thee in them.' Adapting the Protestant rhetoric of a primitive church to apply to pre-Reformation Catholic religious Orders, More critiques post-Tridentine monastic dissension as one element preventing Christian believers from being 'perfectly set together again.[47]

Like More, Constable uses the concept of a unified and holy primitive Church to critique contemporary religious practice, but Constable's tone is one of condemnation rather than hope. She presents her reader not with the possibility of a Church 'perfectly set together again', but with the scandals of post-Tridentine Catholicism. Constable's solution to the problems facing her Church – that 'Preests above all others should take notise of it & indeavour to be serious practisers of that holy exercise [prayer] (from whence they must receave the devine light necessarie to governe themselves & others)' – is followed almost immediately by an explanation of the contents of her manuscript that deflects attention from her opinions and advice:

> but my intention is not heere to teach & instruct them what they are to doe, let them looke on the followinge Collections, which will better doe it & whose Authors are unquestionable, both in their lives & writings, which if they will as seriouslie put in practise as I could wish they would they would then be fitt for the ministerie.[48]

Constable denies any intention to 'teach & instruct' in her preface and directs her readers to the collections and the authors included therein, explaining in the dedication to her brother that she has simply 'united these collections together with some little poore thoughts of mine upon the subject'. But she is grammatically ambiguous here: has she united the collections *to* her thoughts? Or has she united the collections *by means of* her thoughts? Constable's conventional deployment of the modesty topos[49] – her denial of any desire to act as an agent of instruction and her characterization of her thoughts as 'little' and 'poore' – should not distract from her radical assumption of authority through what she calls 'my labour to draw [collections] forth & by uninge them together make them more readie for the vew of those they concerned'. As author and editor, Constable provides the extracts and interpretive framework necessary to direct her religious superiors toward the spiritual practice that she deems most 'fitt for the ministerie'.

Throughout her collections, Constable establishes her own interpretative authority on the basis of her citations and readings of spiritual authorities. In the first pages of the *Considerations for Preests*, almost immediately after she has denied her intention to 'teach & instruct', Constable supplements a quotation with her own enumeration of the qualities necessary for priesthood: 'thus farre St. Denis of Areopagita', she writes, 'to which I adde Behold the Character of Preests & what they ought seriouslie to imitate if they will invest themselves with this sacred dignitie, first a profound humilitie is required of them, secondly a great puritie & sanctitie of life'.[50] She emphatically demands her reader's attention, invoking both scripture and sermon through her rubricated command to 'Behold.' The command simultaneously directs her reader back to the words of St Denis – to the 'Character of Preests' – and forward, to her list of the attributes necessary for the 'sacred dignitie' of priesthood. Constable digests the words of St Denis and organizes them into clear points for her readers, making the matter of his characterization less significant than her additional words on the subject. Similarly, in *Advises*, Constable pairs references to biblical history with a summary of lessons that she would have her readers derive from her scriptural examples. 'The Ecclesiasticall histories', as she interprets them,

> are full of examples of people that could not be converted by the most eminent & learned men that were in those ages, which yet came afterwards to be converted by the meanes of some simple & unlearned men, usinge even simple & ordinarie wordes. from hence we may learne three things.[51]

She combines quotation with commentary, instruction and lists of key points in order to transform her primary texts into the material basis for an analysis of both universal and contemporary spiritual practice and conflict.

Spiritual reading was central to Constable's written collections and to her understanding of contemplative prayer. Like Baker and More, she believed that 'to read or heare read pious bookes is a great motive & spur to perfection.'[52] She even went so far as to claim that:

> god speakes by no externall meanes more then by readinge & it has allwaies seemed more efficacious to me then sermons which is more apt (accordinge to the ordinarie sayeinge) to goe in at one eare & out at another, but serious readinge penetrates to the verie bottome of the hart & workes great effects.[53]

This lovely exposition on the power of reading validates the spiritual practice at Cambrai at the same time that it provides a justification for Constable's activities as reader, author and interpreter. Reading is a form of spirituality: though it is not a substitute for prayer, it nonetheless serves as an interface between God and the contemplative reader. But Constable does not simply authorize her spiritual reading through reference to God's Word: she also contrasts reading with speaking. In her analysis, reading is superior in its effects on the body and the spirit. She locates heard speech in the ears, receptors that allow both entry and exit; the effects of reading, on the contrary, pierce the heart. Constable contrasts what she sees as the passive position of listening to sermons with the active process of 'serious' reading. Since God speaks through reading – especially reading undertaken, in Baker's formulation, 'for the sturring up of your wills' – sermons become largely unnecessary as a means of accessing the Word.[54] Constable implies that sermons, primarily the purview of men in the post-Tridentine Catholic hierarchy, are inferior to written works, which could be produced by literate individuals outside the priesthood.[55] She follows the word of the Pauline injunction that prohibited women from preaching – 'I suffer not a woman to teach, nor to usurp authority over the man, but to be in silence' – but subverts its intent.[56]

Writing in manuscript allowed Constable to provide extensive commentary on the state of her church and the individuals within it. Because Baker's and More's printed writings were available to a much wider readership, their critiques of contemporary Catholicism were necessarily muted in those posthumous publications. David Lunn describes the process of editing Baker for print as akin to blunting the point of a knife: 'much of what Baker wrote was critical, vehement and prejudiced. [...] on the whole Baker's attack on contemporary religious institutions and practice is softened by Cressy into advice'.[57] Constable was not subjected to a similar softening. In her *Advises*, she is explicit in her condemnation of confessors who violate the boundaries of a spiritual relationship: 'it seemes to me to be a very necessarie thinge to recommend to all confessors to take heed of their affections to their penitents, since too manie scandalls have risen from the want of care in this poynt as may be proved by many terrible examples'.[58] The 'scandalls' to which Constable refers plagued the Catholic Church throughout the Reformation, when Protestant pamphleteers and playwrights were eager to attribute sexual relationships to nuns and their confessors. For this reason, printed Catholic books were unlikely to allude to the possibility of such impropriety. Constable, however, effectively turns her warning into an implicit critique of Protestantism. She explains:

> manie times the affections that were begunne in spirit & for spirituall ends if they be not carefullie looked too comes to degenerate & fall into great extremities of the contrarie, it is related in the life of the B. woman Sr Marie of the incarnation, that one told her of an Ecclesiasticke who haveinge not well governed his affections was so transported with foolish love to one of his penitents that he would needs turne hereticke to marrie her.[59]

A confessor who desires his penitent is only one step away from a Lutheran shift to clerical marriage; bad Catholics, in other words, are just unacknowledged Protestants. Without denying the possibility of scandal and corruption within the Catholic Church, Constable turns from an internal focus – on the immediacy of the confessor/penitent relationship – to what she saw as the larger problems facing post-Tridentine Catholicism: the ubiquity of sexual scandal, the intrusion of temporal concerns into spiritual practice, and the encroachments of Protestantism. She writes not for a specific confessor (or priest, or abbess) but so that her reader 'may be able out of this my rough cast thinge to draw a perfect Character of a confessor both for the world & religion'.[60] Despite the fact that her manuscripts were physically tied to Cambrai – all were produced at the monastery and a number of them probably remained there – her writing was not tethered to the monastery and its immediate controversies.

Constable wrote 'for the world & religion' even though she expressed reservations concerning the involvement of monastics in temporal politics and controversies. In her *Reflexions*, she depicts the ideal contemplative life:

> after profession we should meddle no more with worldly busines but totally withdraw our selves from it as if there were no such thinge; after our **vowes** we have no more to doe with any thing & therefore ought to recollect & abstract our selves from all medlinge with terrene things which are not compatible with celestiall wherewith we are only to meddle.[61]

But Constable's celestial concerns were tied to the world, and her inversion of clerical hierarchies becomes most radical when she looks outside the convent. In one of her many negative appraisals of confessors, she reveals that:

> the greatest fault in my mind even in the best directours is that aptenesse & facilitie that they have, to have too greate an opinion & esteeme for their penitents, & to indeavour to make others have the like; I am sure it may be very prejudiciall to the penitent whatsoever it is to the confessor; for my part I have ever esteemed it a greate indiscretion.[62]

In order to posit a remedy for this particular problem, Constable imagines herself in the role of confessor, a position of ecclesiastical authority that was closed to women: 'if I had the charge of all the soules of the world they should never know the opinion that I had of them nor no bodie else at least not to such excesse as ordinarelie is committed.'[63] This is certainly not a moderate response to 'such excesse': Constable presents a hypothetical scenario in which she is the world's leading spiritual authority and director. She then goes further 'to conclude,' offering the impossible: 'if I had as greate a saint as St Paule to governe, I should be verie reserved in manifestinge an opinion.'[64] Rather than simply subverting Paul's restrictions on women's religious authority, Constable imagines a relationship in which she acts as an authority over him – an astonishing rhetorical move for any Catholic, let alone a nun. She has proceeded from a qualitative analysis of her sources, arguing in some cases 'that his doctrine is very well worth the regardinge though perhaps there be somethinge which in rigour might have beene omitted', to the creation of a fictional exemplar who governs all the souls in the world, including long-dead saints, and is based upon her own authorial persona.[65]

Constable's collections invert hierarchical relationships, both in their form – Constable imposes order on the spiritual authorities she cites and presents those ordered collections as advice manuals to her religious superiors – and in their content. Within the collections, Constable offers her readers numerous critiques of the clerical hierarchy that was central to post-Tridentine Catholicism. She refuses to limit obedience to penitents or nuns, instead emphasizing that even confessors owe 'obedience to god & superiours', and deftly sketches the conflicts that may arise between authority figures.[66] 'How both the Abbesse & he [the confessor] can have a full power I cannot understand,' she writes,

> & though it belonges to the Abbesse to have this full power by the rule, & all the lawes devine & humane in the world yet if he will needs have it in my opinion

there should be no Abbesse at all but he could be both confessor & abbesse, for to be an Abbesse in name & not in power, is somethinge hard.[67]

Constable does not suggest a levelling of hierarchies, but she demands that the structural basis for temporal authority be clearly delineated and the boundaries between individuals sharply drawn. Ultimately, she is strangely like her Puritan contemporaries in her adherence to God as the source for all earthly authority, and in her recognition that true obedience sometimes demands temporal disobedience. Writing from the 'calm and peaceful' cloister, Constable critiqued the active lives of her religious brothers – including, quite literally, her brother – and suggested that they might be better able to wield their religious authority if they accepted the contemplative practice proposed by Baker and confirmed by the Benedictine nuns of Cambrai and Paris. Her contributions to Benedictine spirituality, manuscript history and the early modern discourse on female obedience reveal that cloistered English nuns actively engaged in the debates over authority that had been central to England's religious history since the Reformation.

Notes

1. I am grateful for the assistance and hospitality of Sister Margaret Truran at Stanbrook Abbey, Sister Benedict Rowell at Colwich Abbey, and Dom David Foster at Downside Abbey.
2. F. Oakley, 'Christian Obedience and Authority, 1520–1550', in J. H. Burns (ed.), *The Cambridge History of Political Thought, 1450–1700* (Cambridge: Cambridge University Press, 1991), pp. 159–92. Richard Rex focuses on the particulars of the English Reformation in 'The Crisis of Obedience: God's Word and Henry's Reformation', *The Historical Journal*, 39 (1996), pp. 863–94.
3. See, for example, A. Dillon, *The Construction of Martyrdom in the English Catholic Community, 1535–1603* (Aldershot: Ashgate, 2002); P. Lake and M. Questier, 'Margaret Clitherow, Catholic Nonconformity, Martyrology and the Politics of Religious Change in Elizabethan England', *Past and Present*, 185 (2004), pp. 43–90; and A. Walsham, *Church Papists: Catholicism, Conformity and Confessional Polemic in Early Modern England* (Woodbridge: The Boydell Press, 1993).
4. C. Walker's *Gender and Politics in Early Modern Europe: English Convents in France and the Low Countries* (New York: Palgrave MacMillan, 2003) is the only comprehensive historiographical study of the English contemplative convents. Recent articles – typically focusing on specific nuns or orders – include C. Bowden, 'The Abbess and Mrs. Brown: Lady Mary Knatchbull and Royalist Politics in Flanders in the Late 1650s', *Recusant History*, 24 (1999), pp. 288–308; M. Pfannebecker, '"Love's Interest": Agency and Identity in a Seventeenth-Century Nun's Letters', *Literature Compass*, 3 (2006), pp. 149–58; C. Walker, 'Prayer, Patronage, and Political Conspiracy: English Nuns and the Restoration', *The Historical Journal*, 43 (2000), pp. 1–23; and H. Wolfe, 'Reading Bells and Loose Papers: Reading and Writing Practices of the English Benedictine Nuns of Cambrai and Paris', in V. E. Burke and J. Gibson (eds) *Early Modern Women's Manuscript Writing* (Aldershot: Ashgate, 2004), pp.135–56. 'Who were the Nuns? A Prosopographical study of the English Convents in exile, 1600–1800', a project supported by the Arts & Humanities Research Council, promises to spur exciting new research in this field. See http://wwtn.history.qmul.ac.uk/index.html.

5. H. N. Birt, 'Introduction', in *Obit Book of the English Benedictines From 1600 to 1912* (Edinburgh: Mercat Press, 1913), pp. xiii–xli, xxxv.

6. Barbara Constable (1617–84) was the daughter of Sir Philip Constable of Everingham in Yorkshire. Like many of her fellow nuns, she was a member of the Catholic gentry and had siblings who also travelled to the continent to practice their faith. She entered Cambrai on 31 August 1638 and professed two years later. For a catalogue of the nuns of Cambrai see Lady Cecilia Heywood, 'Records of the Abbey of our Lady of Consolation at Cambrai, 1620–1793', in J. Gillow (ed.), *Publications of the Catholic Record Society* (London: Ballantyne, Hanson & Co., 1913), pp. 1–85.

7. For a list of works that Constable transcribed, see the appendix to Wolfe's 'Dame Barbara Constable: Catholic Antiquarian, Advisor, and Closet Missionary', in R. Corthell, F. E. Dolan, C. Highley and A. F. Marotti (eds), *Catholic Culture in Early Modern England* (Notre Dame: University of Notre Dame Press, 2007), pp. 175–82.

8. Downside Abbey Archives (hereafter Downside) MS 82146/629 (1650), Colwich MS 43 (1650), and Downside MS 82145/552 (1653), respectively. Wolfe identifies 'eleven original works and collections' in 'Dame Barbara Constable' (158). Four of the eleven works are in a single volume (*Considerations for Preests*, which includes 'A breefe Treatise of learninge & Preachinge', 'A discourse to Preachers', and 'For Missioners'. I treat the four works as a whole, since the volume has consistent pagination).

9. The appointed chaplain of a convent said mass, administered sacraments, and confessed the nuns. Baker was sent to the convent by the English Benedictine Congregation to provide the nuns with a resource for instruction in prayer and spiritual life.

10. Augustine Baker, OSB, *The Life and Death of Dame Gertrude More*, in Ben Wekking (ed.) (Salzburg: Analecta Cartusiana, 2002), pp.147–48.

11. Augustine Baker, *Directions for Contemplation*, Downside Abbey Baker MS 2, 149.

12. Augustine Baker, 'Concerning the Librarie of this howse', pp. 138–9.

13. P. Spearritt, OSB, 'The Survival of Mediaeval Spirituality Among the Exiled English Black Monks', *The American Benedictine Review*, 25 (1974), p. 295.

14. For an analysis of Jesuit direction of seventeenth-century contemplative convents, with particular reference to Brussels, see Walker, *Gender and Politics*, pp. 134–47.

15. For a brief overview of the controversy, see J. McCann, OSB, 'Introduction', in P. Salvin and S. Cressy (eds), *The Life of Father Augustine Baker, O.S.B.* (London: Burns Oates & Washbourne Ltd., 1933), rpt. in *Salzburg English & American Studies* 20, ed. J. McCann (Salzburg: Institut für Anglistik und Amerikanistik, 1997), xxiii–xxviii.

16. M. Barrett, OSB, '"Such a World of Books": Spiritual Reading in Augustine Baker', unpublished essay. I am grateful to Fr. Barrett for permission to cite from his work.

17. Dame Gertrude More (1604–1633) is the author of *The Spiritual Exercises* (1658), a book that includes examples of her prayer and a spirited defence of Baker. For Baker's book lists, see Beinecke MS Osborn b268, Downside MS 26559 (Baker MS 2), and *The Holy Practises of a Devine Lover or The Sainctly Ideots Devotions* (Paris: Lewis de la Fosse, 1657).

18. Baker, *The Life and Death of Dame Gertrude More*, p. 36.

19. A. Baker, *Sancta Sophia*, edited by Serenus Cressy (Douai: John Patte and Thomas Fievet, 1657).

20. D. Lunn, 'Augustine Baker (1575–1641) and the English Mystical Tradition', *The Journal of Ecclesiastical History*, 26 (1975), p. 271. Clark began editing the manuscripts two decades later, and his work has influenced two recent collections: J. Hogg (ed.), *'Stand up to Godwards': Essays in Mystical and Monastic Theology in Honour of the Reverend John Clark on his Sixty-Fifth Birthday*, Analecta Cartusiana (Salzburg: Universitat Salzburg, 2002), Vol. 204 and M. Woodward (ed.), *That Mysterious Man: Essays on Augustine Baker OSB, 1575–1641, Analecta Cartusiana* 119:15 (Abergavenny: Three Peaks Press, 2001).

21. A few of the nuns' manuscripts have been included in the *Analecta Cartusiana* series. Clark recently edited the *Devotions* of Margaret Gascoigne (*Analecta Cartusiana* 119:28 (2007)) and Julia Bolton Holloway's edition of *Bibliothèque Mazarine 1202* includes material by both Gertrude More and Catherine Gascoigne (*Analecta Cartusiana* 119:26 (2006)).

22. J. T. Rhodes, 'Some Writings of a Seventeenth-Century English Benedictine: Dom Augustine Baker O.S.B.', *The Yale University Library Gazette*, 67 (1993), p. 113. For an important corrective to this tendency, see C. Walker, 'Spiritual Property: The English Benedictine Nuns of Cambrai and the Dispute over the Baker Manuscripts' in N. E. Wright, M. W. Ferguson and A. R. Buck (eds), *Women, Property, and the Letters of the Law in Early Modern England* (Toronto: University of Toronto Press, 2004), pp. 237–55.

23. Walker, *Gender and Politics*, p. 145.

24. See Walker, 'Spiritual Property', especially pp. 242–9.

25. Wolfe, 'Dame Barbara Constable', p. 175.

26. *Ibid.*, p. 162.

27. *Ibid.*, pp. 168, 175.

28. G. More, *The Spiritual Exercises of the Most Vertuous and Religious D. Gertrvde More* (Paris: Lewis De La Fosse, 1658), pp. 19, 58.

29. An example of the manuscript circulation of More's writings can be found in Colwich MS 22, which includes 'The Sixt Confession D.G.'. (123). Walker describes the attempted censorship of the 1650s in 'Spiritual Property'.

30. McCann, 'Introduction', p. xxviii.

31. The remaining manuscript was transcribed in 1681; Wolfe provides the chronological appendix of Constable's manuscripts in 'Dame Barbara Constable'.

32. Wolfe characterizes Constable's signed and dedicated collections as 'original works', but not her translations or her compilations without commentary ('Dame Barbara Constable', p. 158).

33. J. Leclercq, OSB, *The Love of Learning and the Desire for God: A Study of Monastic Culture*, translated by Catharine Misrahi (New York: Fordham University Press, 1982), p. 182.

34. *Ibid.*, p. 183.

35. *Gemitus Pecatorum, Or the complaints of sinners*, Downside MS 82143 (1649), 3–4.

36. *Considerations for Preests*, Downside MS 82145/552 (1653), 197, 213. Constable also dedicated volumes, such as *A Spiritual Treatise, Conteininge Some Advise for Seculars*, to friends and relatives in England. Wolfe provides a detailed analysis of Constable's 'hypothetical and real' readers in 'Dame Barbara Constable', 168–71.

37. *Advises: For Confessors and Spirituall Directors*, Downside MS 82146/629 (1650), pp. 213–14. Her first 'treatise of prayer' was not completed until 1657, and it was dedicated to her married sister living in England.

38. *Advises*, 398, and *Considerations or Reflexions upon the Rule of the Most Glorious Father St Benedict*, Downside MS 82144/627 (1655), p. 191.

39. Wolfe claims that 'none of [Constable's] original writings were ever printed or copied,' and she only cites the copy of *Gemitus Pecatorum* held at Stanbrook (pp. 158, 176).

40. Constable, *Advises*, p. 396.

41. *Ibid.*, p. 380.

42. Wolfe, 'Dame Barbara Constable', 172. In this article and in 'Reading Bells', Wolfe makes much of Constable's 'faults and the impediments these faults presented in terms of successfully prosecuting a contemplative life' ('Reading Bells', 145). I am interested, instead, in Constable's rhetorical deployment of her experience and her use of the modesty topos and other forms of self-abnegation as seemingly paradoxical sources of authority: she adopts an authorial stance that emphasizes her own faults so that she might provide examples and instruction for others.

43. Constable, *Considerations or Reflexions*, pp. 15–16.

44. *Ibid.*, p. 64.

45. Early modern nuns had many sources for information on religious and political life outside the cloister, including letters from family members, visitors to the convent and controversial books printed in England and on the continent.

46. More, *The Spiritual Exercises*, p. 211.

47. *Ibid.*, pp. 66–7.

48. Cf. Constable's dedication to Father Benedict Stapleton in *Advises*, wherein she protests 'nor doe you think I humbly beseech you that I have any intention heerebie to teach you any thinge'.

49. For the modesty topos in a humanist and Protestant context, see K. Dunn *Pretexts of Authority: The Rhetoric of Authorship in the Renaissance Preface* (Stanford: Stanford University Press, 1994). K. J. P. Lowe addresses the use of the modesty topos in Italian convents in *Nuns' Chronicles and Convent Culture in Renaissance and Counter-Reformation Italy* (Cambridge: Cambridge University Press, 2003).

50. Constable, *Considerations for Preests*, p. 2.

51. Constable, *Advises*, pp. 165–6.

52. Constable, *Considerations or Reflexions*, p. 190.

53. *Ibid.*, pp. 190–1.

54. Baker, 'A Treatise, sheweng one, how he is to behave himself in the time of sicknes or corporall infirmitie, and how to prepare himself for death,' in *Sickness Patience Emblems*, Downside Abbey Baker MS 23, p. 306.

55. As Jennifer Summit observes, 'whatever the restrictions that were placed on women's speech in this period [...] women's writing was produced under a very different set of institutional conditions.' See *Lost Property: The Woman Writer and English Literary History, 1380–1589* (Chicago: University of Chicago Press, 2000), p. 8.

56. I Tim. 2:12. For a brief overview of debates on this issue, see K. L. Jansen, *The Making of the Magdalen: Preaching and Popular Devotion in the Later Middle Ages* (Princeton: Princeton University Press, 2000), pp. 54–7.

57. Lunn, 'Augustine Baker', p. 275.

58. Constable, *Advises*, p. 318.

59. *Ibid.*, p. 320.

60. *Ibid.*, p. 381.

61. Constable, *Considerations or Reflexions*, pp. 171–2.

62. Constable, *Advises*, pp. 360–1.

63. *Ibid.*, p. 361.

64. *Ibid.*, p. 366.

65. *Ibid.*, p. 198.

66. From the 'Dedication' to *Advises*.

67. *Ibid.*, p. 435.

7

Power in Piety: Inspiration, Ambitions and Strategies of Spiritual Virgins in the Northern Netherlands during the Seventeenth Century[1]

Marit Monteiro

On 2 February 1682, the feast of the Purification of Our Lady, 19–year-old Clara Adolf celebrated her spiritual wedding (*geestelijke bruiloft*) with Jesus Christ in a ceremony that marked her initiation into the state in life of a **spiritual virgin**. During this ceremony, she received the objects which symbolized her virginity as well as her union with Christ: a scapular, a veil, a belt, a crown and a ring. She now had become a bride of Christ.[2] She was assisted by Maria Hartman and Maria Boede.[3] They all belonged to a group of so-called *filiae spirituales* (spiritual daughters) or *filiae devotae* of the Augustinian missionary Joannes Uutten Eeckhout (1614–1682) and his successors. Uutten Eeckhout served as a priest in a **house chapel** in Amsterdam, called *De Star* (The Star).[4] In 1664 he began recording the spiritual virgins affiliated with this chapel and by 1695 the list numbered over 60 women.[5]

An estimated 5000 women opted for a life as spiritual virgins in the Dutch Republic during the seventeenth century, most of them unmarried but some widowed and therefore called spiritual widows. The majority of them lived either independently, in small groups with like-minded women, or with relatives. Even the virgins who lived in one of the rare communities, such as De Hoek in Haarlem, did not did lead a communal life comparable to convent life or the way of life of **beguines**,[6] but remained economically independent.[7] Some women, as was the case with the spiritual virgins of *De Star*, joined the **Third Order**[8] of the religious Institute to which their **confessors** belonged. The Roman Catholic Church did not recognize this way of life as a religious state. Their simple dark attire denoted that they rejected the world and its worldly pleasures, and gave them, particularly if they were young, an unmistakably religious aura. Yet, their contemporaries – clergy as well as laity, Protestants as well as Catholics – often did not know the actual status of spiritual virgins. The organization of their existence as spiritual virgins depended mostly on their financial position and social status. They lived under the obedience of a priest, who served as father confessor and **spiritual director**, the role Uutten Eeckhout performed for the spiritual virgins of *De Star*.

Spiritual virgins represented the core members of the Catholic Church which struggled to survive after the Dutch Revolt (1568–1648) against the Spanish king Philip II. The nobility of the seven Northern Provinces of the Netherlands opposed his ambition to centralize the administration within his realm, and rejected the persecution of religious dissenters. In turn, they guaranteed the freedom of conscience in the Union of Utrecht, the treaty that in 1579 unified them into the independent Republic of the Seven United Netherlands. They did, however, forbid the public worship of Catholicism and privileged the Reformed Church as the 'public' church, protected and favoured by the state. By the middle of the seventeenth century, an intricate system of bribes to local authorities ensured that the majority of Catholics could privately practise their religion in relative freedom as long as they submitted to the secular authorities and did not publicly offend the privileged Reformed Church.[9] This system of paid tolerance, as well as the considerable local and regional variety with which it was implemented, illustrates that the absence of a strong central secular authority often favoured pragmatic tolerance on a local level.[10] Protestant dissenters as well as Catholics benefited from the pragmatism of local authorities who generally valued keeping the social order over the theological hair-splitting Reformed ministers regularly attempted.[11]

Catholicism survived in the Dutch Republic thanks to the support and patronage of the laity, which included spiritual virgins. They invested time and money, and cultivated their social networks to ensure that Catholics could continue to practise their faith in private behind the façade of a warehouse, an ordinary stately home, or – as in the case of *De Star* – a brewery. This essay examines the particular identity and agency of spiritual virgins. After a review of spiritual virgins' representations in Dutch historiography, this study will dwell on the seventeenth-century debate which expressed the clergy's ambivalent appreciations of these women's status. Finally, it will highlight the extent to which spiritual virgins themselves were able to shape their particular lifestyle.

Historiographical dilemmas: failed nuns or active women religious?

In contrast with the women religious living under perpetual **vows** who were canonically recognized as brides of Christ, spiritual virgins did not retreat to a convent. They challenged the socially and ecclesiastically approved life options for women, which were confined to marriage or convent, aptly summarized in the Latin expression *maritus aut murus*. The **papal bull** *Periculoso* (1298) dictated that women religious were to maintain the *clausura*; they were not allowed to leave their convent other than in case of an outbreak of fire or life-threatening disease. This regulation was once again confirmed by the constitution *Circa Pastoralis* (1566), which expressed the strict attitude of the Council of Trent with regards to female **enclosure**. Male Orders, on the other hand, were granted more freedom to pursue their missionary activities. In the opinion of the Holy See, women religious as a rule needed to be confined to their convents. Religiously inspired women who sought Church approval for more active forms of religious life were vulnerable to sometimes severe penalties, as the case of Mary Ward and the suppression of her Institute in 1631 illustrates.[12]

The contemporary problems of Church authorities with such spiritually ambitious women are mirrored in the traditional historiography, which largely neglected or marginalized them until the 1970s. Interestingly enough the Dutch spiritual virgins never suffered from such a lack of interest. They were part and parcel of the Catholic historiography that from the second half of the nineteenth century attempted to revise the dominant, liberal version of national history which prevailed over the perspectives of other commemorative communities such as the Catholics. This version emphasized the inherently Protestant nature of Dutch identity, emphasizing the religious dimensions of the Dutch Revolt. Interventions of Catholic historians in these politics of memory challenged this master narrative by claiming the 'Dutchness' of the Catholics.[13] The Catholic narrative, mainly devised by clerical authors, made ample room for spiritual virgins as heroines of the true faith who risked their lives and worldly possessions in order to help their Church and its clergy.

Their way of life was generally attributed to the Reformation and the consequent reduction of status of the Catholic Church in the provinces where Calvinism had become dominant. As the Dutch Republic became missionary territory, monastic life came to an end in what became known as the Holland Mission (*Missio Hollandica*). Contemporary observers therefore considered the way of life of spiritual virgins as a substitute available for those who desired a religious life but no longer could enter a convent. Catholic historians commonly subscribed to this explanation, for it fitted in neatly with the apologetic over-tones with which they attempted to put the dominant liberal version of the history of the Dutch Revolt into perspective. Dutch Catholicism was thus portrayed as an exception to the rule of European Counter-Reformation Catholicism, a representation for which the spiritual virgins served as a case in point in two respects. Some historians argued that the religious lifestyle of spiritual virgins and their charitable commitment resulted from the pressure the clergy exerted upon them to gear their religious zeal to an uncloistered religious life instead of entering a convent in the Catholic Southern Netherlands. Others were convinced that these women bore evidence to the severity of the crisis, which accounted for the fact that the clergy became largely dependant upon the laity. In either case, there was little attention to the specific agency of the women involved.[14]

Recently, the interaction and the collaboration between the missionary clergy and the laity in the Dutch Republic has been re-evaluated. In his study *Faith on the Margins*, the American historian Charles Parker ventures to state that the collapse of the ecclesiastical infrastructure allowed Dutch Catholic leaders more freedom in implementing Tridentine reforms than many bishops across Europe.[15]

Parker moreover argues that lay Catholic elites provided the clergy with new sources of patronage and were therefore granted more leverage in Church affairs than lay persons elsewhere in Europe. The laity, with spiritual virgins as core members of the persecuted Church, closely collaborated with priests in mutual, but not necessarily harmonious, dependency. When highlighting the laity's interaction with the missonery clergy, Parker offers a new paradigm of interpretation; he liberates the religious agency of believers from the ecclesiastical interpretations which so far dominated religious history, and which traditionally considered the clergy as the driving force of change.

It is certainly noteworthy that such a shift in analysis had been advocated as early as 1935 by the historian Eugenie Theissing in her dissertation devoted to spiritual virgins.[16] She questioned the by then familiar causal correlation between the Reformation and the unauthorized religious existence of spiritual virgins by pointing out that a chaste, ascetic life dedicated to pious exercises and (semi-)pastoral activities probably met the wishes of many a devout woman in the seventeenth century, even though such an overtly active religious lifestyle was not in keeping with the conception the Catholic Church held of the religious state of women. Theissing advocated a re-evaluation of the intrinsic religious agency of spiritual virgins instead of qualifying them as an invention or instrument of the missionary clergy. Moreover, she pointed to the necessity to interpret this agency in a broader frame of reference, both in time and space. Chronologically, she not only drew some attention to the early Christian examples employed by clerical authors to legitimate the way of the life of uncloistered religious women, but also to the late medieval religious women's movement. Geographically, she pointed out the similarity in object and organization between the Dutch spiritual virgins and groups such as the one led by Mary Ward.

Although her study was considered a welcome contribution to the history of early modern Catholicism, these explanations were largely neglected. Her argument was not taken up until the 1970s when under the influence of feminist theology religious women in history were hailed as champions of feminine power in the Church.[17] Influenced by this feminist trend, the Dutch historian Elisja Schulte van Kessel concentrated on class and gender as the major explanatory factors for the development and defence of the way of life of spiritual virgins.[18] Her case studies focused on spiritual virgins from the higher social classes who, thanks to their wealth and influential social network, could sometimes subtly outrank priests from more modest classes. As far as gender is concerned, Schulte van Kessel's study bears the traces of the paradigms of women's studies and women's history in the 1970s and 1980s. These paid tribute to a radical feminism rooted in Marxist interpretations of the past. In this frame of reference, the domain of religion was considered unequivocally patriarchal, as much as men were considered oppressors by definition, and women their victims.[19] Schulte van Kessel's findings echo these patriarchal preconceptions as she argued that these women attempted to become free of the patriarchal order of society by opting for the virginal state in life, devoted to God and thereby circumventing worldly power structures.

It was not until the 1990s that a more general interest in uncloistered religious women in the early modern era was revived and more sophisticated models for the analysis of their ambitions and agency were developed. The studies by the German historian Anne Conrad and her Canadian colleague Elizabeth Rapley are particularly relevant for the research on spiritual virgins. Conrad focuses on groups who identify themselves with the foundation of Angela Merici and were referred to as Ursulines, as well as on various other groups of women who took their inspiration from the **Jesuits**, often called 'Jesuitinnen' or '**Jesuitesses**'.[20] She pointed to similarities in their organization and objectives, arguing that – whether of an Ursuline or a Jesuit extraction – in their own religious associations women created 'Freiräume' (refuges) from the clericalized ecclesiastical power structures. To my mind, she over-stresses the feminist character of this endeavour by attributing 'ein ausgeprägtes feministisches Bewußtsein' (a markedly feminist consciousness) to the women involved. Yet, particularly noteworthy is her conclusion that these women clearly distinguished themselves from nuns on the one hand, and the laity on the other. Instead, their manifestations expressed an identity and self-image which Conrad defines as clerical, on an equal footing with the clerics who served as their spiritual directors. As we will see, this was not exceptional, for some priests hinted in the same direction in their books of conduct for spiritual virgins, whereas some spiritual virgins also considered themselves to be clerical ('geestelijk') rather than religious ('religieus').

Elizabeth Rapley's argument ties in with Theissing's earlier contention that in predominantly Catholic countries some women also preferred an active religious way of life to the contemplative, cloistered convent life.[21] Her study focuses on France, dealing specifically yet not exclusively with the Order of the Visitation founded by François de Sales (1567–1622) and Jeanne de Chantal (1572–1647). The history of this community clearly illustrates the difficult and rather elusive socio-economic position of unmarried women who were in no way perpetually bound to the **semi-religious** community to which they pledged their allegiance. Rapley too notes a considerable inspiration from the lifestyle and work undertaken by the Jesuits. Although this Order successfully resisted any attempt to instate a female branch, its members nevertheless proved to be willing to advise and assist women who aspired for an active religious life in conceiving **Rules** and constitutions suited to this end. Mary Ward's Institute testifies to this allegiance, as it does to the tenacity of the Holy See in relegating women to their actions *in religiosis*.

The studies briefly discussed here indicate that self-conception and self-understanding serve as fundamental categories for the analysis of women who nominally were not religious, but who nevertheless considered themselves as such. They therefore elude fixed social categories and are analytically defined in ambiguous terms like 'semi-religious'. Medievalist Caroline Walker Bynum aptly pointed out that the notion 'semi-religious' fits neither the aspirations, nor the self-conception of uncloistered religious women. It takes religious life as its point of departure and then implies that the women concerned were not able to meet this standard, to which they, however, did not aspire. It is for this reason that Bynum coined the notion 'quasi-religious'.[22] This term risks underestimating the genuinely religious character of the ambitions of the women involved. Nevertheless, Bynum's point that they did not necessarily model their alternative lifestyle after the monastic mode applies to the case of the Dutch spiritual virgins. Neither form nor status of this specific way of life was fixed. Instead, both their religious regime, and the particular religious character of identity this regime served to underpin, were subject to negotiations between priests and spiritual virgins. The studies of Conrad and Rapley draw due attention to the significance of the alliances of clerics and women who aspired to an active religious life in these negotiations. Between them, there was a mutual dependence which created options for religiously inspired activities of women within their Church. The next section will highlight the opinions of clerics on the state in life of spiritual virgins.

A genuine state in life? Clerical authors on the status of spiritual virgins

In the absence of a general rule for this state in life, **secular** and **regular priests** wrote several pious books of conduct which illustrate how the clergy defined the way of life and the identity of spiritual virgins, and prescribed the authority relations between these women and the priests who acted as their confessors and spiritual directors. The guidelines reflect the parameters set by clerics for the **apostolic** involvement, financial investments and identity of spiritual virgins. Most authors argue that the lifestyle of spiritual virgins was as dignified as the ecclesiastically approved religious state and would ensure the salvation of their souls just as well. Their pleas for a spiritual life outside convent walls may be read as an explicitly formulated alternative for the recognized religious state. According to one of the authors, spiritual virgins lived in a medial state (*middelen staet*), comparing them to 'the animals of which it is said they are part aquatic and part earthly animals that stay neither on the earth nor in the sea'. With his comparison between spiritual virgins and amphibians the author attempted to clarify that the women involved in fact represented a new category in addition to the religious and the laity.[23]

The daily reading of devotional books was considered to be good practice of religion for spiritual virgins.[24] Whether they actually read the books of conduct which dealt specifically with their particular state in life is hard to establish from the sources available. This question is, however, of little importance here, because the books of conduct for spiritual virgins are analysed mainly as normative sources that reflect how the authors, secular and regular priests, defined the way of life of spiritual virgins as well as their position in the Catholic community. This particular genre reflected an apologia for the state in life of spiritual virgins, combined with a set of rules or guidelines suited to an uncloistered religious life based on the **evangelical** counsels of poverty, obedience and chastity. They helped not only to shape but also to legitimize the *modus vivendi* of spiritual virgins.

Between 1570 and 1730, 34 books appeared in Dutch that specifically dealt with spiritual virgins and their lifestyle. The majority of the books (23) appeared after 1650, as the religious divides in the North were consolidated. Most of the books were printed and ecclesiastically approved in Antwerp, and thus primarily meant for a market in this diocese in the Catholic Southern Netherlands, although they found their way to the Northern Netherlands as well. Of small format, they were intended for the regular use of spiritual virgins and their spiritual directors. In two cases it seems that the books were intended for priests with spiritual virgins under their direction rather than for the women themselves. *Scala Jacob virginibus Deo cum proposito perpetuae contintentiae in seculo famulantibus applicata* (1666) by the secular priest Joannes Lindeborn (1630–1696) was in Latin, the *lingua franca* of the clergy but generally not of the spiritual virgins. The Dutch edition, which appeared in 1670, was meant for spiritual virgins themselves. In the case of the *Clooster van Sion* (six volumes, 1662–6) by the secular priest Joannes van Heumen (1611–1673) the form used, that of sermons, suggests that priests formed the intended audience.[25]

Church officials such as the **vicar apostolic** Philippus Rovenius (1573–1651) stated that spiritual virgins were not women religious, although he nevertheless voiced his appreciation for those women who attempted to lead a religious life in the world. One of his successors, Joannes van Neercassel (1625–1686), shared his opinion, yet he was in the habit of putting the spiritual virgins ahead of the ordinary laity, thereby singling them out as core members of the Church. A confidant of Neercassel, the already mentioned Lindeborn, went even further by arguing in his *Scala Jacob* that a celibate life dedicated to God was indeed a state in life. This book was subject to revision on the order of the Roman Congregation of the Index. The censorship imposed upon *Scala Jacob* demonstrates that the clerical debate about the position and status of spiritual virgins in the Dutch Republic was not without consequence for inner-Church controversies about dogma and morals.

Clearly, most authors were aware of their vulnerability in this respect, trying to avoid, for instance, the term 'state in life' when referring to spiritual virgins. Thus, when writing the biography of Sancia Carillo, the Spanish Jesuit Martin de Roa (1561–1637) mentioned that she opted for a virginal life, without, however, denoting this as a particular state in life.[26] Others hesitated less to use the term, yet avoided any direct comparison with the position of nuns. In print, the authors had to reckon with possible censorship, although in practice spiritual directors apparently enjoyed more freedom in defining the status of their subjects. The Augustinian priest Uutten Eeckhout, who admitted Clara Adolf in the ranks of the virgins of the Amsterdam house chapel *De Star* candidly used the definition *status ecclesiasticus*, which vicar apostolic Rovenius in 1648 had reserved for the clergy. This certainly correlates with the findings of Anne Conrad, as mentioned previously. And this definition was put into practice by spiritual virgins, as we will see in the next section.

What is important to note here is that the authors of this specific genre of books developed lines of argument in which they acknowledged the canonically approved status of the nuns, while at the same time providing legitimizations for an alternative way of life for women besides marriage or convent. They claimed that this was a highly respectable life, favoured even by God and thus profitable for personal salvation, provided that women lived by the guidelines prescribed. If all authors agreed that spiritual virgins were not women religious, several argued that their mode of existence certainly was not inferior to that of nuns. Without challenging the canonical hierarchy between nuns and spiritual virgins, they did in fact question the primacy of the convent life as the only approved religious existence for women. Their arguments show that within the seventeenth-century Catholic Church, different views were taken of the status of a holy life in the world without solemn vows or monastic seclusion.

The impact of these books, however, also went beyond laying some theologically defensible foundations for an active religious existence for women. An important objective on the part of the clerical authors was to regulate the day-to-day life of spiritual virgins. Clearly outlined instructions, inspired by approved monastic Rules, structured the entire existence of the spiritual virgin and were meant to assure the religious and honourable character of the life they had chosen for themselves. The intended outcome of this regulation was twofold. On the one hand, the authors wanted to discipline spiritual virgins, so that they would become shining examples of the Catholic community; on the other hand, the state in life of spiritual virgins took on a precise form and substance thanks to these rules and thus became identifiable for others.

Through this system of plain clothing, modest behaviour, intense devotional practices and works of charity, women could make their inner virtuousness and the holy status of their life known to others. The evangelical counsels of poverty, obedience and chastity were put into practice through a regime of piety. This not only reflected the order of things envisioned by the clergy but offered a frame of action as well, from which spiritual virgins could derive their identity. Conceived as a complex of social, devotional and ritual acts, piety offered spiritual virgins an opportunity to express their faith, live their active religious lives and confirm the honourable nature of their lifestyle, which was not embedded in canon law.

With regard to gender, these books clearly illustrate that the God-given order of society could as much serve to assert that women were rightfully subordinated to men as to affirm them in exactly those ambitions which challenged this subordination. According to the authors it was indeed mandated by God that men ruled over women. Yet, they did not fail to emphasize that women could be freed from their inferior social position by opting for the privileged state of virginity. In theory, spiritual virgins had to obey God and their heavenly Bridegroom, Jesus Christ. In practice, this implied the obligation to obey a priest as His earthly deputy. The hierarchical organization of this relationship, however, did not necessarily put the spiritual virgins at a disadvantage. The *vitae* in particular testify to the exceptional bonds some women developed with God, who granted them mystical trances, visions of dreams which, in turn, could serve as sources of authority. As 'experts by experience' these spiritual virgins could, the *vitae* assert, even influence their confessors and spiritual directors. The majority of the spiritual virgins, however, could attain a respectable and even influential position within their local community in a less conspicuous manner. By a public, recognizable display of piety they could propagate their religious conviction at home and in the Church, thereby contributing to the preservation and the dissemination of what they considered to be the true faith.

Gendered parameters of religious life beyond the convent

To be sure, the spirituality prescribed in the books of conduct for spiritual virgins mirrors to a large extent the general post-Tridentine trends in spirituality: the necessity to interiorize faith, to aim at spiritual perfection, to develop an active apostolic attitude and to engage in different forms of charitable care. These trends were held up as worth imitating for clergy, religious and laity alike. They were cultivated in religious associations such as **sodalities** and **fraternities** under the guidance of religious Orders.[27] Within these associations, as well as on an individual level, patterns of religiosity were adapted to one's personal state. What was advocated as particular lay spirituality can be labelled as ascetic and anti-mystical in orientation.[28] Yet, the conduct books for the *filiae spirituales* clearly indicate broader religious repertoires, with **mystical** tendencies which potentially could tip over the balance of power between well-meaning priests in charge of spiritually gifted and ambitious women. Similar repertoires are reflected in the self-fashioned religious careers of Agnes van Heilsbach (1597–1640) and Joanna van Randenraedt (1610–1684). Both women originally wanted to enter a convent but decided against it, Agnes for reasons of health, Joanna because of family responsibilities.

Agnes van Heilsbach arrived in 1624 in Roermond and moved in with the widow of one of the counsellors of the court of the Duchy of Guelders. She was born in Wassenberg, a small town in the duchy of Juliers, a predominantly Lutheran region where Catholicism could be freely **professed**. Her biography illuminates her efforts to free herself from the responsibility to manage the household of her brother, who had entered the priesthood, first by (unsuccessfully) attempting to enter a convent in Cologne, and subsequently by moving to Roermond.

Joanna van Randenraedt was born in Brussels; her father and her brother Willem Hendrik, as well as an uncle from her mother's side, served as counsellors to the Guelders court. The court officials and their families represented the local elite. At an early age Joanna envisioned entering a convent of the Poor Clares, prompted by a preference for austerity due to a profound desire for physical and mental suffering by which she hoped both to emulate and reciprocate the martyr's death Christ had suffered for humanity. Her parents opposed her becoming a nun and her confessor considered the Rule of the Poor Clares much too rigorous for her. She then decided to become a spiritual virgin, convinced as Agnes was that she could best serve God and her fellow-men *in* the world, rather than behind the convent wall, where many of her female friends lived.[29] Agnes van Heilsbach took charge of her and prepared her for her future state in life under the guidance of the Jesuits. Since 1610, the Jesuits ran a college in town, to which a small community of fathers was attached. In the spirit of Counter-Reformation spirituality they founded sodalities and endeavoured to intensify the religious practice of the Catholic community. Their involvement with spiritual virgins seems to have been instrumental to this same end. Van Heilsbach served as a spiritual mother and intermediary between the Jesuit spiritual directors and a small group of spiritual virgins. She also counselled kindred spirits in Antwerp and Brussels who sought her guidance. After Agnes's death in 1638, Joanna van Randenraedt took over this role. Although both women were sometimes ridiculed on account of their extraordinary lifestyle, their confessional zeal, and the astonishing fits of religious experience that – also by their own device – were not kept within the privacy of the confessional, they also rose to some prominence in Roermond.

Both women wrote not only **accounts of conscience**, religious reflections and letters, but also prepared a **spiritual autobiography**. Van Randenraedt, moreover, copied part of the writings of her spiritual mother van Heilsbach, whose hand-writing was almost illegible. These writings, especially the life histories, served as the basis for the monumental *vitae* the Jesuit Daniël Huysmans (1643–1704) published in 1690 and 1691.[30] The women had already burnished their accounts of conscience in their personal life history, presenting their lives as a spiritual struggle for virtuousness in order to deserve God's love. Huysmans further accentuated their subservience to the Church and its clerical representa-tives. Their writings make it clear that the relationship between these women and the Jesuits cannot be summarized so easily.

Through their writings, van Heilsbach and van Randenraedt crafted a reli-gious life for themselves within the setting of their own homes. They willingly submitted themselves to the control of successive Jesuits who served as father confessors and assured the honourable and religious character of their daily lives. Moreover, these priests were theologically equipped to interpret the extraor-dinary spiritual favours bestowed upon the authors. The lengthy accounts of conscience both women wrote on the order of their confessors were originally intended as instruments of control by these priests. Yet, van Heilsbach and van Randenraedt used these reports of their daily life, their dreams, visions and whis-perings to negotiate their own position, status, tasks and authority.[31]

This analysis does not intend to test the veracity of these writings, but rather to comprehend the dynamics of the relationship between these women and their confessors. These dynamics, it is my contention, were inherently gendered. Writing by order of their confessors granted both women a means of expression, yet confronted them with various dilemmas as well. In her study on Teresa of Avila, Alison Weber introduced the notion of the 'double bind' to clarify the unsolvable dilemma that was related to writing on command: proving dignity and humility at the same time. Both characteristics were filled with preconcep-tions regarding gender and status. To Teresa, as Weber points out, it was illusory to think that she could ignore the instruction of her confessor to record her reli-gious experiences, well aware that by complying with his orders, she also risked snubbing his expectations. An illiterate woman like herself was not expected fully to comprehend her own spiritual experiences, yet she was explicitly instructed to describe her way of praying and the ensuing Godly favours. Although she real-ized that she was vulnerable to suspicion of being deluded by the devil, she was also aware that she would never be able to describe her religious practice and experience to the satisfaction of a theologically trained reader. Proving humility constituted a particular problem in this respect, since this was considered a silent virtue, especially for women.[32]

Similar predicaments come to the fore in the writings of the two Roermond women, rather poignantly in 1645 when the truthfulness of van Heilsbach's accounts was questioned by the Jesuit Jacob Wijns (1593–1649), seconded by the rector of the local Jesuits, François l'Hermite (1598–2690). Their theologi-cal training served as the principal tool to test and establish the veracity of these writings. Van Randenraedt had to defend the reputation as well as the legacy of her spiritual mother, who had died seven years earlier. This incident demonstrated that, although both women had Jesuits as their confessors, they also met with resistance from members of the **Society of Jesus**. Wijns bluntly denounced van Heilsbach's writings as mere women's fantasies (*vrouwenfantasien*), for which he did not want to take any responsibility. Van Randenraedt saw herself confronted with a double bind of an existential nature: how could she face up to these theologically trained Jesuits with respect to the truthfulness of the writings of her spiritual mother Agnes without infringing upon their clerical prerogative to interpret these and putting her own position at risk? She escaped by means of her own accounts, in which she cleverly referred to the earlier authorization of van Heilsbach's writings by Wijns's predecessors, whom she characterized as experienced and learned. Finally, she challenged Wijns's authority by claiming that no one should question what came from God: 'I thought that one should not despise any things that stem [sic] from God.'[33] Besides warding off his attack by this counter-attack, she also employed the rhetorical strategy of concession by admitting that some of van Heilsbach's reports indeed must have contained some fantasies. By challenging the Jesuit's authority and at the same time conceding to it, Van Randenraedt managed to preserve her own authoritative position within the local community and among the spiritual virgins under the direction of the Jesuits.

The writings therefore can be considered as instruments of power for both parties involved. Through these writings both women made their confessors accessories to their sometimes very rigid regime of piety. They did not cease to underline that through his supervision, their father confessor was able to help them accomplish their aspiration after a perfect religious existence outside the convent and thereby assure the salvation of their souls. His support, moreover, meant at least a tacit acknowledgement of their informal, ecclesiastically unauthenticated status in life. Moreover, they could underpin their claim to a certain degree of authority in their writings. Christ had singled them out to be His brides, and in their opinion the regular occurrence of dreams, visions and whisperings testified to this extraordinary election.

In describing their experiences, both women were restricted by the operative frame of reference which they shared to a certain extent with their confessors. This referential framework was gendered: the parameters of self-awareness and self-representation were partly determined by social and cultural constructions of femininity and masculinity. Although both women subscribed to dominant ideas of female inferiority in their accounts, they also tried to evade and even undermine these by setting themselves apart from the other members of their sex. Van Heilsbach, for instance, recorded dreams in which she depicted herself as a manly maiden, daring to fight for her faith, being even more courageous than members of the clergy, the Jesuits not excluded. In the year of her death, she recorded a dream in which she rides a horse like a man, firmly holding the reigns in both hands and keeping it under control 'with manly determination'. She leads a wagon full of spiritual virgins, well-known to her, along a rather dangerous road. Apparently, so the description implies, these women lack her qualities of bravery and steadfastness, defined as masculine. Van Randenraedt was in the habit of underlining her position as privileged bride of Christ, conceding to prevailing ideas of the weakness of the female sex by claiming to be in constant need of His support. Her accounts testified to the fact that Christ lent her this support and thereby underpinned her authority. With this rhetoric of concession van Randenraedt not only set herself apart from other women, but also from actual women religious, as her accounts clarified that Christ preferred her over nuns whose moral depravity was contrasted to her own purity. This self-assured image coexisted with passages in her writings that testified to a fundamental insecurity as to whether the life she had chosen would in fact result in the salvation to which she aspired.

Neither of them counted herself among the laity, as would have been appropriate according to Church law. Instead, van Heilsbach and van Randenraedt regarded themselves as 'spiritual' (*geestelijcke*) persons, categorizing themselves on the level of the clergy. Before all, they considered themselves as the daughters of the founder of the Order of the Jesuits, Ignatius of Loyola, and consequently 'sisters' of their spiritual directors. This self-image, which may be defined as 'jesuitic', reflected their claim for equality towards their confessors, as well as their clerical and decidedly pastoral ambitions. These were only partly satisfied by the informal function of 'spiritual mother'. In 1638 van Heilsbach recorded a vision of herself praying after having received communion. A sudden flash of light illuminated her as she took the hand of Saint Ignatius who instructed her to rise and follow. She obeyed and followed him, as she described, well into the heart of God. Van Heilsbach never challenged the fact that Ignatius's sons and daughters had different competences and duties, but never ceased to underline that both their input was instrumental to the salvation of humanity, if only implicitly. At times, her accounts cross the gendered ecclesiastical boundaries, as she describes dreams in which she sees herself distributing food, characterized as coming from God and thereby equalled to the Eucharist. Such dreams seem to indicate that she definitely aspired for priestly dignity and privileges. Van Randenraedt specifically lamented the gendered boundaries: 'Alas, what can I do, if only I were a man.'[34] This implies that had she been born a man, she might have become a priest and would have been able to serve God better than as a woman.

Records of individual and collective religious practices illuminate how van Heilsbach and van Randenraedt with other spiritual virgins tried to break away from the gender-specific restrictions imposed on their activities by (in part self-inflicted) physical suffering. Here, the accounts of conscience show parallels to medieval *vitae* of holy women, eating what was considered uneatable, fasting to extremes, or inflicting corporal punishment upon themselves or even each other. Through suffering with their heavenly Bridegroom, both van Heilsbach and van Randenraedt confirmed their identity as His brides and experienced an actual union with Him, as they also did in the communion which they, unlike lay women and men, attempted to receive on a daily basis.[35]

Their accounts of conscience clearly reflect that spiritual virgins had a multiple identity with gender at its core, an identity which corresponded with the definition offered by the books of conduct for spiritual virgins. As *filiae devotae*, spiritual daughters, they were subordinate to their father confessors. However, as spiritual mothers they presided over other spiritual virgins and felt authorized as well to speak to other members of the laity about their religious life and practice. As brides of Christ they felt confirmed in their identity and invigorated by His power, which they sometimes used against His earthly deputies. They were convinced that they were endowed with divine grace which legitimized their spiritual leadership over others.

Conclusion: the paradox of submission and personal development *in religiosis*

Agnes van Heilsbach and Joanna van Randenraedt opted for a life as spiritual virgins because they were convinced that they could serve God and their fellow human beings better in the world than behind convent walls. Presumably, this motive was not exceptional among spiritual virgins in the Northern Netherlands. Naturally, some longed for the convent life which was no longer possible within the boundaries of the Dutch Republic after 1581. Others, however, aspired of their own accord to a more active religious lifestyle than the Church approved of for women. The changed status and appearance of the Catholic Church in the Northern Netherlands in part enabled them to realize this and to contribute to the preservation as well as the reform of their Church. In this respect, spiritual virgins were not the typical Dutch phenomenon they were made out to be in older, especially apologetic, historiography. In their apostolic goals and vocations they found their counterparts elsewhere in Europe, in the disciples of Mary Ward, the **Sisters** of the Visitation of Annecy or the Filles de la Charité. Their experiences and self-awareness were shaped by the Reformation and the Counter-Reformation, as they considered themselves as belonging to a threatened group of true believers with a specific responsibility to preserve Catholicism. In contrast to these groups, they did not aspire to institutional recognition, whereas the fragile status of the Catholic Church in the Northern Netherlands paradoxically ensured them some ecclesiastical leeway for an active religious life.

Religious insecurity in this region fostered close relationships between priests and core members of the faithful. This situation offered spiritually ambitious women the opportunity to forge alliances with priests who helped them craft an active religious existence. In the absence of a general rule for spiritual virgins, clerics attempted to determine the parameters of this lifestyle. These were reflected in specific books of conduct, which built on a longstanding tradition of praise of the sacred virginal state by the **Fathers of the Church**, but also mirrored the particular post-Tridentine spiritual program: the interiorization of faith in a systematic but personal pious regime, combined with an active, apostolic lifestyle devoted to charity.

These books elucidate that spiritual virgins could preserve their virtue (in the eyes of the public always a weak spot of unmarried or widowed women) by ensuring the religious character of their state in life. Moreover, various religious repertoires are presented in these sources that unequivocally testify to the worthiness of an uncloistered religious life. Obedience to male authority was a *conditio sine qua non* for this lifestyle, arranged and formalized in the relationship of confessor and penitent. This relationship was asymmetrical by definition, yet did not necessarily put the spiritual virgin at a structural disadvantage. It was up to a spiritual virgin to gather the necessary clerical support in order to safeguard a certain degree of autonomy.

The accounts of conscience of Agnes van Heilsbach and Joanna van Randenraedt illustrate that self-determination was best warranted by submission, not to earthly authority but to the supreme reign of God over their lives. In the daily association with their confessor, the combination of humility and concession proved to be an effective course of action. Like other uncloistered religious women, these women exemplify and personify the paradox of submission and personal development within the early-modern Catholic community: whereas the doctrinal authority of the Catholic Church allotted them a position subordinate to men and treated them as minors, they themselves took their faith as a foundation for life fulfilment, identity and activity. On the one hand, religion provided a frame of reference that encouraged women to submit to the social and cultural preconceptions regarding femininity, while on the other hand it provided women with the words and images suited to challenge these very notions on higher religious authority. As the books of conduct for spiritual virgins make clear, this language and imagery did not merely represent the jargon of endurance and obedience that was already partially imposed by prevailing notions about women. These devotional books also incited their intended female readership to action and contained examples of what the energy of religiously inspired women could bring about in the world and the Church. The writings of van Heilsbach and van Randenraedt indicate that some women were indeed susceptible to this kind of encouragement.

Notes

1. This article is based on my published dissertiation *Geestelijke maagden: Leven tussen klooster en wereld in Noord-Nederland gedurende de zeventiende eeuw* (Hilversum: Verloren, 1996).
2. For the use of marriage symbolism among the early Ursulines, see also G. Zarri, 'Ursula and Catherine: The Marriage of Virgins in the Sixteenth Century', in A. Matter and J. Coakley (eds), *Creative Women in Medieval and Early Modern Italy: A Religious and Artistic Renaissance* (Philadelphia: University of Pennsylvania Press, 1994), pp. 236–78.
3. Specific dates of birth and death of Hartman, Boede and Adolf are unknown as yet.
4. This chapel, also known under the name *Het Hart* (The heart), was preserved, restored and turned into a museum, currently known under the name *Ons' Lieve Heer op Solder* (Our Lord in the attic).
5. A. K. De Meijer, OSA, 'Augustinian *Filiae Spirituales* in Amsterdam during the Seventeenth Century', *Analecta Augustiniana*, LX (1997), pp. 49–80.
6. W. Simons, *Cities of Ladies: Beguine Communities in the Medieval Low Countries, 1200–1565* (Philadelphia: University of Philadelphia Press, 2001).
7. J. Spaans, 'Paragons of Piety: Representations of Priesthood in the *Lives* of the Haarlem Virgins', in W. Janse and T. Clemens (eds), *The Pastor Bonus, Dutch Review of Church History*, 83 (2003), pp. 235–46.
8. Spiritual virgins who joined the Third Order were counted among the secular tertiaries.
9. See B. Kaplan, 'Fictions of Privacy: House Chapels and the Spatial Accommodation of Religious Dissent in Early Modern Europe', *American Historical Review*, 107 (2002), pp. 1031–64.

10. C. Kooi, 'Paying off the Sheriff; Strategies of Catholic Toleration in Golden Age Holland', in R. Po-Chia Hsia and H. van Nierop (eds), *Calvinism and Religious Toleration in the Dutch Golden Age* (Cambridge: Cambridge University Press, 2002), pp. 87–101.

11. W. Frijhoff, 'The State, the Churches, Sociability, and Folk Belief in the Seventeenth-Century Dutch Republic', in J. D. Tracy and M. Ragnow (eds), *Religion and the Early Modern State: Views from China, Russia, and the West* (Cambridge: Cambridge University Press, 2004), pp. 80–97.

12. As discussed in Laurence Lux-Sterritt's contribution in this volume.

13. A. van der Zeijden, *Katholieke identiteit en historisch bewustzijn: W. J. F. Nuyens (1823–1894) en zijn 'nationale' geschiedschrijving* (Hilversum: Verloren, 2002), pp. 333–37.

14. Monteiro, *Geestelijke maagden*, pp. 15–18.

15. C. Parker, *Faith on the Margins: Catholics and Catholicism in the Dutch Golden Age* (Cambridge: Harvard University Press, 2008).

16. E. Theissing, *Over klopjes en kwezels* (Nijmegen: Dekker and Van de Vegt, 1935).

17. R. Liebowitz, 'Virgins in the Service of Christ: The Dispute over an Active Apostolate from Women during the Counter-Reformation', in R. Radford Ruether and E. McLaughlin (eds), *Women of Spirit: Female Leadership in the Jewish and Christian Traditions* (New York: Simon and Schuster, 1979), pp. 131–52.

18. *Geest en vlees in godsdienst en wetenschap: Opstellen over gezagsconflicten in de zeventiende eeuw* (The Hague: SDU, 1980); 'Le vergini devote nella Missione Olandese al tempo di Neercassel', in *Actes du Colloque sur le Jansénisme* (Rome: Publications Universitaires de Louvain/Éditions Nauwelaerts, 1977), pp. 187–203 ; 'Gender and Spirit, Pietas et Contemptum Mundi', in E. Schulte van Kessel (ed.) *Women and Men in Spiritual Culture: XIV–XVII Centuries* (The Hague: SDU 1986), pp. 47–68.

19. See also M. Derks, J. Eijt, M. Grever, and M. Monteiro, '*Res Novae*. Evoluties in de historische beeldvorming over katholieke vrouwen,' *Ex Tempore*, 11 (1992), pp.121–33.

20. A. Conrad, *Zwischen Kloster und Welt: Ursulinen and Jesuitinnen in der katholischen Reformbewegung des 16./17. Jahrhunderts* (Mainz: Von Zabern, 1991). See also L. Lux-Sterritt, *Redefining Female Religious Life: French Ursulines and English Ladies in Seventeenth-Century Catholicism* (Aldershot: Ashgate, 2005).

21. E. Rapley, *The Dévotes: Women and Church in Seventeenth-Century France* (Montreal: McGill Queen's University Press, 1990). See also M. De Vroede, '*Kwezels*' en '*zusters*': *De geestelijke dochters in de Zuidelijke Nederlanden*, 17de en 18de eeuw (Brussels: Koninklijke Academie voor Wetenschappen, Letteren en Schone Kunsten van België, 1994).

22. 'The Mysticism and Asceticism of Medieval Women: Some Comments on the Typologies of Max Weber and Ernst Troeltsch', in *Fragmentation and Redemption: Essays on Gender and the Human Body in Medieval Religion* (New York: Zone Books 1991), pp. 53–78.

23. L. Jacobi, SJ, *Der Spieghel der Maeghden, Die inde werelt de godvruchtigheyt met de suyverheyt paren, uyt-ghebeelt in twee H.H. Maeghden, te weten de H. Isaeblla van Vrankrijck* [originally authored by the Jesuit Nicolas Caussin] *en de H. Lydwina* [originally authored by the Franciscan Joannes Brugman] [...]. Antwerp: the widow of Jan Cnobbaert, 1657, 84 (in the original: *die ghedierten diemen seght eens-deels waetersche, eens-deels aerdsche gehedierten te zijn, die noch op d'aerde, noch inde Zee blijven*).

24. M. Monteiro, 'Paragons of Piety: Spiritual Virgins and their Private Devotion in the Northern Netherlands during the Seventeenth Century', in F. von Ingen and

C. Niekus Moore (eds), *Gebetsliteratur der frühen Neuzeit als Hausfrömmigkeit: Funktionen und Formen in Deutschland und den Niederlanden* (Wiesbaden: Harrosswitz Verlag, 2001), pp. 93–112 (*Wolfenbütteler Forschungen 92*). See also C. Niekus Moore, 'Erbauungsliteratuur als Gebrauchsliteratur für Frauen in 17. Jahrhundert: Leichenpredigten als Quelle weiblicher Lesegewohnheiten', in E. Bödeker and Gérald Chaix (eds), *Le livre religieux et ses pratiques/Der Umgang mit dem religiösen Buch* (Göttingen: Vandenhoeck & Ruprecht, 1991), pp. 291–315.

25. Monteiro, *Geestelijke maagden*, pp. 123–33.

26. In Dutch it appeared under the title *Op-rechte Af-beeldinghe van den maeghdelijkcken staet: betrocken op het leven van de Edele en godtvruchtige Sancia Carillo* [...], translated from the Spanish (1615) (Antwerp: the widow of Jan Cnobbaert, 1639).

27. H. Jedin, 'Religiöse Triebkräfte und geistiger Gehalt der katholischen Erneuerung', in E. Iserloh, H. Glazik and H. Jedin (eds), *Reformation, Katholische Reform und Gegenreformation. Handbuch für Kirchengeschichte IV* (Vienna: Herder, 1967), pp. 451–516. See also L. Châtellier, *L'Europe des dévots* (Paris: Flammarion, 1987).

28. F. J. M. Hoppenbrouwers, *Oefening in volmaaktheid: De zeventiende-eeuwse spiritualiteit in de Republiek* (The Hague: SDU 1996), p. 95.

29. Although no allusions are made to the tradition and discourse shaped since the sixteenth century by women like Angela Merici, the similarities in the argumentation are striking. See in this respect Querciolo Mazzonis's chapter in this volume.

30. *Kort Begryp des levens en der deughden van de weerighe Joanna van randenraedt geestelyke dochter onder de bestieringhe der Societeyt Iesu* (Antwerp: Michiel Cnoabbaert, 1690), and *Leven ende Deughden vande weerdighe Agnes van Heilsbagh gheestelycke dochter onder de bestieringhe der Societeyt Iesu* (Antwerp: Michiel Cnobbaert, 1691).

31. See also P. Ranft, 'A Key to Counter Reformation Women's Activism: The Confessor-Spiritual Director', *Journal of Feminist Studies in Religion*, 10 (1994), pp. 7–26; see also E. A. Macek, '"Ghostly Fathers" and their "Virtuous Daughters": The Role of Spiritual Direction in the Lives of Three Early Modern English Women', *Catholic Historical Review*, 90 (2004), pp. 213–35.

32. A. Weber, *Teresa of Avila and the Rhetoric of Femininity* (Princeton: Princeton University Press, 1990). See also the chapter of Elizabeth Rhodes on Teresa in this volume.

33. Cited in Monteiro, *Geestelijke maagden*, p. 263 (in the original: 'Ende mij docht dat men dingen die van Godt quaemen soe niet en mocht verachten').

34. *Ibid*, 322 (in the original: 'Maer helaes, wat kan ick doun, waer ick [maar] eenen man.')

35. These themes in their spirituality are also underlined in the visual culture connected to spiritual virgins. See E. Verheggen, *Beelden voor passie en hartstocht: Bid- en devotieprenten in de Noordelijke Nederlanden, 19de en 18de eeuw* (Zutphen: Walburg Pers, 2006).

8

'Martyrs of England! Standing on High!': Roman Catholic Women's Hymn-writing for the Re-invigoration of the Faith in England, 1850–1903[1]

Nancy Jiwon Cho

In the past three decades, several studies have demonstrated that hymn-writing in the nineteenth century was an accessible literary genre by which English women could inscribe their spiritual experience, publish their theology, raise awareness about their social concerns, and minister to their fellow Christians.[2] However, research on the development of English women's hymn-writing to date has focused on the works of Protestants and overlooked the contributions of Roman Catholics. This is perhaps not surprising in the context of the relatively late development in English Catholic hymnody (see below), which made it less visible than the longer traditions of the Protestants. Furthermore, for much of the nineteenth century – the golden age of hymn-singing in England[3] – Catholic hymnody did not fit into the Protestant model of congregational hymn-singing in church services. As Muir elucidates:

> Nineteenth-century vernacular Catholic hymnody did not evolve in the same way. In the first place it was driven out of Mass and the Office and largely confined to outdoor processions and extra-liturgical services. The latter had a strong devotional streak, which militated against active congregational participation. As a result, for a long time hymns were often the preserve of the choir and treated like anthems and motets. It was only from the late nineteenth century that stronger efforts were made to develop a tradition of congregational hymn singing.[4]

It has consequently been easy for **hymnologists** (who have often emerged from Protestant backgrounds) to disregard Catholic hymns from the larger body of English hymnody. As a result of these factors, no study to date has examined the emergence of Catholic women's hymn-writing in England during the second half of the nineteenth century. This essay aims to address these gaps in women's, literary and religious history by exploring the identities of the women writers, the subjects and messages of their hymns, their intentions in publishing and their differences from the Protestant tradition. In particular, it will follow Catholic women's participation in the re-conversion of England and re-invigoration of the English Catholic Church in the second half of the nineteenth century through the writing and publishing of didactic hymns.

Background: the late development of English Catholic hymnody

While vernacular congregational hymn-singing became popular in England among dissenters and some Anglicans from the eighteenth century, the English hymn did not enter into Catholic worship until the mid-decades of the nineteenth century. This was because, following the English Reformations and the establishment of the Church of England, legislation had been passed which placed restrictions on non-Anglicans. Catholics were particularly affected; Elizabeth I's 1559 Act of Supremacy explicitly stated that Catholics had to renounce allegiance to the Roman Catholic Church, which was understood as a foreign sovereign power; it thereby outlawed Catholicism in England. Under James I and Charles II, the Test Acts, a series of penal laws requiring civic officials to profess the Anglican faith, prohibited Catholics from holding positions such as judicial offices and serving as MPs. As Laurence Lux-Sterritt's essay about the early modern endeavours of Catholic women such as Mary Ward illustrates, the conditions of repression which existed between 1559 and the first Catholic Relief Act of 1778 made it difficult for Catholics to practise their faith on English soil; it was all the more problematic to sing openly about it. As Earle wrote in his essay on Roman Catholic Hymnody, 'In the stormy days of Elizabeth and James I, when the celebration of Divine Service according to the Roman Use exposed both priest and worshipper to the severest penalties, it was not to be expected that Roman Catholic Hymnody could possibly flourish.'[5] Thus, other than the emergence of a few hymns and carols,[6] little attention was given to hymnody by English Catholics in the seventeenth and eighteenth centuries.

After much agitation in the 1820s, particularly from the Irish led by Daniel O'Connell (1775–1847), the Catholic Emancipation Act was passed through parliament in April 1829.[7] This Act stated that Catholics could serve as MPs at Westminster, and hold judicial appointments in ecclesiastical courts and most public offices;[8] thus, civil restrictions were largely removed and Catholics enjoyed greater freedom for public worship. This led to the growth of vernacular Catholic hymnody, both through the writing of new hymns and the translation of a large deposit of Medieval Latin hymns which had been utilized by different religious Orders for the recitation of the Divine Office. The early leaders in the emergence of English Catholic hymnody, through translation and their own compositions, were male converts from the Anglican **Oxford Movement** who brought their love of hymn-singing and skills in hymn-writing with them to the Catholic Church. They included John Henry Newman (1801–1890), the principal contributor to *Lyra Apostolica* (1836) and the author of *Hymni Ecclesiae* (1838); Edward Caswall (1814–1878), author of *Lyra Catholica* (1849); and Frederick William Faber (1814–1863), whose first collection of hymns was also published in 1849.

The emergence of Catholic women's hymn-writing in England

With the gradual popularization of hymns in Catholic worship, women also came to make contributions to the development of an English Catholic hymnody. They achieved this through the writing of hymn texts,[9] mostly in the vernacular, which were then circulated via publication in English Catholic hymnals. For those with poetical talents and aspirations, hymn-writing offered a socially acceptable literary and religious practice for women. As Jay has noted, it was easier for English women writers to publish religious verse than prose during the nineteenth century:

> The manuscripts of notable women writers of the period leave us in no doubt that they indulged in theological speculation, but finding a public voice was harder. A late nineteenth-century survey book, *Religious Thought in the Nineteenth Century*, devoted only eight of its 396 pages to women's contributions. Macmillan was happy to publish Christina Rossetti's poetry but not so willing to put out her books of devotional, moral and **exegetical** reflection on biblical texts and Church offices.[10]

Hymn-writing was considered a 'ladylike' pursuit, as the title of Pitman's first appraisal of the tradition, *Lady Hymn Writers* (1892), demonstrates. The Victorians often differentiated between (forceful, masculine) 'poets' and (gentle, feminine) 'poetesses', and hymns seem to have been perceived as an especially apposite form of women's writing. The high purpose of hymn-writing (to express worship and glorify God) meant that the activity could not be dismissed as a trivial pastime. For serious-minded, religious women, it provided an accessible means by which to speak to the Church and engage with its mission in the world.

Catholic hymns for children

Early Catholic hymnals in England often did not attribute hymn-writers' names, making it difficult to calculate the number of female-authored works. However, a number of publications which do document authorship illustrate that the proportion of female contributors could be surprisingly high. One area in which women were visibly pioneers was hymn-writing for children, which was embraced as an innovative method of delivering moral and religious education. In all denominations, children's hymnody was considered an appropriate arena for women during the Victorian era owing to the common belief that an innate affinity existed between women and children; as Pitman surmised: 'Women – and especially women who were mothers – have excelled in the art of writing hymns for children. Somehow it needs mother-love to interpret divine love to the little ones.'[11] In the English Catholic context, there was another reason why hymns for infants were particularly suitable for women. As previously noted, pre-Vatican II hymns were 'largely composed for the Latin Tridentine liturgy'.[12] As the classical languages were normally omitted from female education, women were largely excluded from the writing of Latin hymns. However, it is evident that hymns for the education of children would be most fitting in the vernacular.

Formby and Lambert's *Catholic Hymns* was the first of a three-part collection entitled *First Series of Hymns and Songs for the Use of Catholic Schools, Families. Collection of Hymns for the use of Choirs and Congregations. Arranged in Order for the Chief Festivals, the Feasts of Saints etc, Throughout the Year* (1853). This work totalling 44 hymns included 14 by women – nine by 'C.M.C.' (Cecilia M. Caddell, 1814–1877), two attributed to 'M.L.' (actually Jane Eliza Leeson, 1808–1881), and three by Sister M.J. (dates unknown). Thus, strikingly nearly a third of this hymnal which was published only a few years after the famous male converts of the Oxford movement had started the process of writing English Roman Catholic hymns was female-authored. This is in sharp contrast to the proportion of women's works included in ordinary anthologies of verse for adults at mid-century; for example, F. T. Palgrave included only one female-authored work out of a total of 132 poems (under 1 per cent) in his Volume 4 (the nineteenth-century verse) of *The Golden Treasury of Songs and Lyrics* (1861).

The personal histories of women who wrote hymns are intriguing. *Catholic Hymns* indicate that they could have very different social and religious backgrounds. Caddell was descended from an old Catholic family through her father, Richard O'Farrel Caddell, of Harbourstown House, Balbriggan, County Meath, Ireland, and her mother, Paulina, was a daughter of Thomas Arthur, the second Viscount Southwell.[13] In contrast, Leeson, born in Wilford, Nottinghamshire, was a convert from the Anglican Church with a background in radical religion; she had been a member of a millenarian group called the 'Catholic Apostolic Church', established under the inspiration of the charismatic preaching of Edward Irving (1792–1834).[14] Despite social and class differences, however, Caddell's and Leeson's hymns shared the same didactic intention in their hymns for children: their works in *Catholic Hymns* promoted the ancient practices and traditions of the faith.

Perhaps in response to her long Catholic heritage, Caddell's hymns repeatedly displayed a wish to reassert the old practices of Catholic devotion, such as the veneration of Mary and the saints, and celebration of Catholic festivals. This intention is testified in her titles 'A child's hymn to the Blessed Virgin', 'St Aloysius' and 'Feast of the Immaculate Conception' and '**Litany** of the passion of Christ'. Caddell's hymns therefore document female concern with, and desire to participate in, the Victorian English Catholic Church's recovery and implementation of ancient Catholic practices. This belief in the importance of not only sustaining ancient Catholic practice but reclaiming it for new generations is also evident in Leeson's hymns.[15] For instance, her 'Victimae paschali laudes' ('Christ the Lord is risen to-day'), included in *Catholic Hymns*, was a translation of a Medieval Latin sequence.[16] As noted above, contemporary women were not usually educated in the classical languages. Leeson, therefore, stands out as a rare example of a woman participating in the Victorian Catholic Church's reclamation of Medieval offices and liturgy. Indeed, this may be a reason why this hymn was included in Catholic hymnals, as it did not discuss specifically Catholic subjects or practices:

1. Christ the Lord is risen to-day:
    Christians, haste your vows to pay:
    Offer ye your praises meet
    At the Paschal Victim's feet;
    For the sheep the Lamb hath bled,
    Sinless in the sinner's stead.
    Christ the Lord is ris'n on high;
    Now he lives, no more to die.[17]

As Richards has explained the 'conversion of England and the restoration of ancient glories' were two central themes of the English Catholic Church from the 1850s onwards.[18] For instance; Ambrose Phillips de Lisle asserted in a letter to the first Cardinal of Westminster, Nicholas P. S. Wiseman (1802–1865) in 1853:

> Nothing could more conduce [sic] towards the conversion of England than the establishment of a glorious solemn cathedral church in London, in which the Divine Office could be carried out with all conceivable glory and magnificence in a way worthy of England's past recollections, and in some degree commensurate with what so many holy servants of God bid us to hope for her future.[19]

While Leeson's translation did not re-establish the ancient Divine Office, its inclusion in *Catholic Hymns* represents another strategy by which one Catholic woman attempted to introduce children to the sentiments and rudiments of faith inscribed in the glorious Catholic past.

Such hymns for children were part of wider Catholic outreach work with the young attempting to ignite revivalism in Victorian Britain and Ireland. Although the spirit of revivalism prevailed in both Catholic and Protestant churches during the nineteenth century, Sharp has argued that the pioneers of large missions to children were Catholics.[20] For instance, John Joseph Furniss (1809–1865), who was one of the earliest members of the English Redemptorists, came to be known as 'the Father of Children's missions, which were almost unknown before his time' for his work conducting 73 missions in England and 11 in Ireland between 1855 to 1862.[21] At the same time, a growing number of 'active' conventual institutes in England devoted their energy to outreach work with poor children throughout the Victorian period. Walsh has highlighted the sharp increase in the number of 'active' institutes from 65 in 1857 to 605 in 1917.[22] Specifically, the children of Irish immigrant workers were identified as those in danger of losing any connection to the Catholic faith. As Sharp asserts:

> What inspired Furniss (and religious **sisters**) was the firm belief that children would be lost to the faith unless they were evangelised at an early age, and that religion was the only antidote to the appalling social and moral state of the cities of England and Ireland, where 'impurity is infiltrated through the eyes and ears of these children until it penetrates the very marrow of their bones'.[23]

As Muir has observed, urbanization prompted by industrialization also meant that, '[i]n effect, major urban churches gradually superceded rural aristocratic chapels as centres of music' throughout the nineteenth century.[24] As Catholic missionaries addressed the needs of the urban poor, the popular practice of hymn-singing became identified as a simple oral and aural instrument by which Catholic philanthropic workers attempted to connect with and educate children.

Easy Hymns and Sacred Songs, for Young Children (1855), published by the self-consciously Catholic publisher Burns and Lambert in London, was a hymnal for infants composed almost entirely of works by women religious. As the preface explained, it contained original hymns written by **women religious** from three convents:

> The little volume owes a large proportion of its contents to the Convent of the Holy Child, St Leonard's on the Sea, Hastings; some pretty songs to the Convent of Sisters of Mercy, Kinsale; besides several new contributions from Sister M.J. and Sister Agnes, of the Convent of Charleville.[25]

This is an unexpected combination of communities: the Convent of the Holy Child only operated in England at this point, while the Sisters of Mercy at Kinsale; and Charleville were clearly in Ireland. However, at mid-century, all these congregations were working actively with children and contributing to the developing education systems of Britain and Ireland.[26] It is difficult to determine whether these particular convents set out to specialize in hymn-writing as a new method of ministering to or capturing the imaginations of children. However, some background information about the congregations helps explain what they hoped to achieve through their hymns.

The Convent of the Holy Child Jesus at St Leonards was founded in 1848 by Cornelia Augusta Peacock Connelly (1809–1879), an American convert from the Episcopalian Church.[27] This convent was, for more than 30 years, the motherhouse of the Society of the Holy Child Jesus (hereafter SHCJ), a religious congregation established with the approbation of Gregory XVI. A short history of the St Leonard's convent explains that the foundation was made:

> at the request of Bishop, later Cardinal, Wiseman. In his efforts for the conversion of England, this prelate had realized the paramount importance of providing educational facilities on national lines for the daughters of the old English Catholic families, as well as for those of the possibly more cultured converts won over to the Church during the Oxford Movement.[28]

For the educated middle and upper-class women religious engaged in the special work of this order, the practice of hymn-writing may have appeared a genteel and accomplished means by which to undertake their mission. It is easy to imagine that hymn-writing would have been deemed a suitable activity for both 'daughters of the old English Catholic families' (we remember Caddell), and the 'cultured converts' of the Oxford Movement. The latter in particular would have been able to draw from their knowledge of Anglican hymnody; the Catholic hymns of

Newman, Faber and Caswall; and **Anglo-Catholic** women's hymn-writing such as Frances Mary Yonge's *A Child's Christian Year* (1841) and Cecil Frances Alexander's extremely successful *Hymns for Little Children* (1848).[29]

One such 'cultured convert' hymn-writer of the SHJC was Sister M.B. who contributed six hymns to *Easy Hymns*. Sister (later Mother) Maria Joseph Buckle (born Elizabeth Buckle, 1822–1902) was one of Connelly's first followers; she entered into the SHCJ in 1848 and was **professed** in 1850. She was from a wealthy Gloucestershire family which had initially embraced Anglo-Catholicism and then converted to Rome with Newman. As an entry in the handwritten book of early necrologies of the SHCJ records:

> Dear Mother Maria Joseph became a Catholic at the time of the **Tractarian** Movement. (She used to tell us how well she recalled the scene when her father an Oxford M.A. came home one day strangely agitated & exclaimed 'Newman has gone over to Rome –' They all shortly afterwards had the same happiness.) [...] Our dear Mth Maria Joseph was highly gifted & a great linguist so was a valuable aid to Our Mother **Foundress** in the establishment of the Training College at St Leonards.[30]

Her hymns included in *Easy Hymns*, such as 'Hymn to the Infant Jesus', 'Holy Joseph, let me sing (Infant's Hymn to St Joseph)' and 'I am a little Catholic', aimed to teach children about Catholic devotional practices and beliefs. Her 'I am a little Catholic' is notable for teaching about the importance of Rome as the seat of the faith, and its hopes for the re-conversion of England:

1. I am a little Catholic,
    And Christian is my name,
 And I believe the holy Church
    In every age the same.

2. The holy ancient Roman Church,
    Enduring firmly still,
 Where Christ her king hath planted her
    Upon St Peter's Hill.

3. Jerusalem she is above,
    Our city and our home;
 But after that same pattern is
    The holy city Rome.

4. Time writes no wrinkle on thy brow,
    For thou art ever young;
 Hail Rome, eternal citadel,
    From whence our Faith has sprung.

5. Once England was the fairest gem
    In all St Peter's Crown
 Oh, may be soon there shine again,
    As once of yore it shone.

Victorian children often memorized hymns as part of their religious education and this hymn, which sounds like a Romanizing creed – 'I believe the
holy Church,/In every age the same' – may have been intended for this use.
Certainly, the hymn was an appealing instructional tool precisely because its
simple **metre** and rhyming patterns made it easier to commit to memory than
prose.

Women's real influence through this ministry is uncertain. Arguably, hymn-
writing for children offered women a powerless audience for their didacticism;
indeed, the genre may have been deemed 'acceptable' for this very reason.
Concomitantly, as D. H. Lawrence reflected in his essay 'Hymns in a Man's
Life' (1928):

> Nothing is more difficult than to determine what a child takes in, and does not
> take in, of its environment and teaching. This fact is brought home to me by the
> hymns which I learned as a child, and never forgot. They mean to me almost more
> than the finest poetry, and they have for me a more permanent value, somehow
> or other.[31]

Simple hymns learnt in youth could remain powerfully with the adult
throughout his or her life.

Catholic Hymns and *Easy Hymns* demonstrate that the English hymn offered,
for members of the recently liberated English Catholic Church, a vernacular
vehicle by which to offer Catholic religious instruction and cultivate the growth
of the hitherto suppressed faith.[32] It is also worth noting that all of the writers
of hymns for children discussed were unmarried and nulliparous. This partially
reflects the demographics of the time: the 1851 census had established, to the
shock of some social commentators, that 'There were in *England and Wales*, in
1851, 1,248,000 women [...] between the ages of twenty and forty years, who
were unmarried, out of a total number of less than 3,000,000.'[33] For single
women (particularly those like Caddell and Leeson who were not members
of religious communities which worked directly with children), hymn-writing
may have offered a means of enacting a motherly role despite lacking biologi-
cal maternity. This poignant possibility would correlate with the patterns of
Protestant women's hymn-writing, which, as I have argued elsewhere, offered
to some unmarried women a meaningful and socially useful alternative vocation
to the traditional roles of wife and mother.[34]

Marian hymns and hymns about female saints

The didactic purpose of hymns, particularly to enforce particular doctrinal ideas,
may be further explored in the Marian hymns of the period. While the history of
devotion to the Virgin extends to the early centuries of Christianity, the nature
of Mary's distinguished status was a particularly pertinent subject for nineteenth-century Catholics, especially when Pope Pius IX made the Immaculate
Conception Roman Catholic dogma in 1854. This meant that it became
dogma for Catholics to believe that Mary possessed sanctifying grace from
the moment of her conception, was born without original sin, and remained

sinless throughout her life. This tenet was enforced throughout the second half of the nineteenth century; in England, Marian devotion was encouraged by the first Cardinal of Westminster, Nicholas Wiseman, who saw greater devotion to the Virgin Mary as a priority of the Roman Church in England.[35] By the later decades of the nineteenth century, catechisms emphasized the significance of Mary with questions relating to the importance of the Hail Mary and her sacred position as Mother of Christ.[36] Thus, a key doctrine for Victorian Catholic women hymn-writers to explore and expound was the special status of Mary in the faith. That Mary became an increasingly important devotional subject – perhaps especially for women – is indicated by the fact, as noted by Muir, that while Edward Caswall's *Lyra Catholica* (1849) included only 35 hymns about or directed to Mary out of a total of 197 (18 per cent), and Faber's *Jesus and Mary. Or, Catholic Hymns* (1849) contained six Marian hymns out of 63 works (9.5 per cent), *Convent Hymns and Music Used by the Sisters of Notre Dame* (1891) contained 58 out of 137 texts (42 per cent) about Mary.[37]

One celebrated writer of Marian verse was Adelaide Anne Procter (1825–1864). Procter was a widely admired writer; she was, under the pseudonym Mary Berwick, the most published poet of Dickens's periodicals.[38] She converted in 1851, and many of her subsequent writings emerged out of her Catholic faith. Several of her poems came to be used as hymns in the second half of the nineteenth century; as a consequence, she was the only woman to be discussed in some detail in Earle's essay on 'Roman Catholic Hymnody' in Julian's *Dictionary of Hymnology* (1907).[39] Her 'The names of Our Lady' offered some history of Mary from the Bible and promoted supplication to her:

1. Around thy starry crown are wreathed
    So many names divine:
    Which is the dearest to my heart,
    And the most worthy thine?

2. Mary, the name that Gabriel spoke
    The name that conquers hell;
    Mary, the name that through high heaven
    The angels love so well.[40]

As a Marian hymn, this work is immediately recognizable as being Catholic; hymns directed to Mary would have been controversial in most Protestant circles except Anglo-Catholic ones during the nineteenth century. Herringer identifies the period 1830 to 1885 as one in which Mary was a particularly polemic figure; when John Keble (1792–1866), the eminent Anglo-Catholic priest and poet wished to include a poem about the Virgin, 'Mother out of sight', in his second book of poems, *Lyra Innocentium* (1844), he was met with grave objections from friends who feared he was near conversion to Roman Catholicism.[41] Even in 1906, when the Anglican *English Hymnal* included a few Anglo-Catholic hymns to Mary, so much controversy was roused with anti-Catholic clerics refusing to use the collection that an abridged edition was produced in 1907. Thus, Procter's hymn may be read as a bold declaration of her Catholic identity. At the same time, it championed and spread doctrinal belief in Mary's special position.

While Marian devotion was by no means a practice confined to women, the tradition offered a poignant and different way by which Catholic women could direct their worship and supplication. Unlike in the Protestant tradition, where celebrations of Mary could quickly rouse suspicion of idolatry, Catholicism offered a powerful female exemplar of the feminine divine, as has been reflected in numerous prayers, songs, hymns, paintings and statues throughout history. Mary was envisaged as the personification of maternal mercy; although she was originally considered a mediator to her son, her role evolved with the centuries so that she came to be a kind of superhuman intercessor, able to influence her heavenly son and obtain almost anything she requested. Procter's hymn thus reminds us that Catholic intercession could operate differently from Protestant prayer, allowing for female (maternal) power as well as masculine (paternal) authority. As a fully human figure, Mary could be deemed more sympathetic to human cares, and capable of greater understanding than the divine Father, Son or Holy Ghost; as Küng has observed, the Madonna was seen as 'the helper particularly of ordinary people, the oppressed, the anxious, the marginalized'.[42]

For Procter, who was a women's activist involved in the foundation of the *English Woman's Journal* in 1858 and the Society for the Promotion of the Employment of Women in 1859,[43] the figure of Mary may also have appealed as a female devotional subject offering the possibilities of a more gynocentric spirituality. As Yeo has argued, Catholicism was attractive to many Victorian feminists, even Protestants and atheists, throughout the Victorian period because of 'its resources for feminising divinity, [and] its icons offering role models to single women'.[44] The privileging of Mary in Procter's hymns reflected contemporary feminist ideas as discussed by Yeo:

> Both [Anna] Jameson [1794–1860] and [Frances Power] Cobbe [1822–1904] indicated their desire to modify a Protestantism which had too excessively masculinised its gods. For them, as for many religious feminists now, this single-gendered godhead […] constricted the development of real women. [… They] insisted on restoring a feminine side to divinity which would, as a corollary, upgrade human femininity which they saw as nurturant tenderess.[45]

Certainly Procter's hymn exalts Mary above the traditional interpretations of Virgin, Mediatrix and New Eve by intimating that she was both the primary and ultimate source of heavenly solace:

3. Mary – our comfort and our hope.
    Oh, may that word be given
    To be the last we sigh on earth –
    The first we breathe in heaven.[46]

With no mention of God in this hymn, only a meditation on the exceptionality of Mary as one whose name 'conquers hell' and the 'angels love so well', Procter could be accused of Mariolatry and having raised the Virgin to a competing position as Goddess against the male-identified God of the Christian faith. Procter's hymn may thus be considered a devotional work containing a consciously feminist statement about the importance of women in Christian society, and articulating the possibilities of the feminine divine. Given Procter's association with Victorian feminist groups, it seems possible that her Marian hymn deliberately sought to encourage thinking singers and readers to recall the significant and valued roles that women have held in the history of Christianity. Her hymn would thus have been instructional on more than one level, teaching about the Virgin Mary's blessedness and promoting devotion to her, but also making feminist Christian commentary by promoting positive ways of thinking about the place of women in the Church.[47]

Indeed, Catholicism appealed to Victorian women not only because of the high position of Mary but also because of its celebration of exemplary women as saints. In the social context of the high proportion of single women in the English population at mid-century, these often-virgin women saints offered inspiring role models of holy devotion and selfless service for some unmarried religious women. Indeed, for Catholic women, hymn-writing could even be a means of honouring modern heroines; for instance, a hymn celebrating the quiet but influential life of Saint Thérèse of Lisieux (1873–1897) was written, shortly after her canonization in 1925, by a **Carmelite nun**:

3. Hidden by Carmel's cloister-wall,
    But e'en more 'hid with Christ in God'
    Love's victim, who, in giving all,
    Her 'Little Way' unswerving trod.
    No earthly cloud e'er came between
    Teresa and her only Love,
    While all unnoticed and unseen
    She lived as Angels live above.

4. And still her prayers make sick men whole,
    To anguished minds bring peace and rest,
    More wondrous still, those healed in soul
    By thousands rise and call her blest.
    Teresa of the Child Divine,
    Styled 'Saint' by Holy Church's power,
    The sacred aureole is thine –
    But still, thou'rt Jesus 'Little Flow'r.'[48]

Despite being a twentieth-century production, this hymn reminds us that, in contrast to the masculine-centred, hetero-erotic tones of Protestant women's hymns directed to Jesus as the lover,[49] hymns directed to female saints (including Mary) by Catholic women could seek to enable a powerful female-centred religious fellowship.

English Catholic patriotism

The hymns hitherto discussed in this essay attempted to teach about the differences of Catholicism from mainstream English (Protestant) religion such as the special place of Rome and belief in the heavenly power of Mary. However, with the growth of the British Empire throughout the nineteenth century, the English Catholics were keen to convey their own sense of patriotic pride. As Richards states:

> The period from Queen Victoria's Golden Jubilee to the aftermath of the Great War, from the heyday of imperialism to its nostalgic survival, strengthened by military victory, inevitably influenced the frame of mind in which Catholics undertook their church building, ordered their ceremonial and even uttered their prayers.[50]

That this patriotism penetrated English Catholic hymnody is evidenced in the works of Sister Mary Xavier (Sybil Farish Partridge, 1865–1917), a woman religious teacher of the congregation of the Sisters of Notre Dame de Namur (hereafter SND) at Liverpool. Her *'In Hymnis et Canticis': Verses Sacred and Profane* (1903) was dedicated 'To the former students of the Liverpool Training College for whom most of these verses were written in memory of many happy years of work amongst them'.[51] This statement, in conjunction with the fact that at least one of her hymns, 'Martyrs of England! standing on high!' was published in the SND's first hymn book *Convent Hymns and Music as used by the Pupils of the Sisters of Notre Dame, Liverpool* (1891), indicates that most of her poetical works were written in the nineteenth century.

Although several of her hymns became popular,[52] the only one directly attributed to her, rather than to the 'SND', was 'Martyrs of England!', which was most frequently accredited to 'S.M.X.' This long hymn, comprised of seven eight-line verses interspersed with variations of a rousing chorus, enlisted the help of the English martyrs to claim England back for Roman Catholicism:

First Chorus

> Martyrs of England! standing on high.
> Warrior-band of the Great White Throne,
> Martyrs of England! hark to our cry:
> Pray for the country you called your own.

> 1. Not as strangers of far-off land;
>   Not as heroes of long ago –
>   Our English speech ye can understand;
>   Our cities, and hills, and fields ye know
>   Nighest to us of the white-robed host;
>   Bound to us as our kith and kin;
>   Get us the love that counts no cost,
>   That knows no fear but the fear of sin.[53]

This hymn follows the example of Faber's 'Faith of our fathers' (1849), 'one of the most popular – and notorious – hymns of the pre-Vatican II era'.[54] This hymn also harked back to the sixteenth and seventeenth-century Catholic martyrs and, as Muir observes, expressed 'a determination to recover losses and dethrone the Anglican Church as the dominant denomination through conversions':[55]

1. Faith of our fathers, living still,
    In spite of dungeon, fire and sword;
    O how our hearts beat high with joy
    Whenever we hear that glorious Word!

    Faith of our fathers, holy faith!
    We will be true to thee till death.

2. Faith of our fathers, we will strive
    To win all nations unto Thee;
    And through the truth that comes from God,
    We all shall then be truly free.
    [...]

3. Faith of our fathers, Mary's prayers
    Shall win our country back to Thee;
    And through the truth that comes from God,
    England shall then indeed be free.[56]

In contrast to Buckle's 'I am a little Catholic' and Wiseman's 'Full in the panting heart of Rome', Partridge's late Victorian work narrated an attachment to England rather than to Rome: 'Our English speech ye can understand/Our cities, and hills, and fields ye know.' Partridge asserted that English Catholics needed to remember their heritage:

2. Many, alas! your blood forget;
    Many your combat do not know.
    We, your children, will pay the debt
    Our thankless country to you doth owe.
    Few are the shrines o'er your scattered dust;
    Grateful hearts are your living fane,
    Your incense our love, and pray'r, and trust,
    Till England honour her Saints again.[57]

Thus, at the turn of the nineteenth century – many decades after the Catholic Emancipation Act – when English Catholics could have forgotten or been unaware of the history of Catholic repression in England, Partridge was teaching her students not to forget the past.

Partridge attempted this several times in *In Hymnis et Canticis*, twice in relation to specific martyrdoms: 'To Venerable Margaret Clitheroe (Martyr)' and 'To the Venerable William Carter, Printer, Martyred 1583'. These works recalled graphic details of the martyrs' persecutions; for instance, Clitheroe's gruesome death is recalled to emphasize the moral fortitude of this remarkable English Catholic woman who died for the faith:

9. Lying with thine arms extended
        Like thy Master crucified,
    Dying for the love of Jesus

      On the day when Jesus died;
  If the stones pressed heavy on thee,
      Other weight pressed stronger yet,
  Love of Margaret for Jesus,
      Jesus' love for Margaret.

10.   As thy mangled body lieth
        Crushed beneath that oaken door,
    Through that door thy soul is passing
        To the bright and distant shore.
    In Christ's diadem of glory
        As a jewel thou art set,
    Pearl of England, pearl of Jesus,
        Blissful Martyr Margaret! (pp. 85–6)

As Partridge also wrote a hymn about Carter, 'To Venerable Margaret Clitheroe (Martyr)' seems to indicate a desire to generally promote remembrance and appreciation of heroic Catholics in English history. However, when this work is compared with contemporary hymns by Protestant women, it is rendered extraordinary because there were no comparable works celebrating modern women in the Protestant tradition. This suggests that the ends of hymnody were somewhat different for Protestants and Catholics in the nineteenth century. Protestant hymnody did not aim to provide a medium to instruct about its history; instead, its primary purpose was to praise and worship (a male-identified) God. As a result, in the Catholic tradition, women could honour their heroines in a way that Protestant women hymn-writers rarely could. In contrast, in the Evangelical tradition at this time, hymns were devotional works of internal faith in keeping with the influential theology of the contemplative **Holiness Movement**; as British Protestants' history of religious practice had been so different, they evidently did not feel the need to defend and remember their heritage in the way that Catholics did.[58]

English Catholics in the Victorian era consciously sought to develop a distinctive hymnody which upheld and promoted their particular beliefs and faith practices. As verse-writing was considered an acceptable feminine activity during the nineteenth century, the emergence of an English Catholic hymnody provided welcome opportunities for willing women to participate in this undertaking. During a time when opportunities for women's work in the public sphere were still limited, the vernacular hymn provided an accessible mode by which women of the faith – lay and in religious Institutes – could participate in the English Catholic Church's drive for renewal and revival, demonstrate their engagement with contemporary societal concerns, and prove their value to wider society. While many published hymns by women could be deemed defensive – guarding the established (conservative) tenets of faith (for instance, their hymnody for children) – sometimes, personal agendas could also stimulate more radical thinking which contained the potential to affect cultural transformation (as in the case of Procter's Marian hymn with its feminist subtext). In the period 1850–1903 then, in England, hymn-writing developed into a potent instrument by which Catholic women could minister to the poor, young and helpless; contribute to the development of an indigenous Catholic identity; widen their opportunities for service in the Church; and publicly vocalize their commitment to the once suppressed faith.

Notes

1. I would like to thank J. R.Watson for his suggestions; Clare Walsh, the Archivist of the British Province Sisters of Notre Dame de Namur, Liverpool, and Sister Helen Forshaw, archivist of European Province Archives of the Society of the Holy Child Jesus, Oxford, for their kind assistance; and the SND and SHCJ for their permissions to reproduce their hymns.
2. See M. Maison, '"Thine, Only Thine!" Women Hymn Writers in Britain, 1760–1835', in G. Malmgreen (ed.), *Religion in the Lives of English Women, 1760–1930* (London and Sydney: Croom Helm, 1986), pp. 11–40; I. Bradley, *Abide with Me: The World of Victorian Hymns* (London: SCM, 1997); J. R. Watson, *The English Hymn: A Critical and Literary History* (Oxford: Clarendon, 1997); N. J. Cho, '"The Ministry of Song": Unmarried British Women's Hymn Writing, 1760–1936' (unpublished doctoral thesis, Durham University, 2007); and P. R. Backscheider, 'Hymns, Narratives, and Innovations in Women's Religious Poetry', in *Eighteenth-Century Women Poets and Their Poetry: Inventing Agency, Inventing Genre* (Baltimore: Johns Hopkins University, 2006), Bradley, *Abide with Me* pp. 123–74.
3. During the nineteenth century, hymns were everywhere: Bradley writes that they appeared 'on postcards and tombstones, on framed posters to be hung at home and in school reading books. Their tunes were played by brass organs and barrel organs and formed the largest single category of subject matter for pianola rolls,' *Abide with Me* pp. xiii–xiv.
4. See T. E. Muir, *Roman Catholic Church Music in England, 1791–1914: A Handmaid of Liturgy?* (Aldershot: Ashgate, 2008), pp. 3, 12.
5. J. C. Earle, 'Roman Catholic Hymnody', in J. Julian (ed.), *A Dictionary of Hymnology*, 2nd edition (London: John Murray, 1907), p. 973.
6. Such as 'Jerusalem, my happy home', and the 'Adeste Fideles'. See Earle for further information.
7. Penal laws discriminating against Catholics had also been enforced in Ireland where about 80 per cent of the population was Catholic.
8. For instance, the offices of Monarch, Regent, Lord Chancellor and Lord Lieutenant of Ireland were still prohibited.
9. Although the verses were often written without specific melodies in mind, because they were characteristically written in widely used metres, they could be sung to any number of appropriate tunes.
10. E. Jay, 'Women Writers and Religion: "A Self Worth Saving, a Duty Worth Doing and a Voice Worth Raising"', in J. Shattock (ed.), *Women and Literature in Britain, 1800–1900*, p. 256. For more on Rossetti see J. Marsh, *Christina Rossetti: A Literary Biography* (London: Pimlico, 1994), pp. 267–69 and pp. 450–54; Jay, 'Women Writers and Religion', pp. 270–71.
11. E. R. Pitman, *Lady Hymn Writers* (London: T. Nelson and Son, 1892).
12. Muir, *Roman Catholic Church Music*, p. 3.
13. Despite being an invalid, or perhaps because of the reflective time it rendered her, Caddell composed a substantial amount of verse and prose (including religious and historical fiction, and contributions to periodicals, including *The Irish Monthly*), which were written from a Catholic point of view.

14. Insufficient information has been recovered about Sister M. J. to compare her personal background.

15. Although we do not know when she started the practice, publications show that she was engaged in hymn-writing by her thirties. Her works were first published in *Infant Hymnings* (date unknown), which was later incorporated into her most successful publication, *Hymns and Scenes from Childhood: Or, a Sponsor's Gift* (1842). She also published religious books for children, including *The Christian Child's Book* (1848) and *Songs of Christian Chivalry* (1848).

16. Some of Leeson's other hymns were also often published in the children's sections of hymnals in the twentieth century; these include 'A Little Child May Know' and 'Gracious Saviour, Gentle Shepherd'.

17. *The Hymn Book: Compiled and Prescribed by the Catholic Hierarchy* (London: Burns and Oates, 1911), p. 42.

18. M. Richards, 'Prelude: 1890s to 1920', in J. D. Crichton, H. E. Winstone and J. R. Ainslie (eds), *English Catholic Worship: Liturgical Renewal in England since 1900* (London: Geoffrey Chapman, 1979), p. 2.

19. Quoted in W. de l'Hôpital, *Westminster Cathedral and its Architect*, 2 vols (London: Hutchinson and Co, 1919), Vol. 1, p. 8. Quoted in Richards, 'Prelude: 1890s to 1920', p. 2.

20. J. Sharp, 'Juvenile Holiness: Catholic Revivalism among Children in Victorian Britain', *Journal of Ecclesiastical History*, 35 (1984), p. 221.

21. *Ibid.*, Quotation from T. Livius, *Father Furniss and his Work for Children* (London: 1896), pp. 173–81.

22. During the same period contemplative orders only increased from 14 to 45. B. Walsh, *Roman Catholic Nuns in England and Wales, 1800–1937* (Dublin: Irish Academic Press, 2002), p. 177.

23. Sharp, 'Juvenile Holiness', p. 222. Quotation from J. Furniss, *The Sunday School* (Dublin: n.d.), p. 6.

24. Muir, *Roman Catholic Church Music*, p. 22.

25. Preface: *Easy Hymns and Sacred Songs, for Young Children*, large edition (Burns & Lambert: London, c. 1855), p. 32.

26. See M. Peckham Magray, *The Transforming Power of the Nuns: Women, Religion, and Cultural Change in Ireland, 1750–1900* (Oxford: Oxford University Press, 1998).

27. For more on Connelly, see J. A. Lancaster, *Cornelia Connelly and her Interpreters* (Oxford: Way Books, 2004).

28. *The Convent of the Holy Child Jesus, St Leonards-on-Sea: Its History, Development and Present-day Activities* (Gloucester: The British Publishing Co., 1936), p. 7.

29. This work included the still popular hymns 'All Things Bright and Beautiful', 'Once in Royal David's City', and 'There is a Green Hill Far Away'.

30. European Province Archives, SHCJ, Oxford: Handwritten Book of Early Necrologies, p. 68.

31. D. H. Lawrence, 'Hymns in a Man's Life', in A. Beal (ed.), *Selected Literary Criticism* (London: William Heinemann, 1956), p. 6.

32. Both these hymnals were published by Burns and Lambert, a firm which disseminated works that nurtured and informed about the Roman Catholic faith, further indicating that these women's hymns were written for the revival of English Catholicism.

33. W. Rathbone Greg, 'Why Are Women Redundant?', *National Review*, 15 (1862), p. 441.

34. This was a central argument of my doctoral thesis, '"The Ministry of Song"'.

35. E. Norman, *The English Catholic Church in the Nineteenth Century* (Oxford: Clarendon Press, 1985), p. 146.

36. See M. Heimann, *Catholic Devotion in Victorian Britain* (New York: Clarendon Press, 1995), p. 113.

37. T. E. Muir, '"Full in the Panting Heart of Rome": Roman Catholic Church Music in England: 1850–1962', 2 vols (unpublished doctoral thesis, University of Durham, 2004), Vol. 1, p. 285.

38. Seventy-three of her poems were published in *Household Words* and seven in *All the Year Round*.

39. Earle, 'Roman Catholic Hymnody', p. 975.

40. A. A. Procter, 'The Names of Our Lady', in *The Complete Works* (London: George Bell and Sons, 1905), pp. 385–88. This abridged version, comprising verses 2, 16 and 17 of the longer original text, is included in the *AMDG* [*Ad Maiorem Dei Gloriam*] *Cantionale,* compiled by J. Driscoll (London: The Manresa Press, 1947), p. 450. *Ad Maiorem Dei Gloriam* is the motto of the Society of Jesus (Jesuits). It means 'For the greater glory of God' and is thought to have been conceived by the founder of the order, Saint Ignatius of Loyola.

41. See C. Englehardt Herringer, *Victorians and the Virgin Mary: Religion and Gender in England, 1830–85* (Manchester: Manchester University Press, 2008), pp. 1–2.

42. H. Küng, *Women in Christianity* (London: Continuum, 2001), p. 55.

43. See G. Gill, 'Adelaide Anne Procter', in *Oxford Dictionary of National Biography*.

44. E. Janes Yeo, 'Protestant feminists and Catholic saints in Victorian Britain', in E. Janes Yeo (ed.), *Radical Femininity: Women's Self-Representation in the Public Sphere* (Manchester: Manchester University Press, 1998), p. 127.

45. *Ibid.*, p. 129.

46. Procter, *AMDG, Cantionale*, p. 450.

47. Several studies on the role of the Virgin Mary in Catholic cultures have shown that Marian devotion could enable girls and women to enter the public sphere; for instance, by participating in Marian festivals or by testifying to apparitions of the Madonna. See D. Blackbourn, *Marpingen: Apparitions of the Virgin Mary in Nineteenth-Century Germany* (New York: Alfred Knopf, 1994); R. Orsi, *The Madonna of 115th Street: Faith and Community in Italian Harlem, 1880–1950* (New Haven, CT, Yale University Press, 1985); and S. Zimdars-Swartz, *Encountering Mary: From LaSalette to Medjugorge* (Princeton: Princeton University Press, 1991).

48. *A Daily Hymn Book: Containing 384 English and Latin Hymns. With a preface by* [...] *Cardinal Bourne* (London: Burns, Oates and Washbourne, 1932), pp. 421–22.

49. Frances Ridley Havergal (1836–1879), an Anglican who was one of the most successful Victorian woman hymn-writers, expressed her dedication to Jesus in terms of heterosexual desire in many of her hymns, including 'I could not do without Thee', 'Jesus, Master, whose I am' and 'Master, Say on!': *The Poetical Works of Frances Ridley Havergal* (London: James Nisbet, 1880).

50. Richards, 'Prelude: 1890s to 1920,' p. 1.

51. Preface: [Sybil Farish Partridge] A Sister of Notre Dame (SMX), '*In Hymnis et Canticis*': *Verses Sacred and Profane* (London: Kegan Paul, Trench, Trübner and Co., 1903).

52. *The Notre Dame Hymn Book* (1905) includes her 'O King and Lord, who dwellest on the Altar', 'Lord of glory/wondrous story', 'How to praise Thee, O Mary we know not' and 'Peal, ye bells, on the summer air'; while *The Hymn Book. Compiled and Prescribed by the Catholic Hierarchy* (1911) contains 'Martyrs of England' and 'Lord, for Tomorrow and its Needs'; and *The Westminster Hymnal: The*

Only Collection Authorized by the Hierarchy of England and Wales (1912), which absorbed *The Hymn Book*, further added 'Little King, so Fair and Sweet'.

53. Partridge, *'In Hymnis et Canticis'*, p. 94.
54. Muir, *Roman Catholic Church Music*, p. 15.
55. *Ibid.*, pp. 15, 18.
56. F. W. Faber, *Jesus and Mary: Or, Catholic Hymns* (London: James Burns, 1849), pp. 133–34.
57. Partridge, *'In Hymnis et Canticis'*, pp. 94–95.
58. For more on the Holiness Movement, see Chapter 5 of D. W. Bebbington's *Evangelicalism in Modern Britain: A History from the 1730s to 1980s* (London: Unwin Hyman 1989). For instance, F. R. Havergal's 'Take my Life, and Let it be' (1874) and 'Like a River Glorious' (1876) are meditative hymns of internal faith offering devotion to God.

9

Expressions of Self-Surrender in Nineteenth-Century France: The Case of Thérèse Couderc (1805–1885)

Kate Stogdon

Thérèse Couderc, co-founder of the Congregation of Our Lady of the Retreat in the Cenacle, was instrumental in initiating new forms of spiritual ministry for Roman Catholic women in nineteenth-century France. This was made possible by the resurgence of female congregations in the context of a fragmented political, social and religious landscape. While most of these religious **sisters** ministered in educational and social fields, the Sisters of the Cenacle specialized in the giving of spiritual retreats according to the Ignatian method. However, despite her contribution to this pioneering work, Couderc seemed to withdraw into a life of increasing invisibility and was noted in particular for her great humility (cited as one of the central reasons for her canonization in 1970). This representation of her as *une grande humble* has been undergirded by her own writings as well as the assessments made about her by contemporaries and subsequent interpreters.

This essay examines Couderc's language and practice of self-surrender, the influences that informed it and the context in which she lived it out. It will highlight the important role played in the sisters' spiritual formation by the seventeenth-century French School of spirituality and by the sixteenth-century *Spiritual Exercises* of Ignatius of Loyola. It is here that a productive tension between surrender understood as self-abnegation and surrender as a passionate following of the heart's desire will be explored. Through the radical surrendering of self the work of God took centre stage, serving to transform Couderc, her sisters and the mission that they carried out. This will reveal how faith practices and spiritualities helped to expand as well as to reinforce the roles stipulated for Roman Catholic women during this time.[1] The primary sources utilized to examine the life and writings of Couderc are drawn from the congregational central archive located in Rome and are the equivalent of private papers. Through a consideration of the history of Couderc's interpretation it is possible to differentiate between materials collected expressly to support the process for canonization and those that enable a more critical reading of her life and writings.[2]

Thérèse Couderc and self-surrender

Thérèse Couderc and Père Etienne Terme (a priest and missionary of the diocese of Viviers 1791–1834) sought to revitalize Catholicism in the Ardèche region through offering the *Spiritual Exercises* specifically for women pilgrims visiting the shrine of Saint Régis at La Louvesc.[3] In the congregational recollections the sisters tended to utilize a reluctant tone to describe their efforts, emphasizing that they acted at Terme's behest. Couderc in particular protested that the sisters did not understand the Ignatian method at all until it was explained to them. However she took care to add that, despite their fears, the sisters did explain the meditations to the women as well as they could.[4] This may be explained by their formation in the habits of humility and self-abnegation. Nevertheless, the significance of their ventures should not be underestimated since this was the first time that Catholic **women religious** in France were encouraged to give the *Exercises* themselves.[5]

In addition, a closer examination of the texts of the congregational archive reveals other tones, such as a strong determination to protect and justify these ministerial developments. The novel work of retreats nearly came to a halt with the sudden death of Terme in 1834 and the appointment as superior of a diocesan priest whom the sisters feared would not have the required expertise to guide them. Couderc took decisive action by writing two letters (one to the Bishop of Viviers and one to the **Jesuit** provincial) to appeal for help, citing the will of Terme which entrusted the congregation to the bishop *and* the **Society of Jesus**. In a personal meeting with Bishop Bonnel (1757–1844), Couderc explained how supervision of the sisters by the Jesuits would enable the stability of the newly established retreat work and gained his consent to her request. This resulted in the ensuing instruction of the sisters on how to give the *Exercises*.

Yet, despite her pivotal role in commencing this ministry and in safeguarding its survival, Couderc appeared to retreat into a relatively hidden life following her resignation as Superior General in 1838. Her reputation for great humility and her silencing within the congregation formed the central thrust of hagiographical accounts written to support the process of canonization. This story buttressed Couderc's representation as an exemplar of heroic virtue in line with the thinking of the Church in the late nineteenth and early twentieth century.[6] Elizabeth Johnson has argued that such constructions of female sanctity have operated as a 'means of ecclesiastical control' which reinforce 'stereotypical feminine virtues'. In this way, risky actions undertaken by women have been translated as obedient submission to hierarchical authorities.[7]

Two factors however facilitated the emergence of a more rigorous evaluation of the written sources of the congregation and therefore a shift in the interpretation of Couderc. Firstly, the transcription and ordering of the primary sources during the 1960s allowed greater access to materials. Secondly, Vatican II's call to religious orders to return to the 'primitive inspiration' of their founders resulted in an appropriation of the insights of Couderc in the light of twentieth century theological and ecclesiological developments.[8] This contributed to the production of more nuanced and factually accurate accounts of Couderc.[9] It has therefore been possible to deconstruct her manufactured image to reveal a more textured picture of this woman and her own sense of priorities. While hagiographical material has focused on the lengthy sidelining of Couderc and her acquiescence to this as evidence of her great humility, the present essay concentrates on how her paradoxical language of self-surrender in fact afforded rather more scope for creative action than might be assumed at first reading.[10]

Couderc's legacy of self-surrender is rooted in her written description of her morning meditation of Sunday 26 June 1864, the account of which she inscribed with the words 'to keep'. She was 59 years of age and living in the community at Tournon. In her preface Couderc stressed that the Lord Jesus had often made her understand how essential it was to surrender the self or to give the self without reserve to the guidance of the Holy Spirit. However, on this occasion she apprehended the *more* of self-surrender.[11] Hearing the church bells summoning people to the celebration of mass, Couderc felt seized by a longing for union with the Eucharistic sacrifice, a feeling of love and gratitude, together with an astonishment that the 'Sacrifice of the Cross' did not sanctify all souls. She wrote down carefully the answer she 'thought' she 'heard': that although the sacrifice of the cross was 'undoubtedly sufficient [...] souls do not correspond. They are not generous enough.' The 'great means' stated Couderc 'whereby one may enter the way of perfection and sanctity is to surrender oneself to our good God.' She then proceeded to spell out the invitation contained in the decision to give oneself to God. Utilizing a tone of paradox, she claimed that while she understood 'the full extent' of its meaning, she could not 'explain' it.[12] She described the way of self-surrender through a series of negations pointing all the time to an excess. She accentuated the vastness of self-surrender embracing both 'the present and the future'. The starkness of this *more* was laid out plainly:

> To surrender oneself is something more than to devote oneself, more than to give oneself, it is even something more than to abandon oneself to God. To surrender oneself is to die to everything and to self, to be no longer concerned with self except to keep it continually turned towards God. Self-surrender is no longer to seek self-satisfaction in anything but solely God's good pleasure. It should be added that self-surrender is to follow that complete spirit of detachment which holds to nothing; neither to persons nor to things, neither to time nor place. It means to accept everything, to submit to everything.[13]

Couderc emphasized that despite the apparent difficulty of this proposition, it was in fact 'easy [...] to put into practice'. The way to achieve this, she had realized, was by the generous giving of oneself 'at the very beginning' and then not shrinking from the consequences of that self-donation, by remembering that one had surrendered oneself. She ended her reflection by her avowal of the 'sweetness and peace' and 'union' experienced by those who 'hold nothing back from the good God'.[14]

In *Se Livrer*, Couderc described her understanding of the gift to be found through the path of a complete self-offering to God. However, within the history of her interpretation, the linking together of self-surrender and Couderc's reputation for humility has tended to result in a truncated view of surrender. Her representation as *une grande humble* is epitomized in what I call her 'shadow text', where she encouraged her sisters to 'do all things [...] in the shadow' and to view themselves as 'the smallest in the Church of the Lord'.[15] This saying of Couderc has been construed as the culmination of a life of self-offerings and contextualized within a progressive deepening of a call to self-denial, suffering and sacrifice.[16] Couderc's self-understanding as a spiritual victim exemplified in her 'Act of Oblation', where she desired to unite herself with the sacrifice of Christ, seems to support such a reading.[17] The expression of her desire to conform herself to the will of God is summed up well in a letter to Me de Larochenégly (1804–1900), Superior General of the congregation between 1852 and 1877:

> I always feel drawn to an entire forgetfulness of myself, to a perfect submission to the will of God, to that detachment from everything which is not God, and it really seems to me that I cling to nothing. I have but one desire: that God may be glorified and that He may especially be by our little Congregation.[18]

The difficulty of Couderc's language of self-abnegation and a possible re-reading of the archival sources has been outlined in 'A Journey with Thérèse Couderc'. A post-structuralist intervention disrupts Couderc's language of self-surrender as self-abnegation by focusing on the whole of her discourse (or language in action). Giving attention to all the texts of her life, actions as well as words, reveals the subtext of 'the work of the Lord' at work within Couderc's script of abnegation.[19] This essay will now focus on the contributory influences of social location and spiritual formation that helped to produce this rupture within her discourse.

The impact of social location

Reading the text of self-surrender in the context of a feminized Catholic spirituality found in nineteenth-century France appears to strengthen the received representation of Couderc as an ideal exemplar of Catholic womanhood. Accounts that support the theory of the feminization of religion during this period in France note the great numbers of women participating in religious practice and their key role in the reconstruction of post-revolutionary Catholicism.[20] Yet such assessments have also been criticized as simply reinforcing contemporaneous prejudices about women, men and their relationship to Catholicism. McMillan argues that gendered stereotypes of a privatized, feminized Catholicism are contradicted by evidence of both religious men and irreligious women and the active participation of significant numbers of women in the public domain.[21] Competing interpretations of the impact of gender on Catholicism at this time means that no straightforward assessment of women such as Couderc can be made. Does the language of self-denial that she utilized to express her understanding of self-surrender point to her characterization as a spiritual victim, as described by Paula Kane, or is there need for greater nuance?[22]

Nineteenth-century manifestations of victim spirituality were plainly gendered, women predominating in the voluntary assumption of suffering. Forming part of a counter-revolutionary French Catholicism, *réparation* worked hand in hand with support for the *restauration* of the monarchy. Kane has argued that spiritual victimhood encouraged contemplation to the exclusion of **apostolic** works and privatized suffering, resulting in an emphasis on interiority within Catholicism.[23] Through the exaltation of physical pain, the suppression of individuality in emulation of the humility of Jesus, and the annihilation of the self, the movement encouraged guilt, scruples and depression. It worked against women's expanding social role within public and Church life by endowing them with spiritual authority while denying them clerical or sacramental authority, and thereby reinforced traditional gendered roles. While Kane acknowledges that this movement could facilitate spiritual renewal for some women she insists that these benefits were outweighed by its emphasis on self-denial. Spiritual victimhood, she concludes, supported 'a socially constructed ideal of extreme suffering as the true expression of the feminine' amongst women who were never actually in a position to reject the symbolism of suffering victim assigned to them.[24]

Couderc can, on the one hand, be identified as exemplifying the notion of the patriarchal construct of true womanhood which served to unite both clerical and anti-clerical protagonists in the battle for the hearts and minds of the French people. This construction of what constituted women's purported natural place, as Perrot has argued, ascribed a moral superiority to women while ensuring their subjugation in the private realm. The exporting of the domestic duties of women beyond the confines of the home has been evidenced as the domestication of politics. However, as Mills has pointed out, the shifting landscape of the fragmented social and political environment resulted in an ongoing negotiation of the so-called separate spheres in which women and men operated. In fact, both Catholic women religious and lay women were at the forefront of providing religious instruction and social assistance for those in need, putting in place by the end of the century a public infrastructure in education, nursing and social care.[25] Their spirituality, it may be argued, was the bedrock of such charitable ministry rather than a privatizing influence. What is noteworthy about the apostolate of the Sisters of the Cenacle is that their expansion of what it was permissible for women to do was carried out in the spiritual domain, threatening to subvert the male priestly control over the cure of souls.[26] While the latter part of the century brought greater restrictions on the sisters' ministry, with an increased emphasis on Eucharistic adoration, their experiments in giving spiritual retreats remained in the corporate memory of the congregation thanks to the written records kept by the sisters.

Thus, Couderc's legacy of surrender is more complicated than Kane's treatment of spiritual victimhood conveys. She was constructed by the spiritual, social and political influences that were brought to bear on her, and utilized the language of self-abnegation and spiritual victimhood. Yet, interlaced with her commitment to following the will of God may be read a determination to enable what she understood as the work of God. This resulted in a tension for Couderc between her desire to submit to the will of Divine Providence and her sense of commitment to the 'work of the Lord' as she described it in her critical letter of 1834 to the Jesuit Provincial.[27] This subtext within her language of submission is also evident at a later period in her life, when she spoke of her difficulty in keeping an attitude of Ignatian indifference about the interests of the congregation.[28] In order to identify the source of this tension, it is necessary to examine the spiritual influences which helped to form her.

Formative considerations

Terme was determined to respond to the religious vacuum left by revolutionary actions against the Church by re-awakening faith in the countryside of the Ardèche. In the formation of the sisters, he emphasized the virtue of self-renunciation but also communicated to them a passion for the purposes of God. Placing God at the centre of his missionary endeavours, he encouraged the sisters to do the same.[29] Terme made a significant contribution towards Couderc's understanding of self-surrender through his Consecration to the Virgin Mary in 1832.[30] Ceding the house of retreats and all associated with it to the Virgin he enjoined the sisters to be 'irrevocably submitted' to her: 'I establish thee, I constitute thee their Superior General [...] we have given thee all, [...] the Superior has abdicated so that all her daughters, becoming orphans, choose thee for their Superior.'[31] Couderc and the sisters signed their assent. The rationale for such subservience is evident in a letter penned to Agnès Barrial.[32] Terme stressed the abasement and humiliation of the self, allied however with a deep belief in the providence of God: 'Always have a great distrust of yourself, because you can do nothing; but always have great confidence in God, in Jesus Christ who is all powerful.'[33] Such abnegation aimed to transform the self into what God desired. This de-selfing was rooted in the notion of docility to the Holy Spirit, enabling the person to be an effective instrument of the will of God. 'Only one thing is necessary,' Terme wrote to Couderc in 1832, 'and that is to will sincerely what God wills.'[34] Drawing on the writings of the seventeenth-century Jesuit Lallemant (1588–1635), a contributor to the 'French School', Terme sought to inspire the sisters to embrace sacrifice through 'a perfect nakedness of spirit' so that they could be 'perfectly possessed by God'.[35] The way to rectify 'self-love' and 'false fears' was through renouncing self-interest and dependence solely on the 'good pleasure of God'.[36]

Terme's commitment to self-abnegation was rooted in his desire to carry out what he thought of as the work of God. Writing to Couderc in 1832, he described his hectic programme of giving missions, preaching, hearing confessions, often depriving himself of sleep and proper nutrition in the process: 'Such is the work of God,' he wrote, 'it is essential I do it.'[37] While he was informed by gendered understandings about what constituted women's work, an important opening in Terme's discourse was facilitated by his judgement that women were *capable* of giving retreats to other women (in fact, it seemed appropriate, necessary even, that they should).[38] To this end, Terme wrote to Pauline Jaricot (1799–1862) offering her the house of La Louvesc and any sisters 'judged suitable for retreat work by our Jesuit Fathers'.[39] This reflected his belief that an Ignatian retreat needed to be carried out privately to 'propose to each soul what was suitable for it according to the time, the need and the capacity of its spirit'. And 'do not tell me', he went on, 'that one cannot find persons capable of giving these retreats to each soul according to its needs. God wishes that this be done.' He pointed to the 'numerous' young people inspired to join religious life at that time.[40] Terme's belief in the 'capability' of women for retreat work proved crucial for the development of the ministry of the congregation as the sisters took up the mantle. Utilizing the language of separate spheres Terme asserted that this retreat work could be facilitated for women only by other women. His words were dangerously counter-cultural, since such ministry threatened to blur the gendered boundaries between lay and priestly ministries within Catholicism.

Nineteenth-century French Catholicism drew much on the spiritual traditions of the preceding three centuries to renew faith, and was particularly influenced by Counter-Reformatory movements, epitomized by the Society of Jesus. Its engagement with the seventeenth-century French School of spirituality, itself a response to the challenges of the Reformation and the Renaissance, gave a renewed impetus to counter-revolutionary attempts to articulate itself in fragmented and volatile times. Through their formation by Terme and the Society of Jesus, the sisters imbibed these influences.

The spirituality of the French School offered, William Thompson has claimed, 'a creative alternative' to the dogmatic theology of the Catholic Reform. It was informed by an apophatic reading of **mysticism** that stresses the unknowability of God, the abstract mysticism of the Rhineland and Flemish mystics and Catherine of Genoa (1447–1510), and the translations of the works of the Spanish mystics and reformers Teresa of Avila (1515–1582) and John of the Cross (1542–1591). This helps to explain a paradox between the language of transcendence and abstraction, on the one hand, and a stress on humanity and a spirituality of the heart on the other. The French School negotiated this tension because its commitment to a rather abstract mysticism (with its total dispossession of self) was tempered by the overriding commitment of the age to the pastoral reform of Catholicism. The central tenets of this spirituality, namely adoration, abasement, adherence, annihilation and abnegation, involved a series of paradoxes which liberated the person from self-interest and enabled the life of apostleship. Such renunciation of self was understood to serve a greater good, by letting go of all that was contrary to the way of Christ.[41]

Couderc's articulation of surrender was inspired by the spirituality of the Jesuit mystics, who combined Christocentrism with an emphasis on the role of the Holy Spirit and the vitality of the apostolic vocation.[42] In particular, her thinking bears the marks of Lallemant with his emphasis on the human void which could only be satisfied by being filled with a divine plenitude, especially in the crucial role he attributed to the Holy Spirit. His description of the practice of 'docility' evokes a picture of total possession and government by the Holy Spirit through 'complete surrender' and 'spiritual renunciation'. Significantly however, this was not an end in itself but a means to be more ordered to Christ through a correspondence with his Spirit.[43] Underlying this spirituality, Buckley has argued, was the synthesis of dialectical tendencies into a 'union between apostolic activity and infused contemplation'.[44] The emphasis on purity of heart and docility to the Holy Spirit found in Lallemant was complemented by the later writings of Jesuit **spiritual director** and preacher De Caussade (1675–1751) and Jesuit spiritual writer Grou (1731–1803), who used the concept of abandonment and spiritual childhood respectively to denote the attitude necessary to progress in the spiritual life.[45] However, Couderc emphasized that self-surrender went beyond self-abandonment, thereby illustrating the influence of Lallemant on her thinking.

The *Spiritual Exercises,* which played such an essential role in the development of French Catholic spirituality, constitute both a record of Ignatius' personal conversion and a tool for enabling transformation in others.[46] The goal of the *Exercises* is to enable the exercitant to grow into complete spiritual freedom, in loving submission to God's vision for all creation.[47] In his 'principle and foundation', Ignatius describes the spiritual attitude of indifference whereby the person seeks to make the will of God their ruling desire: 'Therefore, we must make ourselves indifferent to all created things, as far as we are allowed free choice and are not under any prohibition. Consequently [...] we should not prefer health to sickness, riches to poverty, honour to dishonour, a long life to a short life.' The 'one desire' and 'choice' of the exercitant should be for whatever will promote the praise, reverence and service of God.[48]

Through the dynamic of the *Exercises,* those who pray listen to their deepest desires and seek to follow the will of God. Through the reception of key graces[49] they recognize themselves as loved sinners who can respond to the call of Christ, discriminating between the value systems of good and evil, and testing their degree of spiritual freedom, as they are drawn deeper into the pattern of discipleship according to Jesus Christ. In the 'contemplation to attain the love of God', they pray to be filled with gratitude for what they have received so that they 'may in all things love and serve the Divine Majesty'.[50] As they are sent forth on mission, the exercitants seek to live an ongoing discernment of the will of God in their lives.

Ignatius helped individuals to engage with the inner movements of the spirit, in order to be free to work for the Reign of God. The principle of indifference, while utilizing the language of self-abnegation, promoted a growing interior liberty. Although it was true that the *Exercises* therefore provided a tool to facilitate conversion and to teach people how to pray, Ivens stresses that Ignatius articulated in his *Exercises* a new vision of religious life 'dedicated completely to an apostolic purpose'. The service of God in the world was therefore the hallmark of his spiritual doctrine.[51]

Self-surrender as gift to the good God so that the 'work of the Lord' may be carried out

What then was the link between the apostolic thrust of the *Spiritual Exercises* and Couderc's discourse of surrender? Probing the spirituality which undergirded her choices during the crucial early years of the congregation brings out the role of the 'work of the Lord' and sheds light on the passionate kernel of self-surrender found in her 1864 text. Notwithstanding Couderc's self-deprecating language, the enthusiasm of the early experiments in giving the *Spiritual Exercises* is palpable in the congregational archive.[52] Faced with the crisis of the death of Terme in 1834, the sisters acted decisively to preserve this emerging ministry. Couderc's deferential yet robust letter to the Jesuit provincial where she promised submission but insisted that she could not be 'indifferent concerning the work of the Lord' bears witness to the strength of their feelings.[53] In remonstrating with the Bishop of Viviers over who was to supervise the sisters, it was the apostolate which was most at stake. Josephine Grégoire (1801–1859) commented in her memoirs how Couderc explained to Bishop Bonnel about 'the purpose of the work, of the retreats and their success, of the need for cooperation with the Jesuits, both to form ourselves and for the Exercises of the general retreats, etc.' and that he understood and acquiesced to their reasoning.[54]

Although Couderc comes across in early accounts and letters as knowing her own mind, the formative influence on her of the *Spiritual Exercises* is also apparent. On 14 January 1836 she wrote a letter to Agnès Barrial asking the sisters to begin a novena to Terme to 'obtain for us the grace of being able to succeed in our projects if they are for the glory of God, if not, that he makes them fail'. The sisters were in the midst of deliberations about the division of the congregation according to the sisters' aptitude for either retreats or education. Barrial wanted to be faithful to the early focus on teaching and the situation later necessitated mediation. Couderc accentuated conformity to the 'will of our Divine Master', challenging all the sisters to the disposition of spiritual freedom described in the 'principle and foundation', which seeks to order all things to the praise, service and reverence of God:[55]

> Pray very much to Our Lord that He animate me with His spirit in order that He direct me in all that I do and all that I say and that I work only for His greater glory and the salvation of the souls that He confided to me and of whom He will ask me a rigorous account; on my part I promise you to ask for you the same grace [...] all our affairs are in the hands of God.[56]

Couderc demonstrated a clear sense of responsibility for the congregation and prayed to be animated with the spirit of Jesus Christ so that she could carry out the duty entrusted to her. Later that year, she penned another spirited letter to one of the vicars general who supported those sisters who wanted to retain the village schools. Her firm commitment to the work of retreats was visible in her insistence that teaching remained '*secondary* and *accessory* compared to the aim of retreats which is, according to the letter of the Constitutions *the first, the principal and the most essential one proposed*'.[57] To support her argument Couderc reminded the monsignor that in both his **Rule** and his will Terme specifically referred to retreats as the primary ministry of the congregation. Her capacity for leadership was unequivocal at this stage. Her surprise resignation of 1838, while it can be explained by a number of factors,[58] may also be interpreted as a response to an interior call in the spirit of the *Spiritual Exercises*.

At the beginning of the 'second week' of the *Exercises,* exercitants pray for the grace 'not to be deaf to [Christ's] call, but prompt and diligent to accomplish his most holy will'.[59] Ivens describes a growing intimacy between the exercitant and Christ, which is fundamentally oriented to 'participation in Christ's mission in the world'.[60] In this key meditation, 'the call of an earthly king', those who pray draw on their 'deepest capacity for commitment and unselfishness' in service of a great cause.[61] Cowan and Futrell describe this as 'a concrete taking up again of the "principle and foundation", discovering its depth in the full light of Jesus Christ, so as to order one's life in the service of the kingdom'. Through contemplation of the life of Christ, exercitants learn to conform their lives to the example of Jesus in carrying out the mission of the Father. The consequent renunciation of self is then the result of an impassioned call and response, necessitating an ongoing conversion.[62]

The characteristics of such a conversion may be illustrated by Couderc's private consecration to the Virgin, penned in the months before her resignation. In contrast to Terme's confident dedication of 1832, Couderc wrote during a time of deteriorating fortunes. Her desire, however, to give of herself was all encompassing, as she lamented the 'thousands of times' that she had 'consecrated' herself and then 'taken back' her offering. This time she resolved to consecrate herself 'body [...]. soul [...] mind [...] heart'. Couderc made this offering at a sensitive time in the history of the congregation, acting with a keen sense of authority. She turned to the Virgin to invoke a spirituality of empowerment, in service of the mission. Despite the private nature of this consecration, Couderc's words were far from individualistic: 'I do not consecrate to you only what concerns me personally, I also consecrate to you and beg you to receive among your daughters all my dear Sisters whom I love and whose salvation and perfection I desire as much as my own.'[63] This sense of responsibility was accompanied by a keen awareness of the sisters' ministry as she prayed that the Virgin would protect and help all those who 'practise the holy exercises of the retreat' in their house. Renouncing her legitimate authority as Superior Couderc sought to place all in the hands of her Mother:

> And if you wish that I still keep the name of superior, I wish this only in order to represent you; for I give up today the charge of superior, and whenever I shall be obliged *to perform* any function that this position require of me, I shall ask your permission since I shall have no right of my own to act because I have given you all.[64]

In her use of the verb *Se Livrer* to describe her carrying of authority (to give herself over to the tasks necessary) Couderc manifested her commitment to spiritual liberty. She sought to redirect her authority by invoking a power that expanded the notion of human freedom. The means by which she would do this is made clearer by the final words of her consecration, where she prayed that she would remain 'obedient and faithful to grace' and 'always animated by the spirit of Jesus Christ'. This echo of her words to Barrial the year before reinforces her expression of voluntary radical self-offering and gives some indication of her inner motivation. Couderc entrusted herself, her sisters and

THÉRÈSE COUDERC AND SELF-SURRENDER

those with whom they worked to the providence of God in an attitude of spiritual freedom, articulated as a sacrifice of fullness, not loss, in the belief that the spirit of God would literally breathe life into them all.

Couderc's desire to be spiritually free in order to follow the will of God, articulated in the impassioned words of her consecration, was rooted in a spirituality which was to inform her lifelong discourse of self-surrender. This 'death at the service of life', as de Lassus names it, witnessed to her intimate union with God and made possible an apostolic dynamism.[65] This decision to give herself to God was informed by this spiritual call to follow Christ. The effect of this is described succinctly by Côté: 'To do the work of God gives her life – radically. A passion for the Reign of God runs like a current through all her longing, fusing all her energy into one dynamic.'[66] All of this was encompassed in her one desire, that God be glorified. The work of God was so much of God that, if He did not desire it, then she could not either. 'And this work remains the axis upon which turns all her choices, all her assents, all her renunciations, all her convictions, all her prayer and all her struggle.'[67] By redirecting the focus away from herself she highlighted the centrality of the work of God and the sisters' call.

What was the guiding rationale behind Couderc's description of *Se Livrer* written some 27 years later? What was it that Couderc was so convinced of that she wanted to communicate via the *more* of surrender? Firstly, her words were informed by her intensified belief that she surrendered herself to the 'good God' from whom she wanted to hold nothing back.[68] In 1866 she went on to express as an 'indescribable sweetness' her vision of the 'infinite goodness' of God, which she apprehended on the face of all creation. This revelation of divine goodness made such a deep impression on her she could take no pleasure in anything else for several days.[69] Secondly, Couderc laid great emphasis on the simplicity of her relationship with this God, whom she apprehended as the source of all life and goodness. In a letter to Me de Larochenégly written a few months before she composed *Se Livrer* Couderc described her recent retreat and its profound effect:

> I simply know that I began it with a deep desire to become better, and that I said with all my heart those words: 'My God, here is Thy little servant, be it done unto me according to Thy Will and good pleasure.' Today I close it with these which I learned from the Divine Master, 'My heart is ready, my God, my heart is ready to embrace every manifestation of Thy Will.' I might say that this sums up all I did in retreat – *surrender myself* – God in His goodness did all the rest.[70]

Simplicity, however, should not be misread as simplistic. In fact Couderc reveals here the profundity of a lifetime of seeking to be spiritually free. Her writings illustrate that her desire to offer herself was anchored in a personal relationship with the one she named the 'good God'. Furthermore, by situating her expression of self-surrender within the Ignatian tradition it can be seen that Couderc's longing to surrender to this goodness was, like Ignatius's, fundamentally a response to the gift of God already at work in her. This consciousness of the gratuity of God is revealed in the final exercise of the *Spiritual Exercises*. In the 'contemplation to attain the love of God', exercitants are invited to reflect on how much they have been gifted by God.[71] In response, Ignatius invites them to pray the *suscipe*, the Latin title which Ignatius included in additional material to describe this section of the *Exercises* and translated as 'receive'. Ivens has called this prayer 'an act of handing over, of unconditional surrender, made in love and trust [...] the love-inspired entrustment to God of everything', involving the 'surrender of the whole self' for God to use:[72]

> Take Lord and receive all my liberty, my memory, my understanding and my entire will, all that I have and possess. You gave it all to me; to you I return it. All is yours, dispose of it entirely according to your will. Give me only the love of you, together with your grace for that is enough for me.[73]

What is striking about Couderc's text of self-surrender is that, despite her recurrent language of self-abnegation, this does not contain its real energy. She discarded terms that could not, for her, capture the fullness of her experience of surrendering herself without reserve to God. In emphasizing a positive movement towards the *more*, she exhibited an Ignatian commitment to embracing whatever is 'more for the glory and praise of God our Lord'.[74] God was for her 'everything' and this gave her desire its potency. She did not want to keep her spiritual insight for herself alone, feeling obliged to invite others into this experience of liberty in Christ. The intimate note of *Se Livrer* is at one and the same time a personal testimony and an apostolic missive. This attests to the influence of the Ignatian heritage and also accounts for Couderc's ongoing commitment to carry out the 'work of the Lord'.

Conclusion

Couderc's text of self-surrender was shaped by her formation in the *Spiritual Exercises*, mediated through the spirituality of the French School and expressed in the language of nineteenth-century Catholic spirituality. Her living out of this was also informed by the educational and catechetical concerns of this age, as an increasingly feminized Catholicism encouraged an extension (albeit limited) of women's ministerial possibilities. Utilizing the language of 'true womanhood' and, increasingly, 'spiritual victimhood' Catholic women created meaningful forms of spirituality and apostolate.

As has been suggested, Couderc's expression of self-surrender was informed by an apostolic thrust to be found at the heart of the *Spiritual Exercises* which forms contemplatives in action. Couderc's writings and actions during the course of her life witness to her passionate sense of vocation and a certain tension between her desire to be spiritually free and her conviction that God called the sisters to participate in his work. This essay has argued that she resolved this through a radical dispossession which resulted in this work of God being at the forefront. Consequently, Couderc's practice of self-surrender needs to be understood in terms of the conversion of her self in service of the purposes of God. She was able to take this risk of surrender by entrusting herself to her good God. Her commitment to the work of God contributed to the expansion of Catholic women's ministerial possibilities through the giving of the *Exercises* while also retaining a significant spirituality of self-gift. This is not to deny the ways in which such women were also restricted and undermined by their relationship with the Church and its ecclesiastical authorities. A longer consideration of Couderc's collusion with her own disempowerment is found in 'The Risk of Surrender'.[75] This essay, however, has highlighted the constructive ways in which such women wrested life-giving opportunities out of death-dealing situations because of their passionate belief in the purpose given to them by God.

Notes

1. K. M. Stogdon, 'The Risk of Surrender: *Se Livrer* in the Life of Thérèse Couderc (1805–1885)' (unpublished doctoral thesis, University of Manchester, 2004).
2. These sources are not generally accessible to the general public and are unfoliated and unpaginated. They comprise letters, prayers, recollections, testimonies and narrative accounts. They were written primarily for the members of the congregation to provide a record of the origins. The archive employs a basic referencing system, which has been followed: CA denotes the congregational archive, FT denotes material relating to Mère Thérèse Couderc, FE denotes Père Etienne Terme. For the purposes of dissemination within the congregation some material is also located in collections and has been translated into English. Translations have been done by sisters within the congregation and are generally accepted as accurate. For the purposes of clarity, references refer to the original sources which have been consulted, although detailed examination of translations was beyond the scope of this study. Quotations are given in English in order to make this material more accessible. For detailed analysis of primary and secondary sources on Couderc and the history of her interpretation see, Stogdon, 'Risk of Surrender', pp. 64–94.
3. Ignatius of Loyola (1491–1556), founder of the Jesuits, wrote his *Spiritual Exercises* based on his experience of conversion to the service of Christ and many years of accompanying others in the life of prayer. The *Exercises* consist of 30 days of guided prayer meditations. See M. Ivens, *Understanding the Spiritual Exercises: Text and Commentary* (Herefordshire: Gracewing, 1998).
4. Congregational General Archive (hereafter CA): FT3 T.A.1.3–1–1.2, Thérèse Couderc, 'Souvenirs sur les premiers temps de la Congrégation'.
5. The sisters built on earlier seventeenth-century initiatives for houses of retreats for women but Claude Langlois has cited the distinctive contribution of the Cenacle through the active participation of the sisters; C. Langlois, *Le catholicisme au féminin: Les congrégations françaises à supérieure générale au XIXe siècle* (Paris: Les Editions du Cerf, 1984), p. 472.
6. R. P. G. Longhaye, *La Société de Notre-Dame du Cénacle : Origines et Fondateurs* (Paris: V. Retaux, 1898); H. Perroy, *Une Grande Humble* (Paris: Beauschene, 1928).
7. E. Johnson, *Friends of God and Prophets: A Feminist Theological Reading of the Communion of Saints* (London: SCM, 1998), p. 28.
8. The Second Vatican Council (1962–5) sought to renew the life of the Church; *Perfectae Caritatis*, 28 October 1965 (2), in *Vatican Council II: The Conciliar and Post-Conciliar Documents* in A. Flannery, OP, MN (ed.), (Liturgical Press, 1975) (1984), pp. 611–23.
9. P. de Lassus, *Thérèse Couderc, Woman and Saint 1805–1885: A Few Essays on her Personality and her Spirituality* (New York: St Vincent Press, 1988); G. Côté,

The Cenacle: Its Christological Foundations and Its Spirituality (Paris: Beauchesne Editeur, 1991).

10. It is important to clarify that in fact Couderc's intense isolation and silencing occurred only from 1838 when she resigned until 1842 when she played a vital role in securing a property for the sisters in Lyons. From then on, she regained the esteem of many of the sisters and went on to exert lasting influence in the life of the congregation. See, Stogdon, 'Risk of Surrender', pp. 64–70.

11. The significance of the '*more*' is influenced by the thinking of the *Spiritual Exercises*, which will be brought out later in the essay.

12. CA: FT2 T.A.2.2.1, Thérèse Couderc, '*Se Livrer*' 26 June 1864.

13. *Ibid.*

14. *Ibid.*

15. CA: FT4 Souvenirs sur Mère Thérèse, 'Souvenirs de la R. M. Caroline Ponchon de St André', Mai 1887.

16. A. Combes, 'Les Quatre Offrandes de la Bienheureuse Thérèse Couderc', *La Pensée Catholique*, 59 (1959), pp. 29–38.

17. CA: FT2 T.A.1.2.1.3, Thérèse Couderc, 'Acte d'offrande et d'union'.

18. CA: FT2 LTC, Couderc to Me de Larochenégly, 7 August, 1867.

19. For re-reading of Couderc's humility and methodological considerations see, K. Stogdon, 'A Journey with Thérèse Couderc: Inspiration, Liability or Possibility for Change?', *Feminist Theology*, 16 (2008), pp. 211–29.

20. F. Tallet, 'Dechristianizing France: The Year II and the Revolutionary Experience', in F. Tallet and N. Atkin (eds), *Religion, Society and Politics in France since 1789* (London: Hambledon Press, 1991), pp. 1–28; R. Gibson, *A Social History of French Catholicism 1789–1914* (London: Routledge, 1989), pp. 180–182. However, this phenomenon is not limited to the nineteenth century, as evidenced by E. Rapley, *The Dévotes: Women and Church in Seventeenth-Century France* (Montreal: McGill-Queen's University Press, 1990).

21. J. F. McMillan, 'Religion and Gender', in F. Tallet and N. Atkin (eds), *Religion, Society and Politics in France since 1789* (London: Hambledon Press, 1991), pp. 58, 61–2; J. F. McMillan, *France and Women 1789–1914: Gender, Society and Politics* (London: Routledge, 2000).

22. Victim souls voluntarily embraced suffering as reparation for human sin and, joining with the sacrifice of Christ, they were understood to contribute to the redemption of humanity, by their suffering of the penalties due to sinners; P. M. Kane, 'She Offered Herself Up: The Victim Soul and Victim Spirituality in Catholicism', *Church History*, 71 (2002), pp. 84–5.

23. *Ibid.*, p. 98.

24. *Ibid.*, pp. 112–18.

25. M. Perrot, 'Women, Power and History', in M. Perrot (ed.), *Writing Women's History* (Oxford: Blackwell, 1984, 1992 edition), pp. 160–74; H. Mills, 'Negotiating the Divide: Women, Philanthropy and the "Public Sphere" in Nineteenth-Century France', in F. Tallet and N. Atkin (eds), *Religion, Society and Politics in France since 1789* (London: Hambledon Press, 1991), pp. 29–54.

26. Therefore the constitutions of 1844 (55) specified that the sisters were not to stray into the cure of souls. *Constitutions et Règles des Religieuses de Notre-Dame de la Retraite, ou de Notre-Dame au Cénacle* (1844) (Lyon: Pélagaud, 1855), Chapter 2, Art, 3.

27. CA: FT2 LTC, Couderc to Rev. François Renault, December 1834.

28. CA: FT2 LTC, Couderc to de Larochenégly, 27 May 1862. 'I have reasoned with myself in vain, scolded myself, refused to admit these sentiments, condemned them,

impossible not to feel them. [...] but these thoughts do not cease to afflict me. I thought that I was more indifferent and it seems to me indeed that I am in regard to everything else, but I despair of ever being so in matters which concern this dear Congregation.'

29. Côté, *The Cenacle*, pp. 148–62.
30. This 'devotion' of electing Mary as the Superior of the community was a relatively common devotion amongst religious communities in the late Middle Ages. See L. Lierheimer, 'Female Eloquence and Maternal Ministry' (unpublished doctoral thesis, Princeton University, 1994), p. 416.
31. CA: FT3 T.A.1–4–1.1.1, Etienne Terme, 'Consécration à Notre-Dame', 1832.
32. Barrial was one of the original young women gathered by Terme to respond to the needs for education and faith formation in the diocese of Viviers. In 1836 the congregation was divided into 'school' and 'retreat' sisters and Barrial chose to stay with what she saw as Terme's first work of instruction of the poor.
33. CA: FE1 Letters of Etienne Terme (hereafter LET), Terme to Barrial, 8 September 1831.
34. CA: FE1 LET, Terme to Couderc, 7 December 1832.
35. CA: FE1 LET, Terme to Couderc, November or December 1832. See, A. G. McDougall (ed.), *The Spiritual Teaching of Father Louis Lallemant of the Society of Jesus* (London: Burns, Oates and Washbourne, 1928), pp. 38–9.
36. *Ibid.*
37. CA: FE1 LET, Terme to Couderc, 19 December 1832. Terme refers to the *work* nine times in this letter.
38. Within the Ignatian tradition women were not entrusted with the actual giving of the *Spiritual Exercises*, but could play ancillary roles.
39. CA: FE1 LET, Terme to Jaricot, undated, but written prior to October 1833. Jaricot founded the Society of the Propagation of the Faith and the Association of the Living Rosary.
40. *Ibid.*
41. W. Thompson (ed.), *Bérulle and the French School: Selected Writings* (New York: Paulist Press, 1989), pp. 3–13.
42. Couderc was influenced by the noted Jesuit spiritual directors Surin (1600–1665) and Huby (1608–1693). Surin's *Fondements de la vie spirituelle* (1667) makes numerous references to the virtue of humility as a means to self-emptying in order to be open to the divine life. Huby's main apostolate was the giving of the *Spiritual Exercises*, encouraging retreatants to 'abandon themselves without reserve' to the Holy Spirit. See 'Surin', by M. Dupuy, *Dictionnaire de Spiritualité* (hereafter *DS*), 14, pp. 1311–25 and 'Huby', by Henry Marsille, *DS*, 7, pp. 842–52.
43. McDougall, *The Spiritual Teaching of Father Louis Lallemant*, pp. 27–31, 113.
44. M. J. Buckley, 'Seventeenth-Century French Spirituality: Three Figures', in L. Dupré and D. E. Saliers (eds), *Christian Spirituality: Post-Reformation and Modern* (London: SCM, 1990 edition), pp. 53–63.
45. See 'Caussade, de', by M. Olphe-Galliard, *DS*, 2, pp. 354–70; 'Grou', by A. Rayez, *DS*, 6, pp. 1059–83.
46. When considering the process of the *Spiritual Exercises* the present tense will be used to reflect their status as a living text and the fact that contemporary analysis is brought to bear on their inner dynamic.
47. L. J. Puhl (ed.), *The Spiritual Exercises of St. Ignatius: Based on Studies in the Language of the Autograph* (Chicago: Loyola University Press, 1951), paragraphs 21, 23 (hereafter denoted #).
48. Puhl, *Exercises*, # 23.

49. Grace is understood here as a free, unearned gift of God. Ignatius encourages the exercitant to 'ask for what I want and desire', # 48. Ultimately however he holds that the reception of God's gifts is gratuitous.
50. Puhl, *Exercises,* # 233.
51. M. Ivens, 'Ignatius Loyola', in C. Jones, G. Wainwright and E. Yarnold (eds), *The Study of Spirituality* (London: SPCK, 1986), pp. 357–62.
52. CA: FT8 T.B.1.-1–1.1, Journal, La Louvesc.
53. CA: FT2 LTC, Couderc to Rev. François Renault, December 1834.
54. CA: FT7 301, Joséphine Grégoire, 'Notes sur la Congrégation'. Grégoire formed part of the community at La Louvesc and accompanied Couderc on her visit to the bishop in 1834.
55. Puhl, *Exercises,* # 23.
56. CA: FT2 LTC, Couderc to Barrial, 14 January 1836.
57. CA: FT2 LTC, Couderc to Mgr Lavalette, July 1836. Emphasis in original.
58. De Lassus, *Woman and Saint,* pp. 115–117.
59. Puhl, *Exercises,* # 91.
60. Ivens, *Understanding Spiritual Exercises,* pp. 75–7.
61. Puhl, *Exercises,* # 91–9; Ivens, *Understanding Spiritual Exercises,* p. 79.
62. M. Cowan and J. Carroll Futrell, *Companions in Grace: A Handbook for Directors of the Spiritual Exercises of Saint Ignatius of Loyola* (Saint Louis: IJS, 2000), pp. 67–8.
63. CA: FT2 T.A.1.2.1.1, Thérèse Couderc, 'Consécration à la Sainte Vierge faite le jour de l'Assomption 15 août dans l'église de Notre Dame d'Ay 1837'.
64. My emphasis. To perform is the translation of Couderc's *Se Livrer* in this context.
65. De Lassus, *Woman and Saint,* p. 113.
66. Côté, *Cenacle,* p. 135.
67. *Ibid.,* p. 137.
68. CA: FT2 T.A.2.2.1, Couderc, '*Se Livrer*'.
69. CA: FT2 LTC, Couderc to de Larochenégly, 10 August 1866.
70. CA: FT2 LTC, Couderc to de Larochenégly, 13 February 1864. Emphasis in original.
71. Puhl, *Exercises,* # 230–37.
72. Ivens, *Understanding Spiritual Exercises,* p. 175.
73. Puhl, *Exercises,* # 234.
74. This Ignatian '*more*' (translation of the Latin *magis*) is particularly evident during the election material of the *Exercises,* # 170–89 (179, 180, 182, 189) where the exercitant seeks to make a choice of a way of life.
75. Stogdon, 'Risk of Surrender', pp. 184–225.

10

The 'Mixed Life': Challenging Understandings of Religious Life in Victorian England[1]

Carmen M. Mangion

Introduction

Communities of **women religious**[2] became a vital component of Catholic parish life in Victorian England.[3] The 'works of mercy' of active, simple-**vowed** religious **sisters** whose evangelical efforts took them outside the cloister were numerous and visible in public spaces. This so-called 'mixed life', a religious life of prayer commingled with active evangelization (as teachers, nurses and parish visitors), appealed to women desiring a role within religious life but outside the cloister. The mixed life also appealed to a Catholic hierarchy which was struggling to build a devout Catholic body and in great need of an army of Church workers. While women religious, as visible symbols of Catholicism and celibate women, were contentious in Victorian Britain,[4] their charitable work for the poor was highly regarded by some, including even Protestants typically quick to deride their efforts as 'papist'.[5] As religious sisters taking simple vows, they were classified differently from the cloistered, solemn-vowed contemplative **nuns** who had dominated women's religious life since medieval times.[6] Their mixed life of prayer and 'works of mercy' required a spirituality which accommodated evangelization in public spaces but allowed for a prayerful retreat within the sacred spaces behind convent walls. Religious sisters prized their spiritual lives as well as their evangelical efforts, but reconciling the dual aspects of their vocation had its challenges. This essay will first offer a brief history of this mixed life to place it within the context of the history of women religious. Then it will examine how nineteenth-century women religious understood their spiritual life. Balancing individual desires for personal spirituality with the requirements of the corporate body, whether that corporate body be the religious congregation or the Church hierarchy, required constant negotiation. The obligations of philanthropic work, be they professional or service oriented, led to additional pressures. These challenges are examined here, as are the ways that active women religious maintained the spirituality that they regarded as necessary sustenance for their activities as Church workers.

Spirituality is a problematic term that defies categorization or quantification. It is an abstract term, not easily defined within a historical context and with multiple meanings such that historians tend to speak of spiritualities in the plural to acknowledge not only several meanings but multiple layers of spirituality. For this essay, its meaning comes from the archives of Victorian women religious. It is identified as the core value that gave meaning and purpose to the lives of religious sisters, providing sustenance to their working lives as well as their spirit and soul. Each sister's spirituality developed uniquely in a personal way but would have been influenced by the corporate spirituality of the congregation. This corporate spirituality derived from the founder and was laid down in the congregation's **Rule** and constitutions, those documents that outlined the core objectives of a religious Institute.[7] The founder's personal spirituality was usually at the heart of the corporate spirituality and is often explored by congregation insiders, although rarely is this research widely published. After Vatican II, religious congregations were encouraged to re-examine their heritage and many directed their attention to material in their archives.[8] Some of this research focused on the spirituality of congregation founders has been published. Examples include texts such as Caritas McCarthy's *The Spirituality of Cornelia Connelly: In God, For God, With God* (1986), which explores the lived spirituality of Cornelia Connelly (1809–1879), who founded the Society of the Holy Child Jesus in Derby in 1846. Myra Poole's *Prayer, Protest, Power: The spirituality of Julie Billiart today* (2001) is a more recent example which developed from a feminist appraisal of the spirituality of founder Julie Billiart (1751–1816).[9] Published works on the spirituality of individual women religious have multiplied over the past 20 years and are important contributions to the historiography of Catholic women's spirituality. Scholars, however, have been slow to move from the individual to a more corporate and a more gendered exploration of the spiritualities of nineteenth-century Catholics, male or female, religious, clerical or lay.[10]

This essay will undertake this challenge, by examining one cohort of the Catholic population, women religious, in order to develop an understanding of their spiritualities. The primary sources used to develop this essay on mixed life include nineteenth-century published and manuscript texts written by or about women religious. Published materials such as biographies would typically have been written for the wide body of Catholics and were intended to inspire readers to a greater attentiveness to their own personal salvation. Other published texts, such as the Rules and constitutions, were official corporate sources written for women belonging to a particular congregation. Unpublished records include house annals and correspondence written to instruct or inform religious sisters and not intended to have an audience external to the congregation. A nuanced reading of these documents will allow us to explore how expectations regarding the spirituality of these Catholic women created tensions both amongst sisters within the same congregation and between clergy and women religious.

These documents come from several congregational archives and reflect diverse experiences of the mixed life. This does not imply that the spiritualities of these women spoke with one voice. In fact, quite the opposite, these sources depict a variety of spiritualities that sometimes appear contradictory. This essay will explore the connections between the overall pattern and dynamic of these spiritualities.

Early forms of mixed life

The Roman Catholic Church, through various papal legislation including *Periculoso* (1298), regulations of the Council of Trent (1545–1563)[11] and the three **papal bulls** that followed it, *Circa pastoralis* (1566), *Decori et honestati* (1570) and *Deco sacris virginibus* (1572), was insistent that vowed women religious lead a contemplative life protected by the cloister.[12] Yet Angela Merici (1474–1540) and Mary Ward (1585–1645), as essays in this volume have demonstrated, offered an alternative form of religious life, where contemplation and action were partners in a life devoted to a Church that increasingly required female efforts to meet the spiritual and temporal needs of the Catholic community. In her memorial to Pope Paul V (1551–1621) Mary Ward maintained that the 'sadly afflicted state of England' was in great need of 'spiritual labourers' and 'it seems that the female sex [...] should and can in like manner undertake something more than ordinary in this same common spiritual necessity.' She saw the Institute of the English Ladies undertaking:

> those works of Christian charity towards our neighbour, that cannot be undertaken in convents. Wherefore [sic], we propose to follow a mixed kind of life, such a life as we hold Christ our Lord and Master, to have taught His disciples; such a life as His Blessed Mother seems to have lived [...] and many other holy virgins and widows.[13]

Mary Ward's formulation of religious life, one where women were active evangelizers, was at odds with contemporary understandings of the role of nuns.[14] When she sought Roman approbation of her Institute as a canonically recognized religious Order, the response from Rome was the suppression of her Institute.[15] Despite this, the mixed life on the Continent with its focus on outside action took root; it was not meant as a rejection of the contemplative life but seen as a way of attending to the developing spiritual and temporal needs of the Church.[16]

England's history of religious life did not mirror these continental trends. After the Reformation, English women aspiring to live a consecrated life went by necessity into exile. Most entered English convents on the Continent, where they formed centres of English Catholic piety and 'challenged political, social and religious norms regarding what was appropriate action for contemplative women'.[17] Yet exile and cloister did not lead to the invisibility of these women, as Jenna Lay's article has argued.[18] By the late eighteenth-century, bouts of continental republicanism and anti-clericalism encouraged the mass exodus of English religious Institutes. Twenty-four **enclosed** communities resettled in

England and Wales. For those that were English Orders, this did not always result in a joyous homecoming; for some this return from exile was troubled by difficulties in adjusting to a non-Catholic spiritual and temporal milieu and pressures to adopt more utilitarian functions in addition to their contemplative lifestyle.[19]

The Catholic Relief Acts of 1778 and 1791 and the Catholic Emancipation in 1829 marked the beginning of a more open religious and political climate for Catholics, an environment that was also influenced by the continuing influx of Irish Catholics.[20] In 1850 the restoration of the hierarchy reflected the strengthening of the organizational structure of the Roman Catholic Church in England and Wales.[21] To these important events in the history of the Catholic Church in these countries should be added one more. 1830 was the year that marked the arrival into Britain of the first of the 'modern Orders' of women religious who lived the mixed life, the Faithful Companions of Jesus.[22] They were founded in 1820 in France by Marie Madeleine Victoire de Bengy d'Houët (1781–1858), and their arrival in 1830 was followed by the Irish Presentation sisters in 1836 and the Irish Sisters of Mercy in 1839. Eight additional congregations arrived in the 1840s. So by 1850, when the Catholic hierarchy of England and Wales was established, 11 active congregations were flourishing and managing 42 convents. By 1900, there were 80 congregations with 513 convents in England and Wales and over 10,000 women had entered religious life.[23]

Contemplative and active: separate spheres?

Although these modern institutes were celebrated for the charitable and evangelical work they performed, they were not uncategorically embraced by Catholics. Some Catholic texts compared the contemplative nun with the active sister, pointing to the difficulties of the active sister's life in the world and idealizing the simplicity of the contemplative life. Building on a common trope, the anonymous reviewer of John Nicholas Murphy's (1815–1889) *Terra Incognita* (1873) sets up the dichotomy of the contemplative Mary and the active Martha:[24]

> Even the works of active charity depend upon the hidden influence of prayer, and it may well be, that at the last day before the Great White Throne the contemplative life of Mary, who has chosen the better part, the one thing needful, will have a richer reward, because productive of richer results than the active life of Martha, careful and troubled, as it is, about many things.[25]

This dichotomy positioned Mary's contribution, the life of prayer as 'the better part' and productive of 'richer results' whereas the life of Martha was 'active and troubled'. The reviewer pointed to the 'hidden influence of prayer' that lay behind the sisters' works of active charity. This, as we shall see, was often emphasized by congregation leaders. Yet, he acknowledged the 'richer results' of the contemplative life were not embraced by modernity: 'The world may still profess admiration of our active orders of religious women, but the contemplative orders they consider as little better than barren fig-trees cumbering the earth, for they cannot understand them.'[26] The worldliness of the Marthas, according to this reviewer, meant they were welcomed in Victorian England and encouraged because of their utilitarian charitable work. Historian Linda Wilson makes a similar observation and notes that public approval was given to nineteenth-century non-conformist women whose spirituality was 'active'.[27] This discourse of utility imagined and idealized the practical nature of the work of women religious. For Protestants, the charitable works of women religious had a functional utility as it met the growing concerns of addressing the needs of the poor. Despite the spectre of anti-Catholicism, there were Protestants who supported Catholic philanthropic endeavours, notably those involving care of the aged or medical treatment. The discourse of 'common christianity [sic]' was often utilized to infer a Christian collegiality rooted in action.[28] For Catholics, this utility had an added spiritual motive as it drew Catholics back to the practice of the faith.[29] It is perhaps unsurprising that Victorians valued the active labours of simple-vowed women religious over the prayerful contemplative life at a time when women were visible and active in charitable work which, as argued by Frank Prochaska, altered the shape and course of philanthropy.[30]

This surge in women's participation in philanthropy was reflected in the developments of the active work of Catholic sisters. Francesca Steele (1849–1931), in her introduction to *The Convents of Great Britain* (1902), noted the proliferation of the modern Orders and although she celebrated both the spiritual and evangelical work of these active congregations, she also voiced her regret that 'the age we live in is not favourable to the contemplative life, which throve [sic] better in olden times, when faith was stronger than it is now and the world was less restless.'[31] Steele equated contemplative Orders with strong faith, and as she opined the 'restless' Victorians were somewhat lacking compared to those who had gone before them. Perhaps the understanding of contemplative religious life, rooted in both the primacy of prayer and the ideal of stability, which located the nuns in one convent or monastery, was a reassuring demonstration of spirituality. The imaging of the solemn, silent praying nun was contrasted with the busyness of the active sisters, often visible in public spaces, and whose days were punctuated by prayer and philanthropy.

Reverend Arthur Devine (1849–1919), author of *Convent Life; Or, The Duties of Sisters Dedicated in Religion To the Service of God* (1889), included a short section on the modern orders entitled 'Nuns without enclosure'.[32] He noted that:

> although they are without Enclosure and without solemn vows, they are nevertheless *true Religious*, their Institutes contain what constitutes the essence of the Religious State, and as such they are approved by the Church as true Religious States affording their members the means of sanctity and Religious perfection.[33]

Over the course of four pages, he reiterated four times how active religious sisters were 'true religious' or 'real religious' and concluded that 'they are *not in the least inferior* to the state with solemn vows and Enclosure.'[34] This overemphasis of the value of the mixed life suggests that perhaps not all members of the Catholic faithful equated the mixed life with the 'Religious State'.

Devine's defence of the modern Orders reflected the contested nature of the mixed life. Both the anonymous review of *Terra Incognita* and Steele offered subtle critiques which idealized the contemplative religious life as one separate from the world and unaffected by the temptations and difficulties of modernity. While these were not overtly gendered critiques, there is a parallel with the Victorian discourse of separate spheres that cannot be ignored. This discourse proposed a strict dichotomy with women in the domestic sphere, often envisioned as a protected and sanctified space, and men in the rough-and-tumble public spaces of the world.[35] Contemplative nuns were contrasted with members of modern congregations, active sisters in the world without the protection of the grilles of the nuns' cloister. Such a strict dichotomy between the contemplative and the active spheres of life was not envisaged by the nineteenth-century founders of active congregations as the following section will demonstrate.

The 'mixed life': conflating contemplative and active?

To develop a better understanding of the lived experience of the 'mixed life', we will first turn to the biography of Margaret Hallahan (1802–1868), founder of the English Dominicans of St Catherine of Siena in 1845. She advocated the mixed life for her sisters, whose 'active work' included teaching in parish schools, nursing in their own hospitals and visiting parishioners. According to Hallahan's biographer and successor, Mother Raphael (Augusta Theodosia Drane) (1823–1894), this '"humble, hidden, useful life" of active labour' was 'spiritualized by prayer and a holy intention'.[36] Hallahan argued that the 'strict obligations of religious life are fully compatible with the discharge of active charitable labours,' and behind their charitable activities was 'something higher'. This 'something higher' was the spiritual life of the sisters. Hallahan maintained that 'active work' did not demand that strict religious obligations be eliminated; rather that it was 'such religious obligations themselves which support the work'. Hallahan was critical of congregations that eliminated religious devotions to create more time for their active endeavours.

> Almost every one of what are called the active Orders of the Church, at least those of modern foundation, have yielded up a certain proportion of this principle. It has become a sort of canon in the popular mind, that teaching bodies must be released both from the recital of the Divine Office and from the observation of anything more than the fasts and abstinences of the Church. It is supposed that the discharge of duties, so exhausting both to physical and mental strength, as those which are borne in the hospital or the school, demand the surrender of these and other austerities; and that they to whom God has given the vocation of labouring for the good of their neighbour must make the sacrifice as a matter of course.[37]

Hallahan supported some of the traditional devotional practices of the contemplative life, including saying the Divine Office, which was prayed regularly by the sisters until Bishop Bernard (William) Ullathorne (1806–1889) suggested that it was too disruptive to their charitable endeavours.[38] They replaced the Divine Office with the Little Office of the Virgin Mary, the Office often recited by active congregations as it was shorter and less vocally demanding. In 1866, most likely due to Hallahan's persuasiveness, Ullathorne sanctioned the Dominicans' return to praying the Divine Office.[39] Hallahan argued that the Divine Office was 'the real work' of women religious and that 'for one soul gained to God by their words and exhortations, they might save thousands by their prayers.'[40] She advocated the primacy of prayer over active works, a seemingly contradictory statement given the numerous charitable initiatives of the congregation. Yet Hallahan saw no inconsistency in conflating both modes of life. She maintained, as will be stressed even further in the next section, that the active works performed by the sisters were dependent on a strong prayer life.

Margaret Hallahan was concerned that religious sisters would be over-absorbed in their charitable work and relegate their spiritual life to second place. She argued that being an 'excellent schoolmistress' or a 'first-rate hospital nurse' or being engrossed by the 'bustle and business of her charitable labours, may so have filled up every cranny of her mind, that little room has been left for the exercises of the interior life; and, wearing the habit, she may, after all, have retained but little of the real character of a *nun*.'[41]

Hallahan was not the only leader of a congregation concerned about sisters being overly immersed in their exterior life. The Sisters of Mercy, founded in Ireland by Catherine McAuley (1778–1841) in 1831, also recorded their disquiet about the responsibilities of the 'works of mercy' overwhelming the contemplative life of the sisters. The *Abridgment of a Guide for the Religious Called Sisters of Mercy* (1866), published as a handbook for the Sisters of Mercy, by then located in Ireland, Britain, North America, Australia and Argentina, acknowledged that the 'spirit of our Institute is that of the mixed life'.[42] Besides the usual three vows of poverty, chastity and obedience, the Sisters of Mercy included a fourth vow, which recognized their 'service of the poor, sick, and ignorant'. The *Guide* warned the Sisters that:

> [the] substitution of assumed for real duties is an evil that cannot be too carefully guarded against, as it would eventually change the spirit of the Institute, and thus mar the designs of God on it, and on its members, but [sic] turning them from their real vocation.

Here again, an instructional text cautioned sisters that their 'works of mercy' were not their 'real duties'. The *Abridgment of a Guide* emphasized that:

> Exterior works must not be so multiplied as to deprive the Sisters of the time necessary for the fervent discharge of the spiritual obligations coeval with the Institute; nor should the spiritual exercises be so increased as to absorb the time due to the service of our neighbor.[43]

These instructions make transparent the difficult balancing of philanthropic and spiritual duties.

Mary Potter (1847–1913), founder of the Little Company of Mary, addressed similar concerns.[44] Potter intended to found a congregation devoted to the dying; her original aims, though, were both contemplative and active.[45] She envisioned one congregation with two parts. Contemplative sisters, 'engaged in perpetual intercession for the dying', what she called the 'office of head and heart', formed one part. Their counterpart, the active sisters, were 'employed more in the useful work of hands and feet'. Even more uniquely, she saw women religious moving from contemplative to active or vice versa as their lives developed.[46] Her original intentions were altered by the practical considerations of obtaining diocesan and then pontifical approval for the congregation. In practice, the contemplative intent receded, and the active works in the form of nursing came to the forefront. By the time the Rule and Constitutions of the Little Company of Mary were approved in 1893, they had become 'The Institute of Nursing Sisters'.[47]

The journey from these dual aims to an active nursing ministry began in Nottingham, a diocese short of priests and in dire need of church workers to evangelize the Catholic poor. Bishop of Nottingham Edward Gilpin Bagshawe (1829–1915) understood, and probably even appreciated Potter's spiritual aims, but his primary objective was to obtain a competent workforce and the sisters of the Little Company of Mary were immediately put to work in small parishes teaching, nursing and catechizing. Potter had no difficulties with this practical focus, but maintained that those whose work was of the 'hands and feet' needed a thorough understanding of the congregation's fundamental spirituality. The depth of this spiritual training was questioned by some of the early sisters as well as Bagshawe. Bagshawe's eventual response was to replace Potter with a member of the congregation more amenable to his ideas in 1877.[48] Mary Potter regained control of her congregation two years later but the pressures between balancing the active with the contemplative life did not disappear.

Like Margaret Hallahan and the Sisters of Mercy, Mary Potter sought to infuse the active life of her sisters with a very distinctive spirituality. Religious life was not meant to focus solely on philanthropic work. The constitutions and Rules of the Little Company of Mary began by noting that 'Assiduous prayer, especially for the dying, is no less than corporal attendance on the sick, the principal and characteristic work of the Little Company of Mary.' Yet, in some cases, especially when sisters were nursing patients in their homes, the requirements regarding prayer left some decision making to the judgement of the sister or her superior. Potter purposefully built this flexibility into the Rule, which suggests that the responsibilities of nursing sometimes required the interruption or temporary abatement of spiritual duties.[49] But there were limits. Potter mildly chastised Sister M. Juliana (Julie Towson): 'Am sorry you do not go to Mass in the mornings, as, unless you have to leave your patient alone when dangerously ill, you know it is the rule and necessary for health of soul and body.'[50] Potter also surmised that some sisters appeared to place more emphasis on their charitable responsibilities than their spiritual duties. She reminded the sisters that:

> the first object of our foundation is not to nurse, as so many suppose, and it is not right; too many of our sisters allow them to suppose [sic]. Our first object is to model Calvary and form a united body representing to heaven mirroring that grand work of the Holy Ghost: that mystery of grace – Calvary.[51]

Many women were attracted to religious life specifically because of the 'love of the works'.[52] For some women, perhaps this commitment to caring for the physical needs of their patients was more in line with modeling Calvary than were the spiritual duties required by their Rule. Sadly, there are few documents in the voice of the ordinary sister that address the lived experience of balancing 'works of mercy' with personal spirituality. Yet, hints of the difficulties of balancing the two appear in the following examination of documents written, most likely, by congregation leaders.

The 'mixed life': meeting parish needs

Nineteenth-century records across most congregations give the impression that the active religious life was demanding, with far too much work and too few workers. Convent annals and correspondence mention continual requests to open a convent in needy areas – and regular refusals, often because of insufficient numbers of sisters to staff the ventures or inadequate funding.[53] Women religious became an important component of parish life, often as teachers, nurses or catechists. Clergy were generally appreciative of their efforts but on some occasions sisters noted pique regarding the requirements of their spiritual life. The Coventry annals of the Sisters of Mercy noted that Mother Mary Elizabeth (Teresa Watkins) (1821–1901):

> ventured to represent to Father Pratt that they had their office and spiritual exercises to attend to out of school hours; but he did not seem to understand how they ought to have anything to do but attend to the School work, and replied inconsiderately 'You must remember that you have not come to the best; that place you have left, where you would say office and the rest in the day.'

Watkins replied that it was her 'duty to see that it becomes the same sort of place in these matters'.[54] Watkins was no stranger to these sorts of pressures. In 1855, when superior of the Chelsea convent of the Sisters of Mercy, she wrote to Cardinal Nicholas Wiseman (1802–1865) demanding a change in clergy because of unsatisfactory spiritual care. She argued:

> it matters greatly to us to have that spiritual support which we were all promised in embracing this particular Institute [...] What is the poor nun good for when the Mass & the B. Eucharist is taken from her!!! Believe me, my Lord, it is not without cause I write to you.[55]

Watkins pointed to the Rule and constitutions, authoritative documents approved by Rome, which outlined the spiritual requirements of the Sisters of Mercy and argued that 'spiritual support' was something the sisters were entitled to. When their errant **chaplain** was replaced, the Chelsea annalist noted that the appointment of a new chaplain 'contributed much to the spiritual good and comfort of the Sisters'.[56] Congregation leaders were not silent when parish priests or ecclesiastical superiors failed to provide the quality or quantity of spiritual guidance that they deemed the sisters were entitled to.

There were other examples of sisters who were vocal about the loss of spiritual sustenance. The Daughters of the Heart of Mary noted that their **confessor** 'gave us reasons to think that being much occupied and not understanding our Society very well it would perhaps be better for someone else to have the charge of our souls'. Discussions with Father Frederick Faber (1814–1863) and Cardinal Wiseman followed, and their confessor was replaced.[57] In another example, Peter Kaye (1804–1856), Rector of St Albans, appeared to Sister M. Alphonse de Liguori (Ipheigenia De Paiva) (1818–1884), a sister of Notre Dame de Namur, to be more interested in their charitable work in his parish than their spiritual lives. She noted that he continued 'to take a great interest in us with regard to our temporal affairs but we never have a spiritual word from him'.[58] In one missive she compared him unfavourably to the Redemptorist Fathers who had been their confessors in Clapton: 'We have been twice to confession to Mr. Kaye since he was named; he comes regularly every week. It's very different from having a religious – he says nothing to us.'[59] The Notre Dame sisters implied that secular priests did not understand the spiritual needs of the sisters and that regulars, male congregations of priests and brothers, were better suited as confessors. These complaints should not be seen as an indictment of the insensitivity of all clergy. It is likely that most **secular clergy** were unused to addressing the spiritual needs of women religious. In 1864, Bishop William (Bernard) Ullathorne, himself a Benedictine, stated in a letter to Geneviève Dupuis (1813–1903), founder of the Sisters of Charity of St Paul the Apostle, that some clergy 'from ignorance of what religious life requires, cause affliction and distress to the sisters and imperil the establishments'.[60] At this time, congregations of women religious living the mixed life were still new to the religious landscape, but by the 1880s there were fewer complaints in congregational correspondence and more praise for the spiritual sustenance given by clergy.

Conclusions

This short essay does not pretend to reflect all the perspectives of the mixed life, but it suggests the diversity and continuity of certain themes and issues within religious life. The shift towards the mixed life in Victorian England is yet another example of women's spirituality contributing to the changing landscape of Catholic practice. Founders such as Margaret Hallahan and Mary Potter saw no contradiction or competition between a life of prayer and a life of charitable activity. The life of prayer was meant to feed the souls of the sisters and nurture the activities of the congregation. Martha and Mary, in their view, could coexist. But tensions and conflict did exist amongst the sisters themselves and among women's religious Institutes and the clergy. These anxieties were bound up with the needs of a rapidly growing Catholic Church, a clergy which saw the utility of these groups of women who could responsibly and cheaply meet the developing needs of a parish, and women religious who were drawn to this form of religious life because it united both prayer and philanthropic activity and allowed them to evangelize their fellow Catholics. The rapid growth of these modern Orders with their mixed life testifies to their attractiveness. Congregation leaders addressed these competing demands by advocating a balanced approach to religious life in published texts and congregation correspondence and by negotiating with the clergy as to their spiritual needs.

The history of religious life is not one of continuities and uniformity. The 'mixed life' of Catholic women religious remains a contested and debated terrain. There are those who view twenty-first century religious life as a pale contrast to a mythological past where 'faith was stronger than it is now'. It is all too easy to blame liberalism and feminism for the perceived fragmentation of religious life. As society and its dominant needs change in the twenty-first century, so perhaps we should anticipate that the dimensions of Catholic religious life and its spiritualities will develop along diverse paths. Instead of focusing on rigid ideas of religious life and a uniform spirituality, perhaps it would be more fruitful to acknowledge the ever-changing kaleidoscope of religious life and the existing and potential spiritualities it contains.

Notes

1. I wish to express my gratitude to the archivists at the Westminster Diocesan Archives, the General Archives of the Union of the Sisters of Mercy of Great Britain, the Institute of Our Lady of Mercy Archives, the Archives of the Little Company of Mary, Notre Dame Archives (British Province) and the Archives of the Daughters of the Heart of Mary. Without their assistance, this research would not be possible. I would also like to especially thank Caroline Bowden, Karly Kehoe, Laurence Lux-Sterritt, Rosa MacGinley and Elizabeth West for their thoughtful comments on early drafts of this paper. Their suggestions undoubtedly improved this essay; all errors are my own. Finally, I wish to thank the University of London Central Research Fund and the Economic History Society for financial support.
2. Women religious is the term used to refer to both contemplative nuns, who took solemn vows and lived a life of prayer within an enclosed community, and active sisters, who took simple vows and lived a life of prayer and evangelical work, typically teaching or nursing, outside convent walls. In common parlance these two terms, nuns and sisters, are interchangeable, as indeed they were in the nineteenth century, but under Roman Catholic canon law they have different meanings. Active sisters were organized into religious congregations which were described as 'modern Orders' in the nineteenth century.
3. S. O'Brien, '"Terra Incognita": The Nun in Nineteenth-Century England', *Past and Present*, 121 (1988), pp. 110–40; B. Walsh, *Roman Catholic Nuns in England and Wales, 1800–1937: A Social History* (Dublin: Irish Academic Press, 2002).
4. C. M. Mangion, *Contested Identities: Catholic Women Religious In Nineteenth-century England and Wales* (Manchester: Manchester University Press, 2008), pp. 23, 56–58.
5. C. M. Mangion, 'Religious Ministry and Feminist Practice', in J. De Vries and S. Morgan (eds) *Women, Gender and Religious Cultures* (London: Routledge, 2010), pp. 72–93.
6. This classification was formalized in 1900 with the decree *Conditae a Christo* which defined the juridical nature of religious congregations. M. R. MacGinley, PBVM, *A Dynamic of Hope: Institutes of Women Religious in Australia* (Darlinghurst, New South Wales: Crossing Press, 2002), p. 59.
7. Religious sisters in the nineteenth-century speaking of their 'holy Rule' were often referring to both their Rule and constitutions, a text which did not always contain a distinction between the two documents. Strictly speaking, the Rule was usually identified with one of the four ancient Rules: Augustinian, Benedictine, Franciscan or Basilian. The constitution contained the varying practices of each religious

institute and governed their manner of life. Only religious Orders of solemn-vowed nuns had a Rule in the strictest sense of the term.

8. Vatican II was an Ecumenical Council opened under Pope John XXIII in 1962 and closed under Pope Paul VI in 1965. It addressed the need for *aggiornamento*, a rejuvenation of the practices of Roman Catholic Church teaching. For a contemporary understanding of its impact on women's religious life, see L. J. Suenens, *The Nun in the World: New Dimensions in the Modern Apostolate* (Westminster, MD: The Newman Press, 1963).

9. M. Poole, SND, *Prayer, Protest, Power: The Spirituality of Julie Billiart Today* (Norwich: Canterbury Press, 2001), pp. 1–8.

10. Specific attention to English spirituality can be found in J. M. Gordon, *Evangelical Spirituality* (London: SPCK, 1991) and Gordon Mursell, *English Spirituality: From 1700 to the Present Day* (Louisville: Westminster John Knox Press, 2001). Both include small sections on Catholic spirituality. The gendered aspect of spirituality is explicitly addressed in Andrew Bradstock, Sean Gill, Anne Hogan and Sue Morgan's edited collection on *Masculinity and Spirituality in Victorian Culture* (London: Macmillan, 2000), which covers spirituality in various denominations including Catholicism, and Linda Wilson's *Constrained by Zeal: Female Spirituality amongst Nonconformists, 1825–1875* (Carlisle, England: Paternoster, 2000). Mary Heimann's study on *Catholic Devotion in Victorian England* (Oxford: Clarendon, 1995) links devotions with Catholic spirituality and explores the development of devotional practices in England, arguing that multiple forms of religious observance brought together Catholics in England, whether Irish or English, ultramontane or cisalpine, nominal or practicing, and 'this new English spirituality had a good deal in common with contemporary Catholic developments abroad.' Sadly, this otherwise excellent work does not acknowledge the work of women religious in bringing about this devotional revival nor does it explore the gendered nature of devotional spirituality.

11. The Council of Trent was a conference of bishops, priests and male religious convened to discuss matters of church doctrine and practice. See Introduction.

12. E. M. Makowski, *Canon Law and Cloistered Women: Periculoso and its Commentators, 1298–1545* (Washington D.C.: Catholic University of America Press, 1997); Francesca Medioli, 'An Unequal Law: The Enforcement of *Clausura* before and after the Council of Trent', in C. Meek (ed.), *Women in Renaissance and Early Modern Europe* (Dublin: Four Courts Press, 2000), pp. 136–52. Medioli argues that it is not until after the Council of Trent that the Church becomes consistent about enforcing *clausura*.

13. M. C. E. Chambers and H. J. Coleridge, *The Life of Mary Ward (1585–1645)*, 2 vols (London: Burns and Oates, 1882), Vol. 1, pp. 375–76.

14. Laurence Lux-Sterritt's essay in this volume addresses the Institute of English Ladies in more detail.

15. Despite their suppression, the English Ladies, as a group of religious women (not nuns), were accepted in various continental locales and in England.

16. L. Lux-Sterritt, *Redefining Female Religious Life: French Ursulines and English Ladies in Seventeenth-Century Catholicism* (Aldershot: Ashgate, 2005), p. 3.

17. C. Walker, *Gender and Politics in Early Modern Europe: English Convents in France and the Low Countries* (Basingstoke: Palgrave MacMillan, 2003), p. 7; C. Bowden, 'The Abbess and Mrs Brown: Lady Mary Knatchbull and Royalist Politics in Flanders in the late 1650s', *Recusant History*, 24 (1999), pp. 288–308.

18. Caroline Bowden and Michael Questier's Arts and Humanities Research Council-funded project 'Who were the Nuns?' will make these English women more visible to twenty-first century scholars. The project will identify the membership

of the English convents during their period of exile. For more information see http://wwtn.history.qmul.ac.uk/.

19. M. J. Mason, 'The Blue Nuns of Norwich: 1800–1805', *Recusant History*, 24 (1998), pp. 89–122. Unfortunately, there has been very little published research on the experiences of these religious institutes readjusting to life in England.

20. The Catholic Relief Acts of 1778, 1791 and 1829 removed many of the financial and political disabilities for Roman Catholics (in both Britain and Ireland) and allowed Catholics to practise their faith legally. E. R. Norman, *The English Catholic Church in the Nineteenth Century* (Oxford: Oxford University Press, 1984), p. 35; J. Derek Holmes, *More Roman than Rome: English Catholicism in the Nineteenth Century* (London: Burns and Oates, 1978).

21. V. A. McClelland, 'From Without the Flaminian Gate', in V. A. McClelland and M. Hodgetts (eds), *From Without the Flaminian Gate: 150 Years of Roman Catholicism in England and Wales* (London: Darton Longman + Todd, 1999), pp. 1–20.

22. Two convents (one in York and the other in Hammersmith) of the Institute of Mary had existed in England since the seventeenth century despite penal laws.

23. Mangion, *Contested Identities*, pp. 1, 36–8. The remaining eight were the Society of the Sacred Heart (1842), Sisters of Providence (1843), Sisters of Notre Dame de Namur (1845), the Dominican Sisters of St Catherine of Sienna (1845), Society of the Holy Child Jesus (1846), Daughters of the Heart of Mary (1846), the Sisters of Charity of St Paul the Apostle (1847) and the Daughters of the Faithful Virgin (1848).

24. Martha and Mary are often used to represent the two typologies of religious life. In the bible story of Lazurus's resurrection, Jesus returned to Bethany to celebrate Lazurus's homecoming. Lazurus's sister Martha laboured in the kitchen and served the celebratory meal while her sister Mary listened to Jesus. Martha criticised Mary's inactivity, but Jesus, in the passage written by St Luke comes to Mary's defence, acknowledging she had 'chosen the better portion' (*St James Bible*, Luke 10:38–42). This story, for much of the medieval and early modern period, reinforced the 'higher calling' of the contemplative nun.

25. 'Review of *Terra Incognita, Or Convent Life in England*', *Dublin Review* XXI: XLI [New Series] (1873), p. 136.

26. *Ibid.*, p. 136.

27. L. Wilson, *Constrained by Zeal: Female Spirituality Amongst Nonconformists, 1825–1875* (Carlisle: Paternoster Publishing, 2000), p. 137.

28. C. M. Mangion, 'Medical Philanthropy and Civic Culture: Protestants and Catholics United by a "Common Christianity"', in S. Malchau Dietz (ed.), *Proceedings: The First Danish History of Nursing Conference* (Denmark: Aarhus University, 2009), pp. 107–22.

29. Mangion, *Contested Identities*, pp. 111–34.

30. F. K. Prochaska, *Women and Philanthropy in Nineteenth-Century England* (Oxford: Clarendon Press, 1980).

31. F. M. Steele, *The Convents of Great Britain* (London: Sands and M. H. Gill, 1902), p. 8.

32. I am thankful to Alan Randall, Archivist of St Joseph's Province, Congregation of the Passion, for generously providing me with biographical information on Arthur Devine.

33. A. Devine, *Convent Life; Or, The Duties of Sisters Dedicated in Religion To the Service of God* (London: The Passionists, 1889), pp. 82–3. The emphasis is my own. It is true many congregations were approved by Rome, but this did not make them

canonically religious institutes as Devine infers. Until the apostolic constitution *Conditae a Christo* was issued in 1900, only solemn-vowed nuns were recognised as canonical women religious. R. MacGinley, 'Nuns and Sisters: A Question of Historical Evolution', *The Australasian Catholic Record*, 85:3 (2008), 30–9.

34. Devine, *Convent Life*, pp. 82–5. Italics are my own.
35. The significance of separate spheres has been much debated by historians. See L. Davidoff and C. Hall, *Family Fortunes: Men and Women of the English Middle Class, 1780–1850* (London: Hutchinson, 1987); J. Rendall. 'Women and the public sphere', *Gender and History*, 11 (1999), pp. 475–88; A. Vickery, 'Golden Age to Separate Spheres? A Review of the Categories and Chronology of English Women's History', *Historical Journal*, 36 (1993), pp. 383–404.
36. A. D. Drane, *Life of Margaret Mary Hallahan: Foundress of the English Congregation of St Catherine of Siena of the Third Order of St Dominic* (London: Longmans, Green, Reader and Dyer, 1869), p. 107.
37. *Ibid.*, p. 447.
38. The Liturgy of the Hours, or the Divine Office, is composed of a sequence of public liturgical services based on scriptures. It is prayed in seven parts during the day and once in the night. Performance of the Divine Office was one of the core tenets of monastic life.
39. Drane, *Life of Margaret Mary Hallahan*, p. 470. For those nursing or teaching there were practical difficulties to saying the Divine Office; it was a lengthy set of prayers occurring throughout the day and therefore potentially disrupting the work day. It was vocally demanding, a potential difficulty for those teaching in the class-room. Drane indicates the congregation was given permission to recite the Divine Office two years before Hallahan's death in 1868.
40. *Ibid.*, p. 450.
41. *Ibid.*, p. 448.
42. The Irish Sisters of Mercy, founded in 1831 by Catherine McAuley (1778–1841) established their first English convent in Bermondsey, South London, in 1839. By 1900, 101 convents were in existence in England and Wales and at least 1340 women were professed as Sisters of Mercy. The sisters' 'works of mercy' were wide-ranging, and included education, nursing and catechetics. M. C. Sullivan, *Catherine McAuley and the Tradition of Mercy* (Dublin, Ireland: Four Courts Press, 1995). Mangion, *Contested Identities*, pp. 44–45.
43. Sisters of Mercy, *Abridgment of a Guide for the Religious Called Sisters of Mercy* (London: Robson and Son, 1866), p. 2. In 1864, some of the Irish and English Sisters of Mercy met in Limerick to discuss methods of 'preserving uniformity' in the autonomous convents of the Sisters of Mercy. This meeting resulted in the publication of the *Guide for the Religious Called Sisters of Mercy. Amplified by Quotations, Instructions, &c. Part I. & II.* (1866) and the *Abridgement of a Guide for the Religious called Sisters of Mercy*. The texts held no juridic force but were used in some, but certainly not all, of the Mercy convents. M. Peckham Magray, *The Transforming Power of the Nuns: Women, Religion, and Cultural Change in Ireland, 1750–1900* (Oxford: Oxford University Press, 1998), pp. 121–5; C. C. Darcy, RSM, *The Institute of the Sisters of Mercy of the Americas: The Canonical Development of the Proposed Governance Model* (Lanham: University Press of America, 1993), p. 27.
44. The congregation, founded in 1877, spread to Ireland, Italy, Malta, Australia and North America by 1900.
45. Special thanks to Liz West who suggested further reading for a better understanding of Mary Potter's spirituality.

46. Archives of the Little Company of Mary (hereafter LCM): Conferences 'M', 'Devotion to the Dying', ca. 1874/1875, pp. 1–3.

47. LCM: *Rule & Constitutions of the Little Company of Mary* (1893), p. 1.

48. E. A. West, *One Woman's Journey: Mary Potter Founder – Little Company of Mary* (Richmond, Victoria, Australia: Spectrum Publications, 2000), pp. 101–16. West provides an excellent detailed examination of Mary Potter's difficulties with Bishop Bagshawe and her efforts to obtain papal approbation for the Little Company of Mary. All congregations began under episcopal authority as did the Little Company of Mary. If they remained under the authority of the bishop, they were considered diocesan congregations. Once congregations established their viability as diocesan congregations, they could, if they desired, take further steps to seek papal approbation, referred to as pontifical right, which positioned them under the authority of the Pope in Rome. Mangion, *Contested Identities*, pp. 214–23.

49. LCM: 2/1/1, *Rule & Constitutions of the Little Company of Mary* (1893), p. 30.

50. LCM: Book J, Undated letter from Mary Potter to M. Juliana (Julie Towson), p. 96.

51. LCM: Conferences A, No 21, Undated letter (written after 1885) from Mary Potter to 'my children in the Antipodes'. Also cited in West, *One Woman's Journey*, p. 147.

52. Mangion, *Contested Identities*, pp. 53–88. This chapter discusses the multiple factors that influenced 'choosing religious life'.

53. *Ibid.*, p. 228.

54. General Archives of the Union of the Sisters of Mercy of Great Britain (hereafter RSM Handsworth): 5/200/9/1 'Coventry Annals', 1887, p. 40. London-born Teresa Watkins entered the Sisters of Mercy in Chelsea in 1845 and was professed three years later. She was appointed Superior of the Chelsea convent in 1852. In 1862, she formed part of the foundation team that established the Coventry convent of the Sisters of Mercy.

55. Westminster Diocesan Archives: Wiseman Papers – Series 1 & 2 57a, Letter from Mother Mary Elizabeth (Teresa Watkins) to Nicholas Wiseman dated 3 March 1855. Elizabeth Rhodes's essay in this volume indicates that Teresa of Avila offered similar chastisement of the clergy for their slackness.

56. RSM Handsworth: 7/200/9/2 'Chelsea Annals', 1855.

57. Archives of the Daughters of the Heart of Mary: C3 'London Diary: Clapham 1847–1880', May 1852.

58. Notre Dame Archives, British Province (hereafter SND): BX BB/2 in BH1 F1, Letter from Sister M. Alphonse de Liguori (Ipheigenia De Paiva) to Mère Constantine, Superior General, on 6 August 1850.

59. SND: BX BB/2 in BH1 F1, 'Blackburn Community Matters', Letter from Sister M. Alphonse de Liguori (Ipheigenia De Paiva) to Mère Constantine, Superior General, on 13 September 1850.

60. Letter from William Bernard Ullathorne to Genevieve Dupuis dated 26 March 1864 as cited in J. Champ, *William Bernard Ullathorne (1806–1889): A Different Kind of Monk* (Leominster: Gracewing, 2006), p. 286.

Afterword

Frances E. Dolan

'I'm not religious,' people sometimes say today, 'but I am spiritual.' These essays demonstrate that such a division would have been unimaginable to the women considered here. While in common parlance 'spirituality' is often distinguished from participation in institutional religion, the essays collected here explore the spirituality that was made possible by and in turn animated life in holy Orders. These are not stories of freelance, eclectic spiritual beliefs and practices. Rather, as the introduction advises us, this volume offers a contribution to the history of **women religious** which includes the **spiritual virgins** that Marit Monteiro considers, 'women who nominally were not religious, but who nevertheless considered themselves as such' (p. 119) and the Ursulines, 'lay women who lived a life of prayer and penance in their own homes, without vows or common habit', (p. 5) as Quericiolo Mazzonis explains. For the most part, these women conformed to the restrictions and **Rules** imposed by the Church and their Orders. Their spirituality was made possible by and defined through institutional structures, even when they resisted, appropriated and reformed them. Marguerete Porete, as Rina Lahav shows, transgressed by conforming: that is, by structuring a sermon exactly like the ones men gave. In founding her Institute, Mary Ward similarly provoked controversy by presuming to adapt the **Jesuits'** model of institutional organization for women. As Laurence Lux-Sterritt shows, Ward sought to transform opportunities for women from within the Church and with papal sanction.

If spirituality was, in part, made possible in institutional settings, it is also true, as has been widely argued, that spiritual experiences, including visions and prophecies, enabled women such as Teresa de Jesús to outwit hierarchies, claiming a direct message from God and a transcendent authority. Its effects were paradoxical as many contributors note. According to Monteiro, in her study of spiritual virgins in the Northern Netherlands in the seventeenth century,

> On the one hand, religion provided a frame of reference that encouraged women to submit to the social and cultural preconceptions regarding femininity, while on the other hand it provided women with the words and images suited to challenge these very notions on higher religious authority. (p. 128)

Kate Stogdon explores 'how faith practices and spiritualities helped to expand as well as to reinforce the roles stipulated for Roman Catholic women' (p. 149) in nineteenth-century France. In short, spirituality was made possible inside institutions, and was a spur to reinventing those institutions, a means of pressing against their restrictions and an authority that sometimes exceeded the institutions within which it emerged.

What is spirituality? Not surprisingly, the word does not appear in the glossary, in part because it is so difficult to define. As an object of study, it is impossible to pin down. Spirituality pervades the essays as a concern, but its meaning remains elusive. The few attempts to define it offered here are abstract and open-ended. In their introduction, the editors launch a definition by starting with 'St Paul's reference to "spiritual persons" as those influenced by the Holy Spirit of God' (*Corinthians* 2:13, 15; *Ephesians* 1:13). They concede that 'the general understanding of spirituality' is 'increasingly non-denominational' (p. 1) and their further attempts to define it focus not on what it is but what it does and how it is fostered:

> Today, spirituality is broadly understood to give meaning and purpose to life and to provide a transcendental experience to those in search of the sacred. It can be attained through meditation, prayer or communion with the natural world. This transcendence can lead to a sense of connectedness with something greater than oneself, such as nature, the universe or a higher being. For some, spirituality is thoughtful and passive, while for others it is emotional or action-oriented. Notions of spirituality are not fixed, but rather culturally derived and constantly shifting. (p. 1)

This passage explores the why and the how of spirituality but cannot quite capture the what. In her essay at the end of the volume, Carmen Mangion acknowledges that 'Spirituality is a problematic term that defies categorization or quantification.' For the Victorian women religious on whom she focuses, it was 'the core value that gave meaning and purpose to the lives of religious **sisters**, providing sustenance to their working lives as well as their spirit and soul' (p. 166). It was both intensely personal and communally defined and practised. As these essays show, Catholic spirituality changes from era to era, and country to country, especially as a result of dramatic shifts in the status of Catholics: the Reformation, the counter-Reformation, Dutch Reform and Catholic Emancipation. But however shifting and evanescent it is, these essays yearn toward it as the content of the form of Catholicism; however indefinable, it is the reason these women chose the lives they did, their motive for undertaking the restrictions of life in holy Orders. It is the answer to the question of why women chose the religious life over marriage, Catholicism over other denominations. One might argue that, however historically and culturally specific its meanings and manifestations, spirituality is the reason that many readers will turn to these essays, seeking understanding of a history of spiritual search and discovery. To return to the definition of spirituality in terms of its effects, the essays here, taken together, suggest that what spirituality does is propel believers into religious lives that can be organized around spiritual practice and sustain them therein.

Kate Stogdon's essay on Thérèse Couderc offers particularly compelling inquiry into the paradoxical nature of spirituality whereby submission leads to transcendence, discipline to freedom, and one passionately follows '"the heart's desire" by means of strategic and self-conscious surrender of the self" (p. 181). According to Stogdon, the central tenets of Couderc's spirituality, 'namely adoration, abasement, adherence, annihilation and abnegation, involved a series of paradoxes which liberated the person from self-interest and enabled the life of apostleship' (p. 155). Countering the assumption that religious life oppressed women, Stogdon praises 'the constructive ways in which such women wrested life-giving opportunities out of death-dealing situations because of their passionate belief in the purpose given to them by God' (p. 161). Essays such as Stogdon's suggest that women were particularly adept at finessing the paradoxes of such spirituality, heightening the restrictions their gender already placed on them to amplify their own abjection so as to transcend it. The focus on spirituality here means a refusal of hagiographic idealizations of women in favour of more measured and humanizing assessments of what made even the most pious and remarkable women tick.

While spirituality can be achieved through various practices, it is not reducible to those practices and it can be difficult to access its texture and meaning. But for most of the women discussed here spirituality was a spur to verbal communication. This is spirituality on the record; as scholars we necessarily focus on those spiritual experiences that could be and were put into words. Furthermore, reading and writing were key components of many of these women's spiritual practices. Jenna Lay argues that for the English Benedictine Barbara Constable, 'Reading is a form of spirituality: though it is not a substitute for prayer, it nonetheless serves as an interface between God and the contemplative reader.' Indeed, Constable argued that reading is superior to speaking 'in its effects on the body and the spirit' (p. 108). Similarly, Monteiro argues that 'The daily reading of devotional books was considered to be good practice of religion for spiritual virgins (p. 120) who turned to books to help them provide a shape for their 'irregular' lives. Especially for women isolated from family and co-religionists, reading facilitated communications – and interventions – across walls and oceans and time. Writing allowed women to act as preachers and **confessors**, roles otherwise unavailable to them. It made the contemplative life a form of action and outreach. For example, Nancy Jiwon Cho argues that in the last half of the nineteenth century in England:

> hymn-writing developed into a potent instrument by which Catholic women could minister to the poor, young and helpless; contribute to the development of an indigenous Catholic identity; widen their opportunities for service in the Church; and publicly vocalize their commitment to the once suppressed faith. (pp. 144–5)

While many of the contributors challenge familiar ways of defining and deploying gender, it remains the case that, in most of the essays, 'gender' signals 'women'. We find little attention here to the ways in which Catholic men's spirituality was gendered. Yet in defining themselves as exceptional, as unlike other women, some of these women described their own stoutness of heart as masculine. For example, Monteiro explores how Agnes van Heilsbach and Joanna van Randenraedt 'subscribed to dominant ideas of female inferiority in their accounts' but also 'tried to evade and even undermine these by setting themselves apart from the other members of their sex' (p. 125). Van Heilsbach set herself apart by depicting herself as:

> a manly maiden, daring to fight for her faith, being even more courageous than members of the clergy, the Jesuits not excluded. In the year of her death, she recorded a dream in which she rides a horse like a man, firmly holding the reins in both hands and keeping it under control 'with manly determination' (p. 125)

In this vision, van Heilsbach casts her own leadership and fortitude as manly. Joanna van Randenraedt lamented 'Alas, what can I do, if only I were a man', apparently conceding that if she were a man she could have become a priest in which capacity, according to Monteiro, she 'would have been able to serve God better than as a woman' (p. 126). Of the women discussed here, only Mary Ward, as depicted by Lux-Sterritt, refused to walk the 'tightrope of gendered acceptability' (p. 93), openly defied the assumption that women were inferior to men, and challenged rather than accommodated gender constructions:

> To her, divisions of gender were not relevant to spiritual life and served only to hinder the efforts of the Catholic Reformation. Her failure to see the relevance of gender boundaries was going to prevent Mary Ward from enjoying the same degree of success as Teresa of Àvila. (p. 94)

Lux-Sterritt argues that Ward's Institute was suppressed because, among other reasons, 'it was the gendered expression of a *female* free agent who chose to disregard the criteria of a male-defined orthodoxy' (p. 94). As Lux-Sterritt presents her, Ward stands out in the volume as the boldest critic of femininity as culturally constructed and restrictive – and, interestingly enough, as the least successful at achieving her goals within the confines of the institutional Church.

While the focus here is on exceptional women, many of the essays suggest that Catholicism, despite its commitment to clerical celibacy and sex-segregated religious communities, was fundamentally heterosocial. Anti-Catholic polemic registered the fact of Catholic heterosociality in negative terms: in the salacious assumption of clerical sexual misconduct; in the denigration of male–female friendships as scandals; in contempt for Mariolatry; in distrust of men's dependence on their Catholic wives and mothers.[1] But the essays gathered here give us a positive perspective on relationships between Catholic women and men, especially **nuns** and priests, depicting these relationships as mundane, functional, mutual, necessary, unavoidable. As Elizabeth Rhodes puts it: 'History makes it clear – as do most of the essays in this volume – that without the support of the appropriate men, religious women of reformist ambitions get only trouble' (p. 69). According to Rhodes, 'The spiritually advanced religious man was key to Teresa's reform of female convent life, in which women could not avoid their reliance on men for the sacraments and supervision' (p. 76). Other essays suggest that we cannot really understand Clare of Assisi without reference to Francis, as Anna Welch shows; according to Jenna Lay, we cannot understand Barbara Constable without considering her relationship to Augustine Baker, nor can we understand him and his writings without looking at her. Lux-Sterritt emphasizes the importance of Mary Ward's relationship to her **spiritual director**, Roger Lee, who 'strove to ensure a positive reception for the Institute' by negotiating 'the politics of religion more subtly than his penitent' (p. 87) and thus more successfully. To do so, Lee played to conventions regarding women's submission to a male hierarchy, conventions Ward herself sought to challenge, and brokered 'pragmatic compromises' that Ward refused. Even the economically independent spiritual virgins Monteiro discusses 'lived under the obedience of a priest, who served as father confessor and spiritual director' (p. 116), and as 'accessories' (p. 125) to the women's transgressive choices. Monteiro describes the relationships between these spiritual virgins and male clerics as 'alliances' (p. 127) and 'mutual dependencies' (p. 120), on the one hand, and 'asymmetrical by definition' (p. 127) on the other; there was, between the two, a 'mutual, but not necessarily harmonious dependency' (p. 118).

Because of these mutual dependencies, women's fortunes depended on the fortunes of their advisors and models. Several essays here demonstrate both how inspiring many women found the Jesuit Order's spiritual practice and institutional organization and how dangerous it was for them to proclaim their admiration too openly. According to Lux-Sterritt, Mary Ward underestimated the severity of conflicts between Jesuits and **secular** priests and the role those conflicts would play in the reception of her Order. As a consequence, her 'dedication to the creation of an independent **Society of Jesus** for women, combined with the canonical transgressions this entailed, triggered a violent clerical reaction against her proposal' (p. 84). Similarly, Lay shows that Barbara Constable's Benedictine convent got caught up in controversies over Jesuits and their promotion of 'an anti-authoritarian mode of prayer' among the nuns they advised (p. 101).

If women depended on their male models and advisors, men in turn depended on and sought inspiration from women. In addition, women such as Constable, Teresa and Ward presumed to advise their advisors, as the essays by Rhodes, Lux-Sterritt and Lay all show.

Women sometimes paid a price for their alliances with men. We have seen that this was the case for women who were drawn into controversies around their advisors and their Orders. It has also shaped evaluations of women's achievements after the fact. For example, Barbara Constable, as Lay explains, was:

> a prolific transcriber of the manuscripts of Augustine Baker (1575–1641), Cambrai's formative spiritual director. These authorial activities – writing, collecting and editing manuscripts for the use of her sisters in the convent – were essential to the survival of Baker's teachings and to the revival of medieval contemplative practices. (p. 100)

But while this relationship preserved Baker's legacy, Lay argues, it has worked to obscure the original contributions of Constable and her sisters to 'the seventeenth-century practice and literature of **contemplative prayer**' (p. 102).

Just as these essays demonstrate that we cannot separate the history of women religious from the history of men religious because Catholicism was fundamentally and robustly heterosocial, so they demonstrate that one cannot separate contemplative from active lives, Mary from Martha.² These essays show us a proselytizing, catechizing Church in which women played a zealous role. These are not Catholics clinging to the past but striving to build different futures. Although the Council of Trent made no provision for women religious to become part of a Counter-Reformation push to build, extend and defend the Church, insisting that cloistered contemplation was the only acceptable form of religious life for women, it was nonetheless the case that 'many unenclosed female movements emerged which sought to complement male **apostolic** movements' (p. 184), as Lux-Sterritt points out, Mary Ward's Institute, and Angela Merici's Ursulines being just two. In countries in which there were no Catholic convents, such as England and the Dutch Republic, simply entering a convent required ingenuity, courage and adventure. Furthermore, once there, even cloistered women were embedded in the world and forced by necessity to look and reach outward. For example, Lay argues that Barbara Constable's work transcribing and writing in her cloister 'provided the material and methods to question ecclesiastical structures and policies in the English Catholic community' (p. 100), thus turning contemplation into a form of action. Cho argues that lay and religious Catholic women participated 'in the re-conversion of England and re-invigoration of the English Catholic Church in the second half of the nineteenth century through the writing and publishing of didactic hymns' (p. 132). The women we meet in these essays are prolific writers, critical readers, preachers, founders, leaders, administrators, theologians and philosophers.

As Mangion concludes in her essay, the last in the volume, all Catholics' lives might be called 'mixed': 'Balancing individual desires for personal spirituality with the requirements of the corporate body, whether that corporate body be the religious congregation or the Church hierarchy, required constant negotiation' (pp. 165–6). The women she studies in particular 'saw no contradiction or competition between a life of prayer and a life of charitable activity. The life of prayer was meant to feed the souls of the sisters and nurture the activities of the congregation. Martha and Mary, in their view, could coexist' (p. 174). Since this was not a contradiction in terms for the women we meet in many of these essays, one has to wonder why generations of scholars insisted on sharpening oppositions that were blurred in practice, especially since doing so widens the gulf between clergy and lay believers. The mixed life may require constant renegotiation but it is also a community-building project. Recognizing it in all its messiness can forge connections between clergy and laity, women and men, and across time and space.

The particular challenges facing women religious after the Council of Trent became, according to the essays collected here, opportunities to think outside binaries such as active versus contemplative, clergy versus laity, and marriage versus the cloister. Several of the essays gesture tantalizingly to third, mixed, in-the-middle possibilities. Monteiro discusses a text that describes the uncertain status of spiritual virgins, economically independent, unmarried, uncloistered women, as 'a medial state (*middelen staet*)' not unlike the amphibiousness of 'the animals of which it is said they are part aquatic and part earthly animals that stay neither on the earth nor in the sea'. For Monteiro, this statement acknowledges that spiritual virgins 'represented a new category in addition to the religious and the laity' (p. 120). The statement might also suggest that the spiritual virgin is a category problem in addition to or rather than a new category, and thus calls into question the stability of the existing categories for making sense of experience. In their introduction, the editors say that 'In the same way as they transcend the binary oppositions between **enclosed** and non-enclosed, contemplation and action, religious and secular, these women somewhat point to a spirituality of a "third gender", one in which the dichotomy between male and female was seen as reductive' (p. 16). The 'somewhat' here cautiously pulls the punch, but the editors seize on the potential in the 'medial' amphibious state to which Monteiro draws our attention. The spirituality of a third gender might approach the spirituality of a non-gender to which some **mystics** aspired, a discmbodied spirit that cannot be apprehended or figured through the available terms for human embodiment and relationships. Given that many early modern women never married, why would women who had committed themselves to neither marriage nor the convent could undermine the categories available for making sense of women and their options? A gender system that is so easily unsettled and undermined is fragile even if it is tenacious. The prompt to imagine the in-between, in-the-middle and mixed leads to a question that lingers after these essays: What were the ways in which men religious, too, posed gender category problems?

Notes

1. On Catholic heterosociality as scandal, see F. E. Dolan, *Whores of Babylon: Gender, Catholicism, and Seventeenth-Century Print Culture* (Ithaca: Cornell University Press, 1999; South Bend, IN: University of Notre Dame Press, 2005), especially pp. 45–156; F. E. Dolan, 'Why Are Nuns Funny?' *Huntington Library Quarterly*, 70:4 (2007), pp. 1–26; J. M. Ferraro, *Nefarious Crimes, Contested Justice: Illicit Sex and Infanticide in the Republic of Venice, 1557–1789* (Baltimore: Johns Hopkins University Press, 2008), pp. 158–99; M. Laven, *Virgins of Venice: Broken Vows and Cloistered Lives in the Renaissance Convent* (New York: Viking/Penguin, 2002), pp. 176, 179, 184; and A. F. Marotti, 'Alienating Catholics in Early Modern England: Recusant Women, Jesuits and Ideological Fantasies', in A. F. Marotti (ed.), *Catholicism and Anti-Catholicism in Early Modern English Texts* (Houndmills: Macmillan, 1999), pp. 1–34.
2. An important essay on the mixed life and nuns' engagement in politics not cited elsewhere in this collection is C. Walker, 'Combining Martha and Mary: Gender and Work in Seventeenth-Century English Cloisters', *Sixteenth Century Journal* 30:2 (1999), pp. 397–418.

Glossary

Accounts of conscience: were written by penitents, usually religious or semi-religious persons, on the order of their confessor. They often served as a tool for spiritual guidance offered by the confessor. The prescribed daily examination of conscience served as a framework for the spiritual self-reflection recorded in the accounts.

Anglo-Catholic: describes the people, beliefs and practices belonging to, supporting or characteristic of the movement for the revival of Catholic doctrine and observance in the Church of England, which began at Oxford University in 1833 (see Oxford Movement).

Apostolic: deriving from the teachings of the 12 apostles.

Artes Praedicandi: handbooks instructing the clerics how to preach.

Beguines: lay women who, from the early twelfth century, devoted their lives to prayer and good works without entering the convent. They did not take vows and in the beginning, they did not live in communities, although they would later congregate into beguinages forming lay, yet semi-monastic, religious communities. This way of life reflects the evangelical ardour of the late Middle Ages, as well as the search for other than monastic models for designing a life based on the evangelical counsels.

Breviary: a liturgical book used by members of religious Orders and the secular clergy, containing the texts used for the recitation of the Divine Office (performed at the canonical hours of the day: matins, lauds, prime, terce, sext, none, vespers and compline). From Latin the '*brevis*': 'short'.

Carmelites: ancient religious Order whose female and male branches Teresa de Jesus reformed in the second half of the sixteenth century by drawing its members back to strict standards of religious life around the vows of poverty, chastity and obedience. Female Carmelites were cloistered nuns, meaning that they did not leave their convents after making their final vows.

Chaplain: the appointed chaplain of a convent said mass, administered sacraments and heard confessions.

Clausura: refers to solemn-vowed nuns who live within the cloister. Latin for cloister.

Confessor: refers to the role of Roman Catholic priests related to the Sacrament of Penance. On account of this sacrament men and women, after having examined their conscience on the basis of the guidelines laid down in the Ten Commandments, confess their sins to a priest. He offers absolution of these sins, thereby authorizing them to take Holy Communion. Whereas the laity usually confessed and took communion but once a year until well into the nineteenth century, religious and semi-religious women and men confessed and received communion more often. As a consequence of this practice their confessors took on the role of a spiritual director, providing spiritual guidance and adjustment.

Contemplative prayer: an affective rather than intellectual form of prayer; as such, it bypassed Jesuit exercises of meditation on an image or idea.

Dies natalis: the main feast of a saint, commemorating the day the individual died and was 'born' into eternal life. From the Latin for 'day of birth'.

Enclosure: a 'place set apart' for contemplation. Enclosed nuns did not usually leave the convent or monastery.

Evangelical counsels: or counsels of perfection in Christianity. They are poverty, chastity and obedience. These are not binding upon all Christians, but represent the guidelines for those who wish to aim for Christian perfection. As they formally enter a religious Institute, men and women religious take the three vows concerning the counsels of perfection.

Exegesis of the scripture: can occur in four ways. The *sensus historicus* or *literalis*, the literal sense, interpreted the Biblical text only by simple explanation of the words. The *sensus tropologicus*, the moral sense, provided the meaning of the text that looked to instruct on the correction of morals. The *sensus allegoricus*, the allegorical sense, looked for a meaning other than the literal. This interpretation assumed that the Biblical text had an additional mystical meaning that used exemplification by simile. The *sensus anagogicus*, the celestial sense, was used mystically or openly, to stir and exhort the minds of the listeners to the contemplation of heavenly things.

Exemplum (pl. *exempla*): in manuscript studies, this is a text that was used as a master copy, from which others were copied. From the Latin 'example'.

Fathers of the Church or Church Fathers: the early and influential theologians and writers in the Christian Church, particularly those of the first five centuries of Christian history.

Florilegium: a book composed as a miscellany or collection of extracts from other authors.

Foundress: female founder of convents and/or a religious Order.

Fraternity: Religious association or brotherhood under the direction of the clergy and meant mostly, though not exclusively, for the Catholic laity. From the late Middle Ages fraternities served as a suitable milieu for charitable and devotional activities aimed at securing personal salvation. During the Roman Catholic Counter-Reformation fraternities also provided their members with guidelines for an intensified, partly interiorized lay spirituality, which was concentrated on prayer, veneration of saints, examination of conscience, confession and communion. From the Latin *frater*: brother.

Holiness Movement: a movement which emerged from the 1870s which deeply influenced American and British Evangelicalism. It taught that Christians should aim for a second decisive spiritual experience of conviction beyond conversion. After this, struggle and conflict with faith would be replaced by deep trust and calm in the soul.

Horarium: the daily schedule of women religious. Latin for 'daily hours'.

House chapel: is synonymous with so-called hidden churches. Such churches came into being after the Reformation, when Catholics were forbidden to profess their faith publicly. Their churches were confiscated and made available for the use of the Calvinist church that was recognized as the privileged public Church by the States-General of the Dutch Republic. The Catholic community was forced out of the public domain and into the privacy of homes, where house chapels were found. Around 1680, Amsterdam had well over 80 hidden churches. At first these were scarcely decorated, but by the end of the seventeenth century some of them had evolved into small churches for well over a hundred worshippers.

Hymnologist: a scholar of hymns, their history, use, poetry and music etc.

Inquisition (Roman Catholic): institution founded in the twelfth century whose objective was to assure the orthodoxy of Catholic praxis. The first tribunal of the Inquisition in Spain was founded in 1478.

Jesuits: members of the Society of Jesus.

Jesuitesses (*Jesuitinnen*): an often derogatory reference to women who aspired to lead a religious life modelled after that of the members of the Society of Jesus. Most notable were the followers of Mary Ward, who in 1609 founded the Institute of the Holy Virgin Mary, which was suppressed by the Holy See in 1631. Yet, semi-religious women in the Northern and the Southern Netherlands and Germany were also called *Jesuitesses* or *Jesuitinnen*.

Litany: a prayer performed in every Mass, formed as a series of petitions (to saints) alternating with set responses from the congregation. From the Latin '*litania*' (Greek '*litaneia*'): 'entreaty'.

Meditative or discursive prayer: a form of mental prayer that focuses on an image or idea in an imaginative or analytical exercise.

Mental prayer: non-spoken prayer that can use words pronounced in the mind or no words at all. Mental prayer, considered potentially dangerous because uncontrollable by anyone except the person praying, was a fundamental feature of the Early Modern Catholic Reform, and Teresa de Jesús was one of its champions.

Metre: the pattern of stressed and unstressed syllables in verse.

Missal: a liturgical book used by priests, which contains all the texts necessary to recite Masses throughout a complete year. The missal's structure is normally as follows: the Temporal Cycle (Masses from Advent to the end of Lent, including Christmas); the Canon (the texts for celebration of the Eucharist, performed in every Mass); the rest of the Temporal Cycle (masses from Easter to the last Sunday of Pentecost); the Sanctoral Cycle (Masses for specific feasts and saints, e.g. the Purification of the Virgin, St Francis); the Common of the Saints (Masses for different types of saints, e.g. confessor, bishop, martyr); and Votive Masses (e.g. for the Dead). From the Latin '*missalis*': 'of the Mass'.

Mysticism: the direct experience of the divinity by a human being, traditionally divided into purgation, illumination and union.

Nuns: contemplative women religious who take solemn vows and remain strictly enclosed (cloistered) within the convent. They belong to Orders such as the Poor Clares, Benedictines, Augustinians, etc. Contemplatives live a life of prayer but can also do charitable work; they can educate pupils within the convent, make altar breads or vestments. The term 'nun' is not reserved for the Catholic tradition, but applies equally to contemplative women religious in other Christian and non-Christian creeds.

Octave: liturgical commemoration of a major feast, celebrated on the eighth day after the feast (counting the feast as day one).

Oxford Movement: a movement for the revival of Catholic doctrine and observance in the Church of England. It began at Oxford University in 1833 with the publication of the first of John Henry Newman's 'Tracts for the Times' and had a lasting influence on many aspects of subsequent Anglican church practice. It is also sometimes referred to as Tractarianism or Newmanism.

Papal bull: a type of letter or charter issued by a pope to members of the Church, usually containing a decree or Privilege. It is named for the '*bulla*' or seal that authenticates the document, which was usually made of lead or gold in the medieval period.

Professed women religious: women religious who have taken their final vows.

Propaganda Fide: a Roman congregation, established in the sixteenth century, which was established to meet the needs of missionary activity throughout the world.

Provenance: in manuscript studies, the history of the creation and ownership of a manuscript, supplemented by documentation where possible.

Recusant: a person, especially a Roman Catholic, who refused to attend the services of the Church of England.

Regular clergy: members of the clergy (monks, but also deacons and priests) who obey a monastic rule and take vows of poverty, chastity and obedience. If they perform duties in a diocese on the authority of the local bishop, they are subject to his authority, which takes precedence over that of the monastic superior in cases other than concerning the religious Order.

Rubric: text written in red ink in a manuscript, either as a method of highlighting its importance (as in a calendar), to designate it as a heading or to designate it as instructive rather than to be read aloud. From the Latin '*ruber*': 'red'. Also, 'rubrication', from the Latin '*rubrico*': 'to colour red'.

Rule: rule of life for Orders and congregations.

Sanctoral cycle: the section of a missal which contains the masses for specific feasts and saints (see above, Missal).

Scriptorium (pl. scriptoria): a room in a monastery used for writing manuscripts, usually attached to the monastery's library. From the Latin for 'a place for writing'.

Secular clergy: deacons and priests, who do not belong to a religious order as the regular clergy do. They take vows of chastity and obedience.

Semi-religious: refers to persons who are nominally not religious but consider themselves as such. Although their life style is inspired by those ways of life that are ecclesiastically confirmed as religious, neither they nor the communities formed by semi-religious persons are juridically approved by the Church.

Sisters: active women religious who take simple vows and lived in communities called congregations. They often work outside the convent as teachers, nurses or parish visitors.

Society of Jesus: founded in 1540 by the Spanish Ignatius Loyola (1491–1556), the Society aimed at defending Catholicism in the aftermath of the Reformation; its members were part of the regular clergy but undertook missionary work worldwide.

Sodality: is a pious association comparable to a (con)fraternity in its aim and structure.

Spiritual director (see Confessor)

Spiritual life story: first-person account of a person's life with God, often required as part of a religious woman's general confession in early modern Spain, or when her piety surpassed the limits of standard orthodoxy.

Spiritual testimony: short, first-person account of a spiritual experience, usually required of a female confessant whose extraordinary experiences of God were being tracked by her superiors.

Spiritual virgins: though not all spiritual women were virgins, spiritual virgins held a special place in the Netherlands. These lay women devoted their lives to prayer and good works without entering the convent. They did not take vows or live in communities, thus remaining economically independent.

Thematic sermon: a sermon which became common towards the end of the thirteenth century and had a single point of departure in a form of a single *thema* or quotation from Scripture.

Third Order or tertiaries: during the twelfth and thirteenth centuries an internal hierarchy was established within the religious Orders between the *First Order* or the male branch, the *Second Order* or the female branch of contemplative nuns. and finally the *Third Order* of laity, women and men who were founded third. Members of the Third Order, also called tertiaries, lived according to the Third Rule of a religious Order. Tertiaries were lay members of that Order (e.g. the Franciscans or the Dominicans). Members aimed to live according to the principles of their Order. Some did this in a community and were called regular tertiaries. Others did not, but lived 'in the world' and were therefore designated as secular tertiaries.

Tractarianism (see Oxford Movement)

Translatio: a liturgical feast commemorating the moving (translation) of relics from one location to another. From the Latin for 'transferring, handing over'.

Vicar apostolic: usually a titular bishop who leads an apostolic vicariate: a form of territorial jurisdiction of the Catholic Church established in missionary regions and countries which do not have a diocese. These missionary territories come directly under the pope, who delegates his jurisdiction to a vicar apostolic. From 1622 the supervision of these missions was the responsibility of the *Congregatio de Propaganda Fide* (since 1982 renamed as the Congregation of the Evangelization of Peoples).

Vows: by taking the vows of poverty, chastity and obedience, women and men religious dedicate their lives to God. This constitutes the ceremony of religious profession that marks their entrance into a religious Institute. Those who became a member of a religious Order (e.g. the Poor Clares or the Carmelites) took solemn vows of poverty, chastity and obedience. Those who entered a religious congregation (e.g. religious with an active vocation of service to the needy, the sick or the uneducated, such as the Sisters of Mercy or the Daughters of Charity) took simple vows. While in simple vows, a person maintained the right to own goods (but ceded their administration); in solemn vows a person renounced the right of such ownership. Those who took simple vows were not recognized as true religious until the decree *Conditae a Christo* promulgated in 1900.

Women religious: refers to both contemplative nuns, who took solemn vows and lived a life of prayer within an enclosed community, and active sisters, who took simple vows and whose apostolic work, typically teaching or nursing, occurred outside convent walls.

Further Reading

Ahlgren, Gillian T. W., *Teresa of Avila and the Politics of Sanctity* (Ithaca: Cornell University Press, 1996).

Babinsky, Ellen L., 'Christological Transformation in the Mirror of Souls by Marguerite Porete', *Theology Today*, 60 (2003), pp. 34–48.

Baker, Augustine, OSB, *The Life and Death of Dame Gertrude More*, edited by Ben Wekking (Salzburg: Analecta Cartusiana, 2002).

Bilinkoff, Jodi, 'Confessors, Penitents, and the Construction of Identities in Early Modern Avila', in Barbara B. Diefendorf and Carla Hesse (eds), *Culture and Identity in Early Modern Europe (1500–1800): Essays in Honour of Natalie Zemon Davis* (Ann Arbor: University of Michigan Press, 1994), pp. 83–100.

Bilinkoff, Jodi, 'Introduction', in *Teresa of Avila: The Book of Her Life,* trans. Kieran Kavanaugh, OCD, and Otilio Rodríguez Kavanaugh, OCD (Indianapolis: Hackett Publishing Company, 2008), pp. xi–xxvi.

Bilinkoff, Jodi, *Related Lives: Confessors and Their Female Penitents, 1450–1750* (Ithaca: Cornell University Press, 2005).

Bilinkoff, Jodi, *The Avila of St. Teresa: Religious Reform in a Sixteenth-Century City* (Ithaca: Cornell University Press, 1989).

Bilinkoff, Jodi, 'Woman with a Mission: Teresa of Avila and the Apostolic Model', in Guila Barone, Marina Caffiero and Francesco Scorza Barcellona (eds), *Modelli Di Santità E Modelli Di Comportamento: Constrasti, Intersezioni Complementària* (Turin: Rosenberg & Sellier, 1994), pp. 295–305.

Bitel, Lisa. M., and Felice Lifshitz, *Gender and Christianity in Medieval Europe: New Perspectives* (Philadelphia: University of Pennsylvania Press, 2008).

Blumenfeld-Kosinski, Renate, and Timea Szell (eds), *Images of Sainthood in Medieval Europe* (Ithaca and London: Cornell University Press, 1991).

Bornstein, Daniel, and Roberto Rusconi (eds), *Women and Religion in Medieval and Renaissance Italy* (Chicago: University of Chicago Press, 1996).

Børresen, E. Kari, *From Patristics to Matristics: Selected Articles on Christian Gender Models* (Rome: Herder, 2002).

Bossy, John, *The English Catholic Community, 1570–1850* (London: Darton, Longman & Todd, 1976).

Bradstock, Andrew, Sean Gill, Anne Hogan and Sue Morgan, *Masculinity and Spirituality in Victorian Culture* (London: Macmillan Press, 2000).

Bremond, Henri, *La Conquête de Mystique: Histoire littéraire du sentiment religieux en France*, 11 vols (Paris: Librairie Bloud et Gay, 1925), Vol. 3.

Brown, Sylvia Monica (ed.), *Women, Gender and Radical Religion in Early Modern Europe* (Leiden: Brill, 2007).

Burton, Janet, and Karen Stöber (eds), *Monasteries and Society in the British Isles in the Latter Middle Ages* (Woodbridge: Boydell, 2008).

Bynum, Caroline Walker, *Fragmentation and Redemption: Essays on Gender and the Human Body in Medieval Religion* (New York: Zone Books, 1991).

Bynum, Caroline Walker, *Jesus as Mother: Studies in the Spirituality of the High Middle Ages* (Berkeley: University of California Press, 1982).

Caciola, Nancy, *Discerning Spirits: Divine and Demonic Possession in the Middle Ages* (Ithica and London: Cornell University Press, 2003).

Carey, Ann, *Sisters in Crisis: The Tragic Unraveling of Women's Religious Communities* (Huntington: Our Sunday Visitor, 1997).

Carney, Margaret, OSF, *The First Franciscan Woman: Clare of Assisi & Her Form of Life* (Quincy, Illinois: Franciscan Press, 1993).

Carrera, Elena, *Teresa of Avila's Autobiography: Authority, Power and the Self in Mid- Sixteenth-Century Spain* (Oxford: Legenda, 2005).

Champ, Judith, *William Bernard Ullathorne (1806–1889): A Different Kind of Monk* (Leominster: Gracewing, 2006).

Chicarro, Dámaso, 'Introducción', in Dámaso Chicarro (ed.), *Libro de la Vida by Teresa de Jesús*, 8th edn (Madrid: Cátedra, 1972).

Coakley, John Wayland, *Women, Men and Spiritual Power: Female Saints and Their Male Collaborators* (New York: Columbia University Press, 2006).

Coakley, John, 'Friars, Sanctity, and Gender: Mendicant encounters with saints, 1250–1325', in Clare A. Lees (ed.), *Medieval Masculinities: Regarding Men in the Middle Ages* (London: University of Minnesota Press, 1994), pp. 91–110.

Coakley, John, 'Gender and the Authority of Friars: The Significance of Holy Women for Thirteenth-Century Franciscans and Dominicans', *Church History*, 60 (1991), pp. 445–60.

Combes, André, 'Les Quatre Offrandes de la Bienheureuse Thérèse Couderc', *La Pensée Catholique*, 59 (1959), pp. 29–38.

Corthell, Ronald, Frances E. Dolan, Christopher Highley and Arthur Marotti (eds), *Catholic Culture in Early Modern England* (Notre Dame, Indiana: University of Notre Dame Press, 2008).

Cover, Jeanne, *Love – The Driving Force: Mary Ward's Spirituality: Its Significance for Moral Theology* (Milwaukee, WI: Marquette University Press, 1997).

Crawford, Patricia, 'Women's Published Writings 1600–1700', in M. Prior (ed.), *Women in English Society* (London: Methuen, 1985), pp. 211–82.

Crawford, Patricia, *Women and Religion in England 1500–1720* (London: Routledge, 1993).

Dalarun, Jacques, *Francis of Assisi and the Feminine* (St Bonaventure, New York: Franciscan Institute Publications, 2006).

Dalarun, Jacques, *Uno sguardo oltre: donne, letterate e sante nel movimento dell'Osservanza francescana: atti della I Giorno di studio sull'Osservanza francescana e femminile*, 11 novembre 2006, Monastero Clarisse S. Lucia, Foligno (Assisi, Perugia: Porziuncola, 2007).

Deville, Raymond (ed.), *The French School of Spirituality: An Introduction and Reader* (Pittsburgh, PA: Duquesne University Press, 1994).

Diefendorf, Barbara B., *From Penitence to Charity: Pious Women and the Catholic Reformation in Paris* (Oxford: Oxford University Press, 2004).

Dolan, Frances, 'Why Are Nuns Funny?', *Huntington Library Quarterly*, 70:4, (2007), pp. 509–35.

Dolan, Frances, *Whores of Babylon: Catholicism, Gender and Seventeenth-Century Print Culture* (Ithaca and London: Cornell University Press, 1999).

Dyckman, Katherine, Mary Garvin and Elizabeth Ann Liebert, *The Spiritual Exercises Reclaimed: Uncovering Liberating Possibilities for Women* (New York: Paulist Press, 2001).

Earle, J. C., 'Roman Catholic Hymnody', in John Julian (ed.), *A Dictionary of Hymnology*, 2nd edn (London: John Murray, 1907).

Eickenstein, Lina, *Woman under Monasticism: Chapters on Saint-lore and Convent Life between AD500 and AD1500*, (Cambridge: Cambridge University Press, 1986).

Elliott, Dyan, *Proving Woman: Female Spirituality and Inquisitorial Culture in the Later Middle Ages* (Princeton: Princeton University Press, 2004).

Evangelisti, Silvia, '"We do not have it and we do not want it": Women, Power, and Convent Reform in Florence', *Sixteenth Century Journal*, 34:3 (2003), pp. 677–700.

Foot, Sarah, *Veiled Women*, 2 vols (Aldershot: Ashgate, 2000).

Gauthier, Chantal, *Women Without Frontiers: A History of the Missionary Sisters of the Immaculate Conception, 1902–2007* (Outremont: Carte Blanche, 2008).

Gilchrist, Roberta, *Contemplation and Action: The Other Monasticism* (London: Leicester University Press, 1995).

Giles, Mary E. (ed.), *Women in the Inquisition: Spain and the New World* (Baltimore: Johns Hopkins University Press, 1999).

Gordon, J. M., *Evangelical Spirituality* (London: SPCK, 1991).

Guibert, Joseph de, *The Jesuits. Their Spiritual Doctrine and Practice: A Historical Study* (Chicago: IJS, with Loyola University Press, 1964).

Heimann, Mary, *Catholic Devotion in Victorian England* (Oxford: Clarendon Press, 1995).

Hellinckx, Bart, Frank Simon and Marc Depaepe, *The Forgotten Contribution of the Teaching Sisters: A Historiographical Essay on the Educational Work of Catholic Women Religious in the 19th and 20th Centuries* (Leuven, Leuven University Press, 2009).

Helmstadter, Richard (ed.), *Freedom and Religion in the Nineteenth Century* (Stanford, CA: Stanford University Press, 1997).

Herpoel, Sonja, *A la zaga de Santa Teresa: autobiografías por mandato* (Amsterdam: Rodopi, 1999).

Herringer, Carol Englehardt, *Victorians and the Virgin Mary: Religion and Gender in England, 1830–85* (Manchester: Manchester University Press, 2008).

Herzig, Tamar, *Savonarola's Women: Visions and Reform in Renaissance Italy* (London: University of Chicago Press, 2008).

Hills, Helen, *Invisible City: The Architecture of Devotion in Seventeenth-Century Neapolitan Convents* (Oxford: Oxford University Press, 2004).

Hollywood, Amy, 'Suffering Transformed: Marguerite Porete, Meister Eckhart and the Problem of Women's Spirituality', in Bernard McGinn (ed.), *Meister Eckhart and the Beguine Mystics, Hadewijch of Brabant, Mechthild of Magdeburg and Marguerite Porete* (New York: Crossroad, 1994).

Hollywood, Amy, *The Soul as Virgin Wife, Mechthild of Magdeburg, Marguerite Porete and Meister Eckhart* (Notre Dame: University of Notre Dame Press, 1995).

Holmes, J. Derek, *More Roman than Rome: English Catholicism in the Nineteenth Century* (London: Burns and Oates and Patmos Press, 1978).

Jay, Elisabeth, 'Women Writers and Religion: "A Self Worth Saving, a Duty Worth Doing and a Voice Worth Raising"', in Joanna Shattock (ed.), *Women and Literature in Britain, 1800–1900* (Cambridge: Cambridge University Press, 2001), pp. 251–74.

Kloek, Els, Nicole Teeuwen and Marijke Huisman (eds), *Women of the Golden Age: An International Debate on Women in Seventeenth-Century Holland, England and Italy* (Hilversum: Verloren, 1994).

Knox, Lezlie, 'What Francis Intended: Gender and the Transmission of Knowledge in the Franciscan Order', in A. B. Mulder-Bakker (ed.), *Seeing and Knowing: Women and Learning in Medieval Europe 1200–1500* (Turnhout: Brepols, 2004), pp. 143–61.

Knox, Lezlie, *Creating Clare of Assisi: Female Franciscan Identities in Late Medieval Italy* (Leiden: Brill, 2008).

Langlois, Claude, 'Le catholicisme au féminin', *Archives des Sciences Sociales des Religions*, 57:1 (1984), pp. 29–54.

Laven, Mary, *Virgins of Venice: Enclosed Lives and Broken Vows in the Renaissance Convent* (London: Viking Penguin, 2002).

Lichtmann, Maria, 'Marguerite Porete and Meister Eckhart: The Mirror for Simple Souls Mirrored', in Bernard McGinn (ed.), *Meister Eckhart and the Beguine Mystics, Hadewijch of Brabant, Mechthild of Magdeburg and Marguerite Porete* (New York: Continuum, 1994).

Lieblich, Julia, *Sisters: Lives of Devotion and Defiance* (New York: Ballantine, 1992).

Lincoln, Victoria, *Teresa: A Woman. A Biography of Teresa of Avila*, edited by Elias Rivers and Antonia T. de Nicolás (Albany: State University of New York Press, 1984).

Lonsdale, David, *Eyes to See, Ears to Hear: An Introduction to Ignatian Spirituality* (London: DLT, 1990, 2000 edn.).

Lunn, David, 'Augustine Baker (1575–1641) and the English Mystical Tradition', *The Journal of Ecclesiastical History*, 26 (1975), pp. 267–77.

Lux-Sterritt, Laurence, *Redefining Female Religious Life: French Ursulines and English Ladies in Seventeenth-Century Catholicism* (Aldershot: Ashgate, 2005).

Magray, Mary Peckham, *The Transforming Power of the Nuns: Women, Religion, and Cultural Change in Ireland, 1750–1900* (Oxford: Oxford University Press, 1998).

Maison, Margaret, '"Thine, Only Thine!" Women Hymn Writers in Britain, 1760–1835', in Gail Malmgreen (ed.), *Religion in the Lives of English Women, 1760–1930* (London and Sydney: Croom Helm, 1986), pp. 11–40.

Mangion, Carmen M., 'Religious Ministry and Feminist Practice', in Jacqui DeVries and Sue Morgan (eds), *Women, Gender and Religious Cultures* (London: Routledge, 2010).

Mangion, Carmen M., *Contested Identities: Catholic Women Religious in Nineteenth-century England and Wales* (Manchester: Manchester University Press, 2008).

Marshall, Sherrin, *Women in Reformation and Counter-Reformation Europe* (Bloomington: Indiana University Press, 1989).

Martin, J. John, *Myths of Renaissance Individualism* (New York: Palgrave Macmillan, 2004).

Matter, E. Ann, 'The Personal and the Paradigm: The Book of Maria Domitilla Galluzz', in Craig A. Monson (ed.), *The Crannied Wall: Women, Religion, and the Arts in Early Modern Europe* (Ann Arbor: University of Michigan Press, 1992), pp. 87–103.

Mayne Kienzle, Beverly (ed.), *The Sermon* (Turnhout: Brepols, 2000).

Mazzonis, Querciolo, *Spirituality, Gender and the Self in Renaissance Italy: Angela Merici and the Company of St. Ursula (1474–1540)* (Washington, DC: Catholic University of America Press, 2007).

McCann, OSB, Justin, 'Introduction', in Peter Salvin and Serenus Cressy, *The Life of Father Augustine Baker, OSB* (London: Burns Oates & Washbourne Ltd., 1933).

McClelland, V. A., 'From Without the Flaminian Gate', in V. Alan McClelland and Michael Hodgetts (eds), *From Without the Flaminian Gate: 150 Years of Roman Catholicism in England and* Wales (London: Darton Longman + Todd, 1999), pp. 1–20.

McGinn, Bernard, *The Flowering of Mysticism, Men and Women in the New Mysticism (1200–1350), Vol. III of The Presence of God: A History of Western Christian Mysticism* (New York: Crossroad, 1998).

McMillan, James F., *Housewife or Harlot: The Place of Women in French Society 1870–1940* (Brighton: Harvester, 1981).

Medioli, Francesca, 'An Unequal Law: The Enforcement of Clausura before and after the Council of Trent", in Christine Meek (ed.), *Women in Renaissance and Early Modern Europe* (Dublin: Four Courts Press, 2000), pp. 136–52.

Medwick, Cathleen, *Teresa of Avila, The Progress of a Soul* (New York: Doubleday, 1999).

Mills, Hazel M., 'Women and Catholicism in Provincial France, c.1800–c.1850: Franche Comté in National Context', unpublished doctoral thesis (University of Oxford, 1995).

Mooney, Catherine M., 'The Authorial Role of Brother A. in the Composition of Angela of Foligno's Revelations', in Ann Matter and John Coakley (eds) *Creative Women in Medieval and Early Modern Italy* (Philadelphia: University of Pennsylvania Press, 1994), pp. 34–63.

Mooney, Catherine M. (ed.), *Gendered Voices: Medieval Saints and Their Interpreters* (Philadelphia: University of Pennsylvania Press, 1999).

More, Brenna, 'Feminized Suffering in Modern French Catholicism: Raissa Maritain (1883–1960) and Léon Bloy (1846–1917)', *Spiritus: A Journal of Christian Spirituality*, 9 (2009), pp. 46–68.

Muir, T. E., *Roman Catholic Roman Catholic Church Music in England, 1791–1914: A Handmaid of Liturgy?* (Aldershot: Ashgate, 2008).

Muir, T. E., '"Full in the Panting Heart of Rome": Roman Catholic Church Music in England: 1850–1962', 2 vols, unpublished doctoral thesis (University of Durham, 2004).

Mursell, Gordon, *English Spirituality: From 1700 to the Present Day* (Louisville: Westminster John Knox Press, 2001).

Neal, Marie Augusta, *From Nuns to Sisters: An Expanding Vocation* (Mystic: Twenty-third Publications, 1990).

Nelson, Sioban, *Say Little, Do Much: Nurses, Nuns, and Hospitals in the Nineteenth Century* (Philadelphia: University of Pennsylvania Press, 2001).

Newman, Barbara, *From Virile Woman to WomanChrist: Studies in Medieval Religion and Literature* (Philadelphia: University of Pennsylvania Press, 1995).

Norberg, Kathryn, 'The Counter-Reformation and Women: Religious and Lay', in John W. O'Malley SJ (ed.), *Catholicism in Early Modern History: A Guide to Research* (St Louis: Center for Reformation Research, 1988), pp. 133–46.

Norman, E. R., *The English Catholic Church in the Nineteenth Century* (Oxford: Oxford University Press, 1984).

O'Brien, Susan, 'Religious Life for Women', in V. Alan McClelland and Michael Hodgetts (eds), *From Without the Flaminian Gate: 150 Years of Roman Catholicism in England and Wales 1850–2000* (London: Darton Longman + Todd, 1999), pp. 108–41.

O'Brien, Susan, '"Terra Incognita": The Nun in Nineteenth-Century England', *Past and Present*, 121 (1988), pp. 110–40.

O'Malley, John W., 'Introduction', in Thomas L. Amos, Eugene A. Green and Beverly Mayne Kienzle (eds), *De Ore Domini, Preacher and World in the Middle Ages* (Kalamazoo: Medieval Institute Publications, 1989).

Palazzo, Eric, *A History of Liturgical Books from the Beginning to the Thirteenth Century*, translated by Madeleine Beaumont (Collegeville, Minnesota: The Liturgical Press, 1998).

Palmer, Martin E. (ed.), *On Giving the Spiritual Exercises: The Early Jesuit Manuscript Directories and the Official Directory of 1599* (St Louis: IJS, 1996).

Perry, Mary Elizabeth, *Gender and Disorder in Early Modern Seville* (Princeton: Princeton University Press, 1990).

Perry, Mary Elizabeth, 'Subversion and Seduction: Perceptions of the Body in Writings of Religious Women in Counter-Reformation Spain', in Alain Saint-Saëns (ed.), *Religion, Body and Gender in Early Modern Spain* (San Francisco: Mellen Research University Press, 1991), pp. 67–78.

Petroff, Elizabeth, 'A Medieval Woman's Utopian Vision: the Rule of St Clare of Assisi', in Libby Falk Jones and Sarah Webster Goodwin (eds), *Feminisim, Utopia, Narrative* (Knoxville: University of Tennessee Press, 1990), pp. 174–90.

Petroff, Elizabeth, *Body and Soul: Essays on Medieval Women Mysticism* (Oxford: Oxford University Press, 1994).

Po-Chia Hsia, Ronnie, *The World of Catholic Renewal, 1540–1770* (Cambridge: Cambridge University Press, 1998).

Poole, Myra, SND, *Prayer, Protest, Power: The Spirituality of Julie Billiart Today* (Norwich: Canterbury Press, 2001).

Porete, Margaretae, *Speculum Simplicium Animarum*, edited by Paul Verdeyen (Corpus Christianorum, Continuatio Mediaeualis, LXIX) (Turnhout: Brepols, 1986).

Porete, Marguerite, *The Mirror of Simple Souls*, translated by Ellen L. Babinsky (New York: Paulist Press, 1993).

Porete, Marguerite, *The Mirror of Simple Souls*, translated by Edmund Colledge, J. C. Marler and Judith Grant (Notre Dame: University of Notre Dame Press, 1999).

Raughter, Rosemary (ed.), *Religious Women and Their History: Breaking the Silence* (Dublin: Irish Academic Press, 2005).

Rhodes, Elizabeth, '"What's in a Name": On Teresa of Ávila's Book', in R. Boenig (ed.), *The Mystical Gesture: Essays on Medieval and Early Modern Spiritual Culture in Honor of Mary E. Giles* (Burlington: Ashgate Press, 2000), pp. 79–106.

Rhodes, Elizabeth. 'Mysticism and History: The Case of Spain's Golden Age', in A. Weber (ed.), *Teresa of Avila and Spanish Mysticism* (New York: MLA, 2009), pp. 47–56.

Richards, Michael, 'Prelude: 1890s to 1920', in J. D. Crichton, H. E. Winstone and J. R. Ainslie (eds), *English Catholic Worship: Liturgical Renewal in England since 1900* (London: Geoffrey Chapman, 1979).

Scaraffia, Lucetta and Gabriella Zarri (eds), *Women and Faith: Catholic Religious Life in Italy from late Antiquity to the present* (Cambridge: Cambridge University Press, 1999).

Schutte, Anne Jacobson, 'Inquisition and Female Autobiography: The Case of Cecilia Ferrazzi', in Craig A. Monson (ed.), *The Crannied Wall: Women, Religion, and the Arts in Early Modern Europe* (Ann Arbor: University of Michigan Press, 1992), pp. 105–18.

Schutte, Anne Jacobson, '*Per Speculum Enigmate*: Failed Saints, Artists, and Self-Construction of the Female Body in Early Modern Italy', in Ann Matter and John Coakley (eds), *Creative Women in Medieval and Early Modern Italy: A Religious and Artistic Renaissance* (Philadelphia: University of Pennsylvania Press, 1994), pp. 185–200.

Sells, Michael, 'The Pseudo-Woman and the Meister: "Unsaying" and Essentialism', in Bernard McGinn (ed.), *Meister Eckhart and the Beguine Mystics, Hadewijch of Brabant, Mechthild of Magdeburg and Marguerite Porete* (New York: Continuum, 1994).

Shagan, Ethan (ed.), *Catholics and the 'Protestant Nation': Religious Politics and Identity in Early Modern England* (Manchester: Manchester University Press, 2005).

Sharp, John, 'Juvenile Holiness: Catholic Revivalism among Children in Victorian Britain', *Journal of Ecclesiastical History*, 35 (1984), pp. 220–38.

Sheils, W. J. and Diana Woods (eds), *Women in the Church, Studies in Church History* (Oxford: Basil Blackwell, 1990).

Sheldrake, Philip (ed.), *The Way of Ignatius Loyola: Contemporary Approaches to the Spiritual Exercises* (London: SPCK, 1991).

Shell, Alison, *Catholicism, Controversy and the English Literary Imagination, 1558–1660* (Cambridge: Cambridge University Press, 2006).

Simons, Walter, *Cities of Ladies: Beguine Communities in the Medieval Low Countries, 1200–1565* (Philadelphia: University of Pennsylvania Press, 2001).

Sluhowsky, Moshe, *Believe not Every Spirit: Possession, Mysticism, & Discernment in Early Modern Catholicism* (Chicago: University of Chicago Press).

Spear, Valerie, *Leadership in Medieval English Nunneries* (London: Routledge, 2005).

Strasser, Ulrike, 'Catholic Nuns Resist their Enclosure', in Nancy Auer Falk and Rita M. Gross (eds), *Unspoken Worlds: Women's Religious Lives* (Belmont: Wadsworth, 1989), pp. 207–20.

Strasser, Ulrike, 'Early Modern Nuns and the Feminist Politics of Religion', *Journal of Religion*, 8:4 (2004), pp. 529–55.

Strasser, Ulrike, *State of Virginity: Gender, Religion, and Politics in an Early Modern Catholic State* (Ann Arbor: University of Michigan Press, 2004).

Strasser, Ulrike, 'The Cloister as Membrane: Recent Convent Histories and the Circulation of People and Ideas', *Gender History*, 19:1 (2007), pp. 369–75.

Strasser, Ulrike, 'The First Form and Grace: Ignatius of Loyola and the Reformation of Masculinity', in Scott H. Hendrix and Susan C. Karant-Nunn (eds), *Masculinity in the Reformation Era* (Missouri: Truman State University Press, 2008), pp. 45–70.

Suenens, Leon Joseph, *The Nun in the World: New Dimensions in the Modern Apostolate* (Westminster-Maryland: The Newman Press, 1963).

Traub, George E. (ed.), *An Ignatian Spirituality Reader* (Chicago: Loyola Press, 2008).

Tutino, Stefania, *Law and Conscience: Catholicism in Early Modern England, 1570–1625* (Aldershot: Ashgate, 2007).

Van Dijk, S. J. P. (OFM) and J. Hazelden Walker, *The Origins of the Modern Roman Liturgy* (London: Darton, Longman & Todd, 1960).

Van Dijk, S. J. P. *The Sources of the Modern Roman Liturgy: The Ordinals by Haymo of Faversham and Related Documents (1243–1307)* (Leiden: Brill, 1963), Vols. 1–2.

Van Whye, Cordula (ed.), *Female Monasticism in Early Modern Europe: An Interdisciplinary View* (Aldershot: Ashgate, 2008).

Verdeyen, Paul, 'Le Procès d'inquisition contre Marguerite Porete et Guiard de Cressonessart (1309–1310)', *Revue d'histoire ecclésiastique*, 81 (1986), pp. 47–94.

Walker, Claire, 'Combining Martha and Mary: Gender and Work in Seventeenth-Century English Cloisters', *Sixteenth Century Journal*, 30:2 (1999), pp. 397–418.

Walker, Claire, *Gender and Politics in Early Modern Europe: English Convents in France and the Low Countries* (New York: Palgrave MacMillan, 2003).

Walker, Claire, 'Spiritual Property: The English Benedictine Nuns of Cambrai and the Dispute over the Baker Manuscripts', in Nancy E. Wright, Margaret W. Ferguson and A. R. Buck (eds), *Women, Property, and the Letters of the Law in Early Modern England* (Toronto: University of Toronto Press, 2004), pp. 237–55.

Wallace, David, 'Periodizing Women: Mary Ward (1585–1645) and the Premodern Canon', *Journal of Medieval and Early Modern Studies*, 36:2 (2006), pp. 397–453.

Walsh, Barbara, *Roman Catholic Nuns in England and Wales, 1800–1937: A Social History* (Dublin: Irish Academic Press, 2002).

Walsham, Alexandra, *Church Papists: Catholicism, Conformity, and Confessional Polemic in Early Modern England* (Woodbridge: Boydell Press, 1993).

Weber, Alison, '"Dear Daughter": Reform and Persuasion in St Teresa's Letters to Her Prioresses', in Jane Couchman and Ann Crabb (eds), *Women's Letters Across Europe, 1400–1700* (Aldershot and Burlington: Ashgate, 2005), pp. 241–61.

Weber, Alison, 'Spiritual Administration: Gender and Discernment in the Carmelite Reform', *Sixteenth Century Journal*, 31:1 (2000), pp. 123–46.

Weber, Alison, *Teresa of Ávila and the Rhetoric of Femininity* (Princeton: Princeton University Press, 1990).

Weber, Alison, 'The Three Lives of the *Vida*: The Uses of Convent Autobiography', in Marta V. Vicente and Luis R. Corteguera (eds), *Women, Texts and Authority in the Early Modern Spanish World* (Burlington: Ashgate, 2003), pp. 107–27.

West, Elizabeth A., *One Woman's Journey: Mary Potter Founder – Little Company of Mary* (Richmond, Victoria, Australia: Spectrum Publications, 2000).

Wiesner-Hanks, Merry, *Convents Confront the Reformation: Catholic and Protestant Nuns in Germany* (Milwaukee: Marquette University Press, 1996).

Wiesner, Merry E, *Women and Gender in Early Modern Europe* (Cambridge: Cambridge University Press, 2000).

Wolfe, Heather, 'Dame Barbara Constable: Catholic Antiquarian, Advisor, and Closet Missionary', in Ronald Corthell, Frances E. Dolan, Christopher Highley and Arthur F. Marotti (eds), *Catholic Culture in Early Modern England* (Notre Dame: University of Notre Dame Press, 2007), pp. 158–88.

Wolfe, Heather, 'Reading Bells and Loose Papers: Reading and Writing Practices of the English Benedictine Nuns of Cambrai and Paris', in Victoria E. Burke and Jonathan Gibson (eds), *Early Modern Women's Manuscript Writing* (Aldershot: Ashgate, 2004), pp. 135–56.

Wood, Jeryldene, *Women, Art and Spirituality: The Poor Clares of Early Modern Italy* (Cambridge: Cambridge University Press, 1996).

Yeo, Eileen Janes, 'Protestant feminists and Catholic saints in Victorian Britain', in *Radical Femininity: Women's Self-Representation in the Public Sphere* (Manchester: Manchester University Press, 1998), pp. 127–148.

Index

accounts of conscience, 68, 123–4, 126, 128, 187
Adolf, Clara, 115, 121, 128
Alan of Lille, 41–3, 45, 47
Alexander IV, 30, 32
Alexander, Cecil Frances, 137
Angelics, 64–5
Anglo-Catholicism, 137, 139, 187
Anthony of Padua, 19, 22, 26–7, 31–2, 34
  liturgical feasts, 27
Antwerp, 120, 123
apostolic poverty, 29
Apostolorum Apostola, 46
Armstrong, Regis, 29
Artes Praedicandi, 41, 43, 45, 187

Babthorpe, Mary Ann, 85, 88–9, 92, 97
Baker, Augustine, 100–5, 108–9, 111, 112, 183, 184
Barnabites, 64, 65
Bartoli, Marco, 20
beguines, 7, 9, 53, 66, 83, 86, 115, 187
Benedict XIII, 6
Benedict XIV, 17, 95
Berwick, Mary *see* Procter, Adelaide Ann
Bilinkoff, Jodi, 72, 77, 78
Boede, Maria, 115
Bonaventure of Bagnoregio, 21, 26, 27, 30, 32, 33, 34
Boniface VIII, 3, 4, 85
Borromeo, Carlo, 5, 53, 65, 66
bride of Christ, 52, 53, 55, 57, 59, 61, 115, 116, 122, 125, 126
Bridget of Sweden, 65
Buckle, Elizabeth (in religion Maria Joseph), 137, 143
Burns and Lambert, 136, 146
Bynum, Caroline Walker, 6, 8, 9, 33, 119

Caddell, Cecilia M., 134, 136, 138, 145
canon law, 10, 122, 175, 191
Carillo, Sancia, 121

Carmelites, 68, 69, 76, 78, 82, 141, 187, 191
Carter, William, 143–4
Carvajal, Luisa de, 86
Caswall, Edward, 133, 137, 139
Catherine of Bologna, 66
Catherine of Genoa, 67, 155
Catherine of Siena, 65, 78, 82
Chantal, Jeanne de, 119
children, 15, 55, 88, 107, 133–8, 143, 144, 146
Circa Pastoralis (1566), 4, 117, 167
Cistercians, 29
Clare of Assisi, 2–4, 11, 19–21, 23–35, 65, 183
  canonization, 19, 25, 30
  formula vivendi, 28
  Franciscan status, 2–3, 28–32, 33–4
  and gender studies, 21–2, 27, 30, 31, 33–4
  historiography, 19–21, 31–3
  liturgical feasts, 22, 22, 25–6, 32, 33–4
  Rule, 29–31, 32
  San Damiano, 2, 19, 20, 24, 25, 28–9, 30, 33
  Santa Chiara (basilica), 19, 25
Clement VII, 66
Clement XI, 85, 92, 94
Clitheroe, Margaret, 143–4
Coakley, John, 78, 82
Cobbe, Frances Power, 140
Company of Christian Doctrine, 53, 65
Company of Divine Love, 65
Company of St Ursula (also Ursulines), 5, 7, 11, 51–63, 66, 67, 83, 85, 86, 87, 89, 96, 119, 128
confessor, 2, 5, 21, 22, 23, 27, 54, 57, 59, 66, 69, 70–8, 81, 82, 91, 100, 103, 105, 109–10, 115, 116, 120, 122–8, 173, 174, 182, 183, 187, 188, 191